Interrogating Democracy and Human Rights

Interrogating Democracy and Human Rights

The Telangana People's Movement

Jagannatham Begari

RAWAT PUBLICATIONS

Jaipur • New Delhi • Bangalore • Hyderabad • Guwahati • Kolkata

ISBN 978-81-316-0598-1

Published by
Prem Rawat for **Rawat Publications**
Satyam Apts, Sector 3, Jawahar Nagar, Jaipur 302 004 (India)
Phone: 0141 265 1748 / 7006 Fax: 0141 265 1748
E-mail: info@rawatbooks.com
Website: www.rawatbooks.com

New Delhi Office
4858/24, Ansari Road, Daryaganj, New Delhi 110 002
Phone: 011 2326 3290

Also at *Bangalore, Hyderabad, Guwahati* and *Kolkata*

Typeset by Rawat Computers, Jaipur

Printed at Nice Printing Press, New Delhi

To my late parents

Contents

Foreword

Telangana, one of the regions of Nizam State, which, after the Police Action in 1948, became a part of Andhra and subsequently merged with the state of Andhra Pradesh in 1956. It is important to note that from the beginning, people of Telangana resisted its merger with Andhra Pradesh. Therefore, even after the merger, they continued to aspire for separate state. According to them, an uneven development and neglect adversely affected the region. This perception kept their desire alive to have the separate state and this echoed in different ways and forms of struggles. Telangana being part of Nizam State, Urdu medium dominated the education, as a result, the young people were lagging behind both in English and Telugu in comparison to the regions of Coastal Andhra and Rayalaseema and lost job opportunities to a great extent in the post-Nizam period, as a large number of people from Andhra region were posted in government jobs in Telangana. This was, probably, shock for the people, particularly educated youth of Telangana, which created the fear that they do not have opportunities in their own region. This could be the beginning of discontent and triggered cascade effect which gave rise to people's agitations and struggles leading to the people's movement at large for a separate state. Cumulatively, these events turned into turmoil in Telangana leading to the violation of human rights. Against this background, the present book interrogates democracy and human rights.

An attempt has been made to describe the trends in democracy, human rights and people's movements to probe the parliamentary politics in India and also to evaluate the domain of rights and the way they have contributed to the protection and promotion of human rights. The evolution of rights has been probed from different perspectives, viz., liberal, feministic, Ambedkarian and Marxian. The book has brought into focus the modern society, constituted by three sub-systems: economic, politico-administrative and socio-cultural.

The author argues that the crisis in one sub-system induces the crisis in other sub-system and dissipates it into the system as a whole, which manifests in varied new forms at macro level. Economic crisis, for example, can take either political form or even a cultural form. State intervention, in the course of its mitigation, may get entangled with the economic crisis in the political cobweb. It is further illustrated that the state when began to rely more on 'experts' to resolve the political problems, such exercises many a time became futile or the crisis gets further aggravated making it difficult to find the solutions. Such crises are perennial in India.

During the sixty years of independence, several movements sprang up in India because of social-economic disparities and their complexities, uneven distribution of resources, and intra- and inter-regional disparities which seem to be transformed into social and political movements. In addition, the corruption and lack of political will and concern are further likely to create distrust in the minds of masses. According to the author, the entry of some of the socially insensitive people into state legislatures eroded the sanctity of democracy and its associated values which made difficult to achieve the social and economic equilibrium. Further, the adopting of economic reforms in 1991 shifted the focus from social development to economic growth. As a result, poor became poorer and rich, richer, making India as a rich country of poor people. The social issues and problems gained significance mainly for electoral purposes. Unfortunately, in the absence of effective and preventive measures, pain of the poor and underprivileged persisted. The interest of farmers and other vulnerable sections was ignored and overlooked. In the era of globalization, the state has withdrawn its welfare role. On the other hand, the globalization provided an opportunity for elites and propertied class to become dominant in the making of policies and their implementations.

The author is right when he says that rural population, particularly poor, adversely affected, whereas the corporate sector flourished. During the era of liberalization and globalization, India has produced more than 60 billionaires. According to the recent report (2013) of Credit Suisse Research Institute, the number of millionaires in India is expected to increase by 66 per cent in the next five years to 3,02,000 by 2018 from presently 1,82,000. It may be mentioned that at least for the last three years, according to the budget papers, tax concessions (revenue foregone) provided to the corporate and other rich, are to the tune of more than Rs 5 lakh crores per year. Despite such incentives, the overall growth of industrial production has not been substantive and has declined to a great extent. On the other hand, the rich and their well-wishers criticized the government for giving subsidies to the poor. It is matter of shame that on an average more than 16 thousand farmers are committing suicides per year. Since 1995, around 2.5 lakh Indian farmers have taken their lives. It is all result of globalization (for more details, see the findings of P. Sainath on this issue). According to the National Sample Survey Organization (NSSO), for 2009–10 and 2011–12, 9.1 million jobs were lost by rural women in the case of subsidiary work (short-term supplementary work). There was also a huge decline of 2.7 million jobs in two years. In this context, it is pertinent to note that in 1983 about 34 per cent of women in rural areas were working which subsequently declined and now it stands at 25 per cent. These few examples are indicative of increase in gap between the rich and the poor.

The book highlights that democratic and independent India has generated enabling conditions, permitting some dalits to occupy the offices of power. However, no significant change in their socio-political status at the grassroots could be seen. Among other things, the regular phenomenon of patronization and co-option of dalits by dominant castes could also be seen. At the same time, because of increasing access to education, a large number of Dalit youths, by the 1990s, joined to the mainstream and started taking interest in the mobilization of their brethern and resisting discrimination. In this process, many non-dalits too joined and supported their struggle. During the present era of globalization and liberalization, one also observes the emergence of civil society organizations in a large number, taking several issues. However, human rights should come first and then civil rights. Malcolm X, a renowned US black leader, used to say that without human right, civil right has no meaning; therefore, the civil society organizations should fight with more determination for human rights, particularly of SCs, STs and OBCs. The author rightly suggested that the civil society organizations should join the movements against social discrimination. A full-length chapter has been devoted to explicate the assertions of dalit youth in the villages of Allapur and Jhadimalkapur in the district of Medak in Andhra Pradesh and responses of the state to it. These cases highlighted their struggles against the atrocities as well as fight to attain the equality, liberty, fraternity and dignity, for which Dr B.R. Ambedkar relentlessly fought. These are necessary conditions of substantive democracy.

The protest movements did influence the process of democracy, especially in the last decade of the 20th century. These movements sprang up widely to assert democratic rights and the state policies in India. The politics of protest movements became an alternative way for many people to exercise influence over government and seek redressal for their grievances. Protests awakened people and attracted them towards civil society activism at one level and politicization of the people at another level. The civil society mobilization of the masses into political activism influenced the governmental policies. The people's movements in India have been demanding state to see that formal democracy moves towards substantive democracy. It is known that the state tries to suppress the movements by using force rather than contextualize the problem and evaluate the socio-economic, politico-cultural, historical and institutional problems persisting in the country. The book explicates that the politics of India has moved from its democratic spirit or trust in politics to politics of suspicion. The book also reflects on the role of media and technology, which is under the control of a few elite dominant classes and do not really represent the voices of people. Media in our country works for its own and the elite interests, which ironically is against the spirit of the media.

The book further traces the root causes for movements dealing with various social issues like poverty, deprivation, discrimination and nature of politico-administration. It also attempts to understand the attitude of legislature, law enforcement agencies and judiciary. This book has probed into the new and emerging domain of knowledge and traces the theoretical discourse on movements and their relevance in strengthening democracy by creating the consciousness among the masses and classes. It also interrogates the people's agitations, their forms, participation of the people, socio-economic conditions of the activists, their demands and the response of the state. The study highlights several agitations which have taken place in Andhra Pradesh. The findings from the studies of popular strikes reveal that as governance has become complex, the executive has stopped responding whereas the judiciary has started interfering in the affairs of the executive and legislature both. It made all sections, including employees and caste-based groups, extremely unhappy with the state apparatus and made them to take part in agitations. In a democracy, the faith in the impartiality of the institutions is an important characteristic but in the contemporary times, according to the author, it is missing. While, on the one hand, the legislature and executive have both lost their credibility, on the other hand, the people's faith in judiciary to solve their problems is increasing. Such a state of affairs is not good for the future of democracy in India.

This book has critically assessed the Telangana movement and its history. The state of Andhra Pradesh has a distinct place in the history of social movements in India. It had witnessed several movements: peasant, dalit, tribal, women, Naxalite, anti-liquor and civil rights movement apart from the Telangana movement. The Telangana movement is not merely the demand for statehood but also the demand for economic and cultural autonomy from Andhra region. The rebirth of Telangana movement in the 1990s first raised the question of distribution of land, self-respect, self-rule and then equal share in the political and economic domains along with the bifurcation of the state. The region is located in the western part of Andhra Pradesh; it was formerly part of the state of Hyderabad, ruled by the Asaf Jahi dynasty (the ruler popularly known as the Nizam) from the 18th century until 17th September 1948. The dynasty emerged from the ruins of the medieval Qutub Shahi kingdoms and later on Mughal rule and formed a polygonal tract occupying the centre of the Deccan Plateau. The Nizam's State comprised three linguistic regions: Telangana, Marathwada and Karnataka. For the purpose of administration, the entire state was divided into four *subas*: Warangal and Medak (Telangana), Aurangabad (Marathwada) and Gulbarga (Karnataka). The Telangana region that formed as a part of the Nizam's dominions represented the unique Deccan culture. While India achieved independence in 1947, the Hyderabad State did not get freedom until September 1948. After the Police Action, the state was merged with the Indian Union. In 1956, the region was merged with the Andhra regions and became part of Andhra Pradesh based on the language, i.e., Telugu. It may be noted that from the beginning there was resistance for its merger. The Telangana, in one way or the other, has been demanding for the separate state. In the united Andhra Pradesh, people of Telangana continued to have a widespread feeling that the aspirations of the Telangana people were undermined in all spheres, i.e., social, economic and political. The violation of agreements like Gentlemen Agreement, Six-Point Formula, Five-Point Formula and Mulki Rules and Presidential Order to safeguard the interests of the Telangana region by the ruling classes from the region of Seema-Andhra in Andhra Pradesh added fuel to fire and kept the Telangana issue burning.

To critically interrogate India's democracy, the book further traces the electoral politics and civil society activism around the agitation for separate statehood to Telangana. The issues, other than political developments and the concerns that are involved in the movement, have been critically analysed to provide a deeper insight into the dialectics and dynamics of democracy. Although, from the beginning, people aspired for a separate state, there was not a strategy or organized movement for the same. Instead, this issue was raised now and then by the opinion makers from different corners to spread the message and awaken the people. This continued almost till the 1990s, without any political platform. However, the year 2001 appeared to be the turning point in the history of Telangana movement as a political party (TRS) took this issue and believed that separate state can be attained only through political process and it chosen the strategy of lobbying for the cause of Telangana initially. At the same time, there was widespread belief in favour of mass mobilization which should be started from the grassroots.

Therefore, few events including famous hunger strike by the president of TRS in 2009 fully sparked off the Telangana agitation. Subsequently, it forced the Union Government to declare Telangana as a separate state. It is important to note that it brought the mobilization at the grassroots level. A large number of people, mainly rural poor and unprivileged sections of the society, joined the movement. Importantly, their participation in the agitation awakened them for their rights and fight against class domination, caste discrimination and deprivation. Intellectuals, artists and writers from these sections played an important role in awakening and creating consciousness among the masses who suffered for centuries due to the caste hierarchies. This awareness gave birth to a new political culture. It led to realize that the territorial state for the region is not enough as it further benefits the political elites and the socially privileged classes. Hence, the book argues that the people of Telangana, particularly subalterns, need democratic Telangana to uphold their rights and strive for equality, liberty and fraternity which are denied in the integrated Andhra Pradesh. The book further analyses the role of subaltern classes – dalits, tribals and minorities – in the Telangana movement through songs, writings and other cultural activities.

Now, the creation of Telangana as a separate state has been announced by the government. Expectedly, the strong protests have been registered from Coastal Andhra and Rayalaseema. There is complete shutdown in both the regions and the people are indoors. Ministers at the Centre have resigned. Similar revolt in ruling government at the state is also witnessed. Opposition leaders, particularly of regional parties, have gone on hunger strike. The time is great healer! We will wait for outcome. Although not decided the final date, some or the other day Telangana as a state would become a reality for which youths and unprivileged sections of society had fought and made sacrifices. Many gave their precious lives for the cause of separate Telangana. It needs to watch how their sacrifices are honoured and space is created and/or provided in political, economic and social domains to those people who contributed in taking the Telangana struggle to a logical end. It is likely that the political power might be concentrated in the hands of a few belonging to elite, rich and upper castes. In event of such possibility, the neglect of aspirations of large masses, particularly of poor and unprivileged, probably would ignite the revolt for their honour, dignity and share in power against the powerful. It is not necessary that this time the movement would be peaceful.

I am sure that the book will be useful and informative for those who study or believe in political economy and social democracy as well as those who understand and feel the pains and sufferings of people. It may or may not be a coincidence that this book is being published when Andhra Pradesh is in turmoil.

Professor R.K. Kale
Vice Chancellor
Central University of Gujarat, Gandhinagar, India

Acknowledgements

This work, undoubtedly, would not have been possible without the support of my supervisor, Prof. G. Haragopal. He has been a constant source of motivation and inspiration as a mentor and he has always taken a keen interest and inquisitiveness in my research and facilitated me in developing the interest in academics, in general, and research, in particular. I express my deepfelt sincere gratitude for his astute guidance, constructive and sagacious suggestions and untiring patience at the every stage of my research work. I am thankful to my teacher and supervisor, Professor G. Sudarshanam, professor of political science & Coordinator; Centre for Human Rights, University of Hyderabad. He has equally abetted me not merely in publishing this book, but facilitated me when I was in difficulties and need of support. I wish to thank Dr Vanamala ma'am for the love and affection that she has exhibited towards me. I am grateful to my teachers Prof. Prakash Chandra Sarangi, Prof. Arun Kumar Patnaik, Shri. B. Chandrasekhar Rao, Professor P. Easwaraiah, Dr K.Y. Ratnam, Dr K. Laxminarayana (Economics), Dr G. Nagaraju (Sociology) and Dr R. Ramdas for their perpetual reassurance at the Department of Political Science, University of Hyderabad. I wish to express my thanks to Dr Ajay Gudavarthy (JNU), Dr G. Vijay (HCU) and D. Sukumar (DU) whose astute advice provided me to enquire into the domain of knowledge critically. I also wish to thank all my teachers who taught me throughout my studies.

My heartfelt thanks to all my respondents who have really facilitated me to cognize the nature of leadership, the state apparatus and assessing the relevance of the Telangana Movement. I had a great time in interacting and discoursing with scholars like, Professor Mungekar (former Planning Commission member), Professor Gopal Guru (JNU), Professor Manoranjan Mohanty (DU), Professor A.S. Narang (IGNOU), Professor P. Krishnan (Bangalore University) and

Professor M. Kodandaram. I express my deepest heartfelt thanks for their suggestions and guidance. Special thanks to Arundati Roy (writer) who really contributed to my academic endeavours. It was possible to complete my doctoral thesis as well as this book, because of late Professor K. Jayasankar. I owe my deepest heartfelt thanks to him for his constant source of inspiration and long hours interaction with him at his residence on the Telangana Movement as he was part of the movement since beginning, 1950s. It would be impossible to write democratic aspirations, concerns, and assertions of the people of the region without interaction of the people who are part of the people's movements, particularly Telangana Movement. I thank all my respondents and opinion makers whom I interviewed during my field visits. I thank all the activists, writers, singers and students who really helped me in constructing my thoughts on the notion of democracy, human rights and domain of movements.

I record my special note of thanks to Professor R.K. Kale, Vice-Chancellor, Central University of Gujarat as he is a pronounced source of inspiration for me. After joining the University, he has been unremittingly reminding me of my academic endeavours and heartening me to publish my doctoral work. It is because of his guidance, I was able to revive my doctoral work and publish it. I thank N. Rajaram, Dean, School of Social Sciences, Central University of Gujarat and all my colleagues of the Central University of Gujarat for their persistent care in publishing this book. I also acknowledge adoration and fondness of my students and scholars from the Centre for Gandhian Thought and Peace Studies and Centre for the Studies in Society and Development.

I also thank my father-in-law Papaiah and mother-in-law Shobha Rani, brother-in-laws – Naresh, Suresh and Praveen for their heartfelt wishes. I appreciate the bliss of Hannu and Chinnu and I thank the other family members of Napari. I express my gratitude to my sister Gangamma and brother Sanjeev for their constant support in all my academic endeavours. Without their love and affection, it would not have been possible to see this research work in a book form. I thank my sister-in- law Manjula and I acknowledge the love and affection of my upcoming family gems: Krishna Veni, Ravishanker, Shivaleela, Uday Kiran and Kiran Kumar. It is pleasure to record the support, love and affection of my life partner Shailaja who stood by me all the time. Without her adoration and fondness, this would not have been possible to publish my research work in this book form. My loving and affectionate son Medhansh and daughter Saniksha are always there and whose smiling and kindling faces always provides me stimulation to carry out all my academic activities. Without the support of my parents (late), it would not have been possible for me to come to this level and achieve whatever that I have achieved in my life. I know though they do not require any formal thanks but it is a great occasion for me to recall once again their adversities and hitches that they had to undergo for the furtherance of me and my family members. I humbly bow my head and thank them. I know they are always with me with their showering of blessings on each of my activities.

I really express my heartfelt gratitude for the martyrs who have sacrificed their lives for the cause of Telangana separate state.

However, the onus of errors and omissions, if any, is purely that of mine.

Jagannatham Begari

Abbreviations and Translations

AICC	All India Congress Committee
AP	Andhra Pradesh
APCC	Andhra Pradesh Congress Committee
BHEL	Bharat Heavy Electricals Limited
BJP	Bharatiya Janata Party
CISF	Central Industrial Security Force
CM	Chief Minister
CMP	Communist Party of India
CPI (ML)	Communist Party of India (Marxist-Leninist)
CPI	Communist Party of India
CPI-M	Communist Party of India (Marxist)
DGP	Director General of Police
ESMA	Essential Services Maintenance Act
GO	Government Order
JAC	Joint Action Committee
KCR	Kalvakuntla Chandrasekar Rao
KU	Kakatiya University
LPG	Liberalization, Privatization and Globalization
MIM	Muslim Ittadhul Musalmaan
MLA	Member of Legislative Assembly
MMTS	Multi Model Transport System
MP	Member of Parliament
NCAER	National Council of Applied Economic Research
NGO	Non-Governmental Organization

NTR	Nandamuri Taraka Ramarao
OBC	Other Backward Classes
OU	Osmania University
PG	Post Graduation
PSU	Public Sector Undertaking
RTC	Road Transport Corporation
SC	Scheduled Caste
SEZ	Special Economic Zones
SHRC	State Human Rights Commission
SRC	States Reorganization Commission
ST	Scheduled Tribe
TDP	Telugu Desam Party
TEEJAC	Telangana Electricity Employees' Joint Action Committee
TEJAC	Telangana Employees Joint Action Committee
TJS	Telangana Jana Sabha
TNGO	Telangana Non-Gazetted Officers
TPJAC	Telangana Political Joint Action Committee
TRS	Telangana Rastra Samithi
TSJAC	Telangana Student Joint Action Committee
TSS	Telangana Sadana Samithi
UDHR	Universal Declaration of Human Rights
UPA	United Progressive Alliance
VC	Vice-Chancellor
YSR	Y. Samuel Rajasekhara Reddy
YSRCP	Y.S. Rajasekhara Reddy Congress Party

Translations

Adivasis	Tribals
Aikya Cultural front	United Cultural Front
Azam-Jahi cotton mills	Cotton industry
Bandh	Strike
Batakammas	Feminine expression of protest specific to Telangana women
Bathukamma Utsavams	Festival of Batukamma (deity) goddess
Bonalu	Offering to deities
Dharmasastra	Scripts of *dharma*
Dharnas	demonstrations
Dheekhashibirams	place for relay strikes
Dhoom-dhams	Name of a cultural programme.
Doctors Gharjana	Doctors Roar
Doddu Komuranna	Name of a Dalit leader
Doordarshan	National Television Network
Ethnic	Separate cultural group
Ganesh Nimajjanam	Immersing Ganesha idol into the water
Garjanas	Hullabaloo
Hussain Sagar	A lake located at Hyderabad
Jal	Water
Jameen	Land
Jantar Mantar	A place in New Delhi where dharnas are frequently held
Jati	Sect
Jungal	Forest
Komaram Bhim	Name of the Tribal leader
Maha Padayatra	Marathon walk
Manavadikara	Human rights
Manya Rastram	Tribal state
Moharam festival	Festival of Muslims
Mulkis	Locals
nimajjanam of Bathukamma	Immersion of idol of Goddess Bathukamma
Padayatra	Tour on foot/March-past

Palle-Palle Pattalapaiki	Every village on to the rail tracks
Parliament Muttad	Attack on Parliament
Patnam Roadpi Poyyi	Cooking on the roads of Hyderabad city
PoliKeka	lion's roar
Rachha Banda	A place to discuss in the village
'Rail Roko'	Stop the trains
Rangoli	Colour formations
Rasta roko	Blocking road
Rayalaseema	A region within Andhra Pradesh
Sadarana dharma	Natural rights
Sadharana	Common
Sakalajanula Samme	Everybody on strike or Mass strike
Samayka	United
Seema-Andhra	Andhra and Rayalaseema regions of Andhra Pradesh
Shava yatras	Processions carrying the dead body
Tandas	Tribals locality
Telangana Nagara	Beating the drum to awake the people of Telangana
Telangana Sambaralu	Festival of Telangana
Telangana Talli	Mother Telangana
Telugu Talli	Mother Telugu
Vanta-varpu	cooking and eating in public places
Varnashrama	Four-varna system
Vidyarthi Garjana	Students' roar
Vishalandhra	United Andhra
Yatra	Tour

1 Introduction and Theoretical Framework

This study is an attempt to critically grasp the notions of democracy and human rights. There are many studies on the theme but, this study is different as it lays emphasis on democracy and human rights based on a regional movement that has been debated in the realm of academics and outside the academics. The evolution of rights, legally enshrined in Europe in the 19th century, had an enormous impact on other parts of the world. India, of course, is a signatory to a majority of human rights agreements and pacts. India has been playing a major role in the United Nations in protecting and promoting human rights and its constitutional promises to secure the rights of all sections and strive for equality, liberty and fraternity. However, India is still witness to caste, class, gender, religious, cultural and regional disparities. These conflicts have resulted in a spurt in people's movements in the country. To handle these conflicts, the state is always avoiding the confrontation instead of solving the problem through peaceful negotiations. To study the nature of state: confront conflicts and consensus, the paper is based on case studies of protest movements in Hyderabad and the forms that they used during the time of protest. It gives us a clear idea about the nature of the state and its approach towards people's aspirations. This study also analyses whether such movements strengthen, democracy or weaken democracy. Are such movements a process to strengthen the notion of democracy? The Telangana separate state movement in the country is taken as a case study. It is in this context that the study is divided into eight chapters.

After this introductory chapter, the second chapter deals with contextualizing the notions of democracy and human rights. Then, the third chapter reveals the evolution of movements from historical and theoretical perspectives. The fourth chapter focuses on India's democracy whereas the focus of the fifth chapter is to understand the protest movements in Hyderabad city in order to explore the relevance of protests in a democratic country like India. The sixth chapter makes an attempt to assess the rising consciousness among Dalits in Medak district of Andhra Pradesh. The Telangana statehood movement has been discussed in the seventh chapter and the last chapter has concluding remarks.

Human rights and democracy have historically been presenting varied notions and parallel concepts, but they are basically interrelated and interdependent. Democracy refers to government by the people, and human rights refer to universal rights that apply to all individuals in all societies. However, both human rights and democracy as concepts are dynamic and diverse, and both the ideas have led to a discourse that recognizes their mutual relation. Definitions of democracy have expanded beyond the traditional procedural democracy to the ideals of a substantive democracy. Likewise, human rights framework has begun to further develop conceptions of social, economic, and cultural rights, in addition to civil and political rights. Thus, the notion of human rights expands to human security and freedom at the collective, as well as individual, levels. These expanded definitions present opportunities for recognizing the convergence of the theories and fields related to human rights and democracy. If one attempts to contextualize the concept of democracy, one needs to analyse and contextualize the concept.

The term 'democracy' has been used as a generic term and has undergone a series of changes in meaning. Democracy, as evolved by the Greeks in the 4th century BC, meant direct rule of the assembled people. Democracy was then widely projected as a form of government which provided a just society.[1] It entailed a system which ensured the participation of the ignorant masses and decisions were made on the basis of the majority view. This majority principle was not considered as a substitute to the system of rule by the monarchs. After the American and French Revolutions, human society arrived at the principle or form of representative government. Modern democracy is often equated with liberal democracy. It developed in the Age of Enlightenment in the 18th century in opposition to the divine rule of the monarchs and the idea that all people are created equal and questioned the foundation of political authority based on noble blood. One of its main concerns was promotion of individual rights. Its cornerstones are equality, liberty, justice and limited government. This modern form of liberal democracy has been enlarged mainly by capitalism and its commitment to and promotion of individual rights.

However, since democracy is used as a generic term, it cannot be equated with liberal democracy. George Sorenson pointed out that democracy is a 'dynamic entity that has many different definitions', as a result of which 'its meaning remains subject to debate'. Democracy has now come to acquire the most widespread ideological legitimacy in the world as a form of government. Despite its worldwide appeal, it is not free from controversies. This is so, since democracy is invariably a work in progress.[2]

The concept of 'democracy' includes the principle of self-determination of people and an expression of the people's sovereignty. In democracy, people hold the right to set up any political system with their sovereign power and the people's will is expressed through free and fair elections. The citizens exercise their right to elect representatives and also the right to be elected. The people also have the right to freedom of expression, press and association. The rule of law is considered essential to ensure respect for fundamental freedoms and human rights. Unless the will of the people is satisfactorily expressed, free elections and elected governments will not be effective and meaningful. One way that democracy could be rendered effective is with attempts to strive for human dignity and create a human rights culture in society which allows people to develop fully. With the help of human rights, qualities like pursuit of knowledge, development of talent and sharpening of conscience of humans would develop and satisfy their material and natural needs. Human rights are based on mankind's increasing demand for a life in which the inherent dignity and worth of each human person receives respect and protection. In the language of United Nations, human rights are rights that are inherent in our nature and without which one cannot live as a human being. In this background, the interrelationship between democracy and human rights is determined by effectiveness of the state structure, the political system, enforcement of human rights and ensuring a democratic spirit.[3] Both democracy and human rights are important. It is argued that realization of human rights is possible only in a democratic state as the rights discourse has been borrowed from liberalism and rights are new to humanity with the evolution of opposition to Feudalism and bourgeoisie dominance. These developments gave the scope for the United Nations Declaration of Human Rights, which strives for the promotion of rights of all nations, institutions and individuals.

Since the representative institutions of politics – political parties, elections, legislatures, etc., – have lost the initiative of responding to the growing demands, the issues of redefinition and renegotiation of relationships are being raised and fought outside the pale of institutional politics. D.L. Sheth says, 'Contesting in micro politics (grassroots movements, social movements, non-party political formations, mass-based organizations, social action groups and movement groups) has become significant in redefining nationalism and achieving national society'.[4] He also argues, 'When the global discourse of democracy has become dimensional, the neo-liberal model of market democracy became universally a desirable model. In India, a majority of people are opposed to it. When the Indian state has begun to link itself to the vertical hierarchy of global economic and political power, strong counter political and social movements have emerged in India at the local and national levels. The people's movements are very active in different parts of the country for over three decades working on various issues'. He further argues: 'the long-term goal of micro movements is to democratize, transform democracy'.

In 1990s, many micro-movements aligned together and formed larger alliances to protest against the Indian state on the issue of globalization, even as they got in direct confrontation with the institutions and organizations which represented the global economic and political power. The micro-movements in India represent a varied and much more complex phenomenon. There are several movements in India like on gender issues, against globalization, and on regional and sub-regionalism issues started by grassroots activists. Thus, scholars like Suhas Palshikar argue that regionalism demands for linguistic states, autonomy movements and separatist struggles constitute an important terrain of agitations. Their analytical response is to treat all such agitations as essentially democratic expressions. The second type of response would be to look at such movements as expressions of protests among ruling classes. And, the third response treats autonomy movements as expressions of ethnic identity. Historically, movements for the formation of states constituted appropriational aspirational democratic claims and only a mild transformative element.[5] Deepak Nayyar speaks of exclusion from markets at different levels. Individuals, social groups, regions and nations, landless, illiterate, the lower classes, the handicapped, etc., who are at a disadvantage, are subjected to systematic exclusion from livelihood. Deepak Nayyar further argues that exclusion reflects the limitations of representative politics.[6] The scholars who adhere to the theory of political development consider that the rising aspirations of the people are not adequately met by existing political institutions, which are rigid or incompetent. As the gap widens between the two, it results in 'political instability and disorder', leading to a mass upsurge. The parliamentary form of government, as a political institutional device, has proved to be inadequate to continue or expand concrete democratic rights of the people. The movements and protests of people will continue till adequate political institutional forms for the realization and exercise of concrete democratic rights are found.[7]

In this regard, it is important to stress the limitations of representative governments. It is necessary to acknowledge that the electoral process is losing credibility because of the ominous trends emerging in the conduct of free and fair elections. The increasing number of election-related killings, the incidence of malpractices, and the uncontrolled use of money and mafia power witnessed during the last few general elections are eating into the vitals of the electoral system. The entry of confirmed criminals into state legislatures, representing various political parties, seems to spoil some of the grandeur and dignity inherent in the democratic image of India. The criminalization of politics continues to gain political legitimacy, its unlawfulness notwithstanding. The menacing trends in the electoral practices are, however, not a threat to the very survival of parliamentary democracy because it is still localized and manageable. In reality, these drifts are an expression of the expanding nature of democratic participation. Hence, there is a scope and the need for participatory politics.[8]

To further comprehend democracy, it is essential to elucidate the concept of participatory democracy. Political participation signifies the active involvement of individuals and groups in the governmental processes affecting their lives. In other words, when citizens themselves play an active role in the processes of formulation and implementation of public policies, this activity is characterized as political participation.[9] Participation is the manifestation of a collective consciousness of public interest. According to O.P. Gouba, within political participation, there are two kinds of participations: conventional and unconventional. Unconventional participation is nothing but protest. It is a statement or action expressing disapproval of or objection to something. It is also an organized public demonstration expressing strong objection to an anti-public policy adopted by the state, and civil disobedience. For instance, signing a petition, attending a peaceful demonstration, joining a protest march or forming a human chain. Public protest in a non-democratic set-up like could be passive resistance and civil disobedience. Participation could be interest group activity, political campaigning, initiative and recall. Conventional participation includes voting, standing for office, campaigning for political parties, organizing elections, public hearing, forming advisory councils and referendum, national festivals, Republic Day parade, cleanliness drive, essay competitions, debates, forming human chains, illiteracy eradication movements, community development, etc.[10] Since the study focuses on politics of participatory democracy, it is necessary to assess the notion of the freedom.

Understanding the Notion of Freedom

The word 'freedom', with its synonym 'liberty', has a strong admiring connotation. Freedom is also a synonym of self-determination. It has therefore been applied to whatever actions, policies, or institutions may be deemed valuable, from obeying the law to attaining economic affluence. There are several freedoms: freedom of choice, social freedom, economic freedom, political freedom, cultural freedom, religious freedom, and so on.[11] Freedom is the constitutive value of European political life, in which slaves, lacking freedom, must submit to a master, while free men, being equal in respect of being free, constitute for themselves a government which secures order by law, and not by the unchecked will of a master. Freedom, argued Thomas Hobbes, is 'the silence of the law', and in this tradition, by contrast, freedom has always resided in the ability of individuals as judges of their own best interests, to order the lives within a structure of rules which are clear, predictable and known to all.[12] The issue of rights is important because it has become the ratchet of European social and political development; philosophers and politicians alike make use of slogans and images developed from the contrast between slave and freed. 'Man is born free and everywhere he is in chains' is how Rousseau's *Social Contract* begins, while Marx and Engels end the *Communist Manifesto* by telling workers that they have nothing to lose, but their chains. Hegel argued in his *Philosophy of History* that universal freedom has been the great achievement of the modern Germanic world. This doctrine launched the idea of liberation. But whereas freedom and liberty refer to the removal of arbitrary interferences with the way an individual governs his/her life, liberation was the project of removing all conditions thought to frustrate human satisfaction. It stands for a vision of human life in which desire flows freely and uninterruptedly into satisfying action.[13]

'Rights are those conditions of social life without which no man can seek, in general, to be himself, at his best' is one of the pioneering observations by no less a person than Harold J. Laski. There is no denying the fact that human rights are an essential element of human life. Without these, a man is no better than a slave. These play a dominant role in the process of humanization. Justice is the keyword for every society and human rights are integral to the concept of justice. Justice implies fairness. Dealing fairly with a person is what justice is. There is upholding of rights, if there is justice. In fact, without justice, a society is covered with darkness. According to Felix Wilfred, 'Human rights are a question of regulating right relationships in society among individuals or group's relationships – which are humanizing, and hence fair and just. It may be said that 'human rights' is not a new coinage. It is pertinent to evaluate the meaning and definition of the concept of human rights. Human beings are rational beings and possess certain rights which are commonly known as human rights. Since these rights belong to them because of their existence, they become operative with birth. Human rights, being birth-rights, are, inherent to all individuals, irrespective of their caste, creed, religion, sex and nationality. These rights are absolutely essential as they are concerned with freedom and dignity and are conductive to physical, moral, social, and spiritual welfare. They are essential as they provide conditions for material and public upliftment.'[14]

Mill analyses the domain of individual liberty. He regards utility as the ultimate appeal on ethical questions. In his famous essay on liberty, Mill describes a principle which argues that 'the sole end for which mankind is unwarranted, individually or collectively, in interfering with the liberty of action on any of their number, is self-protection which should determine the extent of legitimate control of the society over the individual'. The principal purpose for which power can be rightfully exercised over any member of a civilized community, against his/her will, is to prevent harm to others, either physical or moral. Mill further regards that the society, whether on the plea of popular ethos or majority rule, should not interfere with the free development of the capacities of individuals to exercise their rights. If this capacity is exercised with courage and imagination that one may know the best that life has to offer only by an independent thought and creative power. Mill assumes that every individual has the capacity for rational thought and action. While certain individuals might have greater opportunities to develop, the potentiality for such development is distributed throughout the entire population. Hence, the emphasis of Mill was on education as an integral part of the political process.[15] Mill, therefore, regards liberty of thought and discussion as an important aspect of individual's rights. 'If all mankind minus one were of one opinion, and only one person was of the contrary opinion, mankind would be no more justified in silencing that one person, than, he, if he had the power, would be justified in silencing mankind.' Hence, Mill's argument is that freedom of thought and discussion entitles us to hold an opinion with some confidence is the knowledge that it has withstood searching hostile criticism. Thus, the pursuit of truth is made to coincide with the enlightened pursuit of self-interest. He pleads for free development of individuality, free from the tyranny of popular opinion and social customs. Each individual should be free to form his own opinions and work out his own plan of life.[16]

Karl Marx has developed a cogent view of human rights. His writings contain only a passing reference to human rights. It is, however, true that Marx has not written an elaborate treatise on human rights but on the basis of his early writings, it is possible to evolve a comprehensive picture of Marx's views on human rights. Marx completely departs from the liberal traditions in dealing with human rights. The liberals view rights as an end in itself and examine rights in isolation from the social conditions in which they are located. Marx rejected such an understanding of human rights. He developed an elaborate critique of the liberal argument and presented his views on freedom in opposition to the liberal perspective.[17] Marx defines freedom as the ability to use labour power creatively as an end in itself, in cooperation with other individuals, under conditions collectively planned. Freedom consists in using one's own labour to do things that gives satisfaction. Productive activity is not taken under the threat of deprivation. But such freedom cannot be realized as long as inequalities exist in the civil society. According to Marx, abolition of classes creates an egalitarian society and only the working class can eliminate classes. But mere overthrow of the dominant classes is not sufficient, as the working class too has to dissolve itself into a universal class or a classless society. Marx has completely rejected the liberal theory of rights because rights in an unequal society would only legitimize inequalities. Of course he agrees that rights contribute to the destruction of structural inequalities, but rights have failed in emancipation of individuals from the power relations of the capitalist society. Rights are best granted only as freedom to pursue interests within the framework of capitalist relations. As Marx said, 'Man was not freed from religion, he received religious freedom. He was not freed from property, but he received freedom to own property. He was not freed from egoism of business, he received freedom to engage in business.' Marx, therefore, argued that real freedom, i.e., freedom to realize one's own potentialities through social support is possible only when a classless society is established.[18]

The study also intends to look at the notion of freedom. As Howard Davis observed, in contemporary times, the concept of 'freedom' in a political context is ardently contested and debated. The definition of the term 'political freedom' simply allows individuals and groups to influence the development of the law or government policy either directly or indirectly through public opinion. Political freedom is exercised both by the people voting in elections and by taking part in marches and demonstrations of various kinds. These matters are fully dealt with by works on elections and in works devoted to the mainstream of civil liberties and human rights law. Political freedom is characteristically conducted collectively. Of course, individuals can conduct their own personal campaigns, but political success and prominence invariably involve organized parties, pressure groups, corporate activity, charities, local councils, trade unions and other public bodies. This means that individuals rarely have personal control over the political causes they espouse, but need to pursue them through organized activity and accept collective decisions on political matters. Political freedom includes not only speeches, but also other forms of action.[19] It is also postulated that human beings enjoyed unrestrained freedom in the state of nature. Surrender of a part of the freedom was a part of the contract. This surrender was in exchange for security. Thus, guaranteeing the right to security, in a way, has come to define the basic function of the state. It is precisely for these reasons that the state has been given the power to use force but the force can and should be used only in the way that the procedure mandates. The procedure is evolved in pursuance of the objectives for which the state came into being. Therefore, the essence of any law should necessarily be the concern for the right to life and security of every individual. And every law is an expression of that part of human nature which privileges the security over unrestrained freedom.[20]

The jurisprudential equilibrium rests not only on the nature of the state, which is dependent on the quality and character of the rulers, but also on the levels of contentment, quality of life, the nature of social institutions and instruments of civil society in mediating the relationships in the society. However, it has been the human experience that the 'equilibrium' is never everlasting. It is always open to challenge and, therefore, the possibility of disequilibrium. It is not that the restlessness in the society is new to human experience. It has always existed in one form or the other; what distinguishes the contemporary means of expressions of restlessness is the level of force and forms of violence. The invention of firearms and their widespread availability in the global market brought in altogether new challenges to the system maintenance. One of the significant, but anticipated, fallouts of these trends has been the end of the state monopoly of force (which distinguishes the state from other institutions). In liberal theory, the origin of the state is conjectured as a product of social contract arrived at through the consent of the individuals. The contract was necessary as relations between human beings were mediated through force and it was that arbitrary force in the state of nature that was brought under the regulation of law. It also maintains that every human being is endowed with reason and since reason is superior to raw emotions and uncultivated impulses, it has been possible to arrive at the acceptance of supremacy of law.[21]

Evolution of the Notion of Rights

The question of rights and its discussion can start with the origin or nature of the earlier rights. The theoretical and philosophical debates suggest that natural rights were the earliest form of rights. What are these natural rights? In simple terms, the right to life was the earliest right to be recognized or that which human beings became conscious of. This right came to be considered as an inalienable right. As Jacques Maritan put it, 'The human person has rights because of the fact that it is a person, a whole, a master of itself and its acts and which is not merely a means to an end, an end which must be treated as such by virtue of natural law, the human person has the right to be respected, is the subject of rights, possesses rights. These are the things which are owed to a man'. These 'inalienable' rights, over a period of time, acquired deeper meaning and larger dimensions.[22] The consciousness of freedom and therefore of rights stems from the ability of the human being to confront nature. For, none of the other species is endowed with the ability to comprehend the laws of nature, nor take advantage of these laws of nature as human persons do. The inalienable rights, called natural rights, came into existence when human life was vulnerable and there was no protection whatsoever. Survival of life itself was problematic at this stage. The problems leading to the solutions and resolutions throwing up the problems got linked with the nature of production. Then, he added, 'it was this logic that led to the formulation that rights are not natural, but social'.[23]

The rights existed in a limited form in the early Greek and Roman civilizations or even in the ancient Asiatic civilizations, but the beginnings of the rights, as understood in the modern sense, could be traced to Magna Carta of the early 13th century. Human history witnessed the modern revolutions that were fought by the people to assert their rights and liberties. In the process, they had to oppose the then existing orders and achieve their rights. The puritan revolution gave the Magna Carta for the humanity in 1613. The English Revolution in the 17th century had shown how constitutional liberties were achieved through the bill of rights, and levying taxes and raising an army could be done only with the consent of parliament. This revolution naturally influenced other revolutions all over the world. The American War of Independence gave the Declaration of Rights. It proclaimed that 'all men are created equal' and emphasized inalienable rights, popular sovereignty and the right to revolution. The French Revolution can be considered as a significant step towards the establishment of individual liberties. This revolution was against the absolute monarch and the feudal oppression of French aristocracy. It gave rise to the middle class and universal values like doctrine of equality, and it gave popular sovereignty and right of the people to govern themselves. The First and Second World Wars further strengthened the rights discourse. All these revolutions and wars played an important role in the emergence of human rights. Further, the Industrial Revolution gave a new momentum to human history. It gave scientific discoveries like the flying shuttle, spinning Jenny and powerloom that helped the industry to grow steadily, and Davy's safety lamp and cotton industry, etc., and renaissance and reformation.[24]

In 1945, the United Nations Organization (UNO) came into existence for world peace and the Universal Declaration of Human Rights provided the foundation for the modern concepts of human rights. It further strengthened universal values like freedom, equality and dignity of human being, right to life, liberty and security of person, annihilation of all forms of slavery and strict prohibition of arbitrary interference of the state in the privacy of family, freedom of movement and equality of rights of men and women. Apart from all, there was the freedom of opinion, freedom of expression, peaceful assembly, right to social security and right to work. In the changed world political economy, it was necessary to enact the international Covenant on Civil and Political Rights (1976), international Covenant on Economic, Social and Cultural Rights (1976) and Developmental Rights (1986). The Vienna Declaration, adopted at the World Conference on Human Rights in 1993, expanded the notion of human rights.[25]

This philosophical and historical scenario explains that all the revolutions and wars strived for the promotion of rights, and upheld the dignity of the general masses against feudalism and monarchy. These encouraged other nations and individuals and institutions to fight, protect and promote rights.[26]

Indian Democracy: Emergence of Struggles and Notion of Human Rights

There are scholars who argue that the evolution of human rights was not confined to Western countries and the roots can be traced in ancient India too. That kings, poets, writers, ancient philosophers upheld the rights discourse. Technological progress too added to India's human rights evolution.

Mahendra P. Singh argues that a large section of the society, particularly in Asia and Africa, raised doubts about the universality of human rights and that their concerns are different from that of the West. And that there is an argument for reconsideration, rethinking and redrawing the universality of human rights which arises from Christianity. In India, religious traditions such as Judaism, Islam, Confucianism, Buddhism and Hinduism spoke about human rights and values before the West talked about them. He argues that a few studies on human rights demonstrate the relevance of religious tradition in understanding the idea of human rights. It is argued that the issue of religion coincides with the social and cultural traditions. Indian culture gives priority to duty and not rights. This is in contrast to universal rights as they give priority to rights rather than duties. He further argues that Indian civilization is a surviving and existing civilization with a history spanning over 4,000 years, whereas no other country has such a long cultural continuity. People from different areas around the world migrated to India. Intermixing of so many racial, ethnic, religious and other identities resulted in the creation of a unique culture, which can be called broadly the Indian identity. The Indian Constitution designates it as 'the rich heritage of our composite culture'. Apart from its territorial and demographic dimensions, the identity is reflected in the Vedas between 6,000 and 100 BCE and then onwards there is a continual flow of rich literature from Brahmanas, Upanishads, Smritis and Puranas. These diversities of India gave the scope for human rights before Western nations developed the idea.[27]

Hinduism in India flows from the oldest ancient texts of Vedas, Agamas and Upanishads that continually stress divine truth. They are universal and the religious beliefs are the way of life. The *Manava Dharma Sutra* (Treatise on Human Duties) addresses the existence of good and evil, wisdom, duty (*dharma*) and good conduct *(sadachara)* toward other's suffering. Indian culture too stresses selfless concern, charity and sympathy for the hungry, the sick, the homeless, and the unfortunate. All human life is considered sacred, to be loved and respected. The other traditions such as Judaism, Buddhism, Confucianism, Christianity and Islam together make significant contributions to the evolution of international human rights. Indian culture also lays stress on values, normative standards and ideals, universal sense of obligation toward humankind, and discussions about rights and duties. Mahendra P. Singh quoted Paul Lauren: 'The seeds of human rights exist as much in the ancient Indian tradition as in any other, even though their expression may be different.' The current usage of the Sanskrit word '*adikara*' is used for 'right' and '*manavadikara*' for 'human rights'. The *dharmasastra* speaks more of human duties than of rights. The concept of *dharma* is equivalent to the notion of right. He also explained *varnashrama* and *sadharana dharma*. Though *varnashrama* reflects inequalities, *sadharana dharma* strives for truth, humanity, self-control, ritual purity, uprightness, generosity, compassion, discrimination, forbearance, absence of envy, abstention from violence, freedom from anger, abstention from theft, restraint of the appetites and freedom from meanness. Despite its rather anaemic social history, common *dharma* still provides the strongest ideological plank from within the tradition to all those who are marginal, weak, exploited, and protesting. In the absence of performance of that duty, no right could be expected. He also argues that the spiritual aspects of Indian tradition, *sadarana dharma*, lay stress on living in harmony with nature and other beings, not being guided all the time by self-interest, but caring for the interest of others. Indian tradition, Mahindra P. Singh argues, strives for solving conflicts rather than creating conflicts. The evolution of the idea of human rights in Hindu religion has something to contribute to human rights. For that, political action required for the realization of human rights in India and morality is the basis of all rights and duties in all the traditions expressed in religious texts, philosophical writings or otherwise. *Dharma* in Indian tradition creates the moral base for the rights.[28]

The long tradition of accepted heterodoxy in India has many other sources. It is necessary to see how much heterodoxy there has been in Indian thoughts and beliefs from very early days. A Buddhist emperor of India, Ashoka, in the 3rd century BCE, emphasized the need for tolerance and the richness of heterodoxy and gave the scope for conducting debates and disputations on oldest rules with the opponents on all occasions. Though India's tradition is male dominated, still women's presence in both political leadership and intellectual pursuits has not at all been negligible. This can be seen in Upanishads, that were composed in about the 8th century BCE. The arguments presented by women speakers in epics and classical tales conformed to peace-loving but encouraged women.[29] Indeed, the challenge to religious orthodoxy has often come from spokesmen of socially-disadvantaged groups. Brahminical orthodoxy was challenged by Buddhism and Jainism as well and their literature contains expositions of protest and resistance. This response not only reflects human equality, and captures the nature of the arguments used to undermine the claim to superiority of those occupying exalted positions.[30] There's the tradition of medieval mystical poets and exponents like Kabir, Ravidas, Mira Bai, Andal, Daya-bai, Sahajo-bai and Ksema from the working class – who were influenced both by the egalitarian of the Hindu Bhakti movement and by the Muslims Sufis – and who argued for rejection of social barriers.[31]

In the history of India, Buddhists had a great commitment to public reasoning and social progress. The Buddhist councils tried to settle disputes between different schools of thought and also addressed the demands of social and civic duties, and furthermore helped to consolidate and promote the tradition of open discussion on contentious issues.[32] The toleration of diversity has also been explicitly defended by strong arguments in favour of the richness of variation. Asoka and Akbar contributed to the public reasoning.[33] Indian texts include elaborate religious expositions and protracted defence. They also contain lengthy and sustained debates among different religious schools. Kautilya's classic treatise on political economy and governance, Arthasastra, is a secular treatise.[34] Since Renaissance, the Industrial Revolution and the Enlightenment of the 18th century, most of the scientific progress has actually occurred in the West. But these scientific developments drew substantially on earlier work in mathematics and science done by the Arabs, the Chinese, the Indians and others.[35] It is not hard to see that the possibility of scientific advance is closely connected with the role of heterodoxy. The history of scientific contributions across the world – the experiences of Copernicus, Galileo, Newton, or Darwin – has many examples of the part that resolute heterodoxy had to play in scrutinizing and, when necessary, rejecting the views that are accepted as standard. Indian science and mathematics that began in the Gupta period (*Aryabhata* in fifth century, *Varahamihira* in the sixth, and *Brahamgupta* in the seventh) benefited from the tradition of skepticism and questioning which had been flourishing in India at that time.[36] From the early centuries of the first millennium, the status of knowledge in the world was altered. Indian trigonometry and astronomy influenced the world. In fact, Indian mathematics and astronomy had a particularly profound impact on Arabs and Iranians. These astronomical advances also involved sharp departures from the established religious orthodoxy. It is in this broad context that one can see the importance of the contributions made by India's argumentative tradition to its intellectual and social history.[37]

Akbar spoke for religious neutrality on the part of the state more than 400 years ago. The tradition of secularism can be traced to the trend of tolerant and pluralist thinking that begun to take root before Akbar. Amir Khusrau's writings (14th century), the devotional poetry of Kabir, Nanak Chaitanya and others got support of Emperor Akbar. Akbar also practised as he preached – abolishing discriminatory taxes imposed earlier on non-Muslims and inviting many Hindu intellectuals and artists into his court. Akbar was precisely codifying and consolidating the need for religious neutrality of the state. Akbar emphasized in his defence of a tolerant multiculturalism the role of reasoning. He arranged for discussions involving not only mainstream Hindu and Muslim philosophers, but also Christians, Jews, Parsees and Jains.[38]

T.S.N. Sastry argues that the history of movements is not a new phenomenon; it had roots in ancient, medieval and modern periods, that could be seen in the pre-independent era. The transition from the medieval to modern period resulted in an exceptional change in Indian history. With the advent of British rule in India, a new era started which created ripples in the political and legal spheres, leading to imposition of British political and legal culture in India. There had been a long history of struggles in India against exploitation, colonial rule and cultural backwardness. With that experience, along with the impact of international human rights discourse, India became a major partner in human rights organizations, covenants and conventions. The framers of the Indian Constitution incorporated the human rights values in the Constitution. The British government in India had not only deprived freedom to the Indian people, but also exploited the masses and ruined India economically, politically, culturally and spiritually. As a result, there was a strong resistance and demand for fundamental freedoms – civil and political. The British rulers discriminated against Indians in matters of political and civil liberties and rights. They resorted to arbitrary acts such as brutal assaults on unarmed *satyagrahis*, deportation, etc., against Indians fighting for national independence, equal justice and economic equality.[39]

British rulers also enacted some laws against injustices. Under the regime of British government in India, several laws were enacted though their interests were involved in them like Punjab Alienation of Land Bill of 1899 to check the moneylenders; Factory Act of 1891, which sought to limit the working hours of women and children; the Bengal Tenancy Bill 1882; the Government of India Act, 1919, the Government of India Act of 1935 that were steps towards wider political representation, whatever the intentions may have been. Building roads and railways was encouraged and helped people to develop and led to increasing consciousness of their rights.[40] After witnessing the colonial rule, it became necessary for every Indian to be aware and vigilant about the recognition, protection and implementation of human rights, as they are not only basic issues and freedoms, but also inalienable for them to lead a civilized life.[41]

After independence, India's Constituent Assembly drafted the Constitution, which adopted the genius of the vision, need, recognition, protection and enforcement of human rights – lying in the freedom struggle – which culminated in the form of fundamental rights and Directive Principles of State Policy. The Preamble, Fundamental Rights, Directive Principles of State Policy, newly-added Fundamental Duties, reservation for the Scheduled Castes and the Scheduled Tribes, special provisions for Anglo-Indians and OBCs are important provisions in the Indian Constitution from the human rights point of view. The study of human rights with reference to the Indian Constitution reveals that the Constitution enshrines almost all human rights provided in various international conventions, covenants and treaties, such as Civil and Political Rights and Economic, Social, and Cultural

Rights, 1966.[42] Since the study focuses on democracy in general and Indian democracy in particular, it is necessary to focus on Indian democracy and its success, progress and failures.[43]

Indian Democracy: Formal and Substantive

Rajeev Bhargava maintains that democracy came to India because of the freedom struggle against the British rule for centuries. Thus, Indians came to have their own Constitution which borrowed some provisions from liberalism. It is argued that the character of the democracy, in one significant sense, just had to be liberal not only because of its commitment to civil liberties, but also because of its vision of equality and social justice. The predominant cultural character of nationalism, its traditional proclivity and the importance of collectivities forced the Drafting Committee of the Constitution to move beyond individualist liberalism, in order to understand the conflict between constitutive attachments and personal liberty, between group disadvantage and personal merit. All these factors shaped the character of the emergent secular-democratic state of India. The written Constitution of India is the result of both deliberations in the Round Table Conferences and of political struggles. Indian democracy is committed to civil liberties that flow directly from acceptable norms of dissent and availability of political liberty within the confines of a liberal state. As early as the beginning of the 19th century, Rammohan Roy protested against a regulation curtailing the freedom of the press. He argued that a state that is responsive to the needs of individuals and ready for intervention on their behalf makes available to them the means by which such needs are communicated and therefore, must permit unrestricted liberty. Likewise, Mahatma Jyotirao Phule struggled for education for women and development of agriculture.[44] Assessing the nature of democracy in India, it is necessary to explore its peculiarities, constitutive characteristics and differences with the West. The idea of equal citizenship and equal rights was linked in the West with the unfolding of modernity. It was premised on the constitution of a specific notion of the self as an autonomous, self-reflective, independent individual who could act according to his or her own wish and will.[45]

Modern democracy was established on the ruins of an ancient regime in which rights and roles of individuals were always predetermined by their location within their social hierarchy. Democracy could not develop without emancipation of the individual from the elite communities.[46] In India, the battle for democracy is being fought not under the sign of individual rights alone; it is powered by the struggles of oppressed communities. Javeed Alam analyses how the struggles of Dalits, backward castes, Muslims and women have critically shaped the nature of Indian democracy, redefined its meaning, structuring the peculiar political culture of its operation. The collective claims of these communities have provoked violent social conflicts and dramatic changes in political alignments. Alam argues how social issues inevitably shape the politics of India.[47] India saw one of the longest freedom struggles in the world. Its limits were those imposed by the bourgeois outlook and preferences of the dominant leadership. Nevertheless, one significant feature of the national movement was the constant pressure exerted by the radical urge among the people within. The anti-feudal struggles of the peasantry formed the most important component of the radical impulse. The other has been the unending quest of the most wretched in India, Dalits, to overcome untouchability and disabling conditions which have disfigured the social personality of India. The spiritual and philosophical greatness of India remains diminished to the extent that untouchability remains in our midst. These two struggles of peasants, in general, and Dalits, in particular, also provide a link with the agrarian disturbances and rebellions prior to the beginning of the nationalist phase in Indian politics, all of which were repressed with little or no sympathy from the emerging elite.[48]

Javeed Alam argues that India has not totally failed as the Indian system is different from that of Western countries since India is a combination of caste, varied cultures, languages and different religions and regions. All these are the barriers for Indian democracy to become an egalitarian society. It is in this context that one has to understand Indian democracy. For the past six decades, India has been relatively successful in sustaining its democratic institutions. The country has held regular elections, institutionalized a multiparty system and divisive politics. Along with these features, the people enjoy freedom of speech and free media. But another side of Indian democracy is that it failed to ensure the provision of minimum basic needs to all its citizens, which leads to a denial of the conditions under which the equal rights of citizenship may be meaningfully exercised.[49]

One can see how the Indian democracy at one level has a high level of abstraction: a commitment to democratic procedures, free elections, free press, and basic set of liberal rights such as freedom of expression, but the point is that these are subject to opposing interpretations. The other side of Indian society is the composition of several castes, ethnic groups and regional identities; their demands are always based on the necessities of their own and they may not think of other groups or regions. But the culture of democracy gives the right to freedom of association, writing an essay and they can even question the state machinery. These methods give a compass for the deepening of democracy. The complex issues raised by regional identities in India became weaker. Whenever India has tried democratic accommodation, it has succeeded. The state subverting ethnic violence, in places like Punjab and Kashmir, has invariably been fuelled by authoritarian moments in the Indian state. Indeed, democracy's biggest triumph is that it has proven to be effective, perhaps the only mechanism for holding India together. It is true that one of the reasons for the relative success of its democracy, and its hanging together as a nation, has been profoundly due to the cross-cutting character of cleavages within Indian society that has made collective action on a large scale, to overthrow the state, quite difficult to mount. But democracy has both brought out conflicts into the open and provided an effective mechanism for accommodating them. India has succeeded as the society is 'diverse in unities', which means in the Indian society, every one is able to imagine the relation with others in his/her own way. The success of democracy is not dependent on the presence of democracy alone, the role of creative political choices is also important. But conflicts are a way of getting different groups to participate and there is an immense process of incorporation of hitherto excluded groups.[50] Other scholars argue that post-liberalization, the problems of rural areas and professions increased, the poor became marginalized and rich became richer, reservations got shrunk, and backward regions have been neglected. Hence, it is argued that the inclusion of excluded sections remained unimpressive. It is also essential to study the politics in early post-independence India. Though many sections participated in the freedom struggle, but the elite dominated in politics.

After independence, the bourgeoisie gained the leadership position to take part in the development of India. By aligning with the landed gentry, due to its structural weaknesses and fear of the radical impulse in society, the bourgeoisie has become the leading force. The large land owners were the reservoir of the most conservative trends in Indian politics, with a surplus of coercive power, which often gets mobilized to beat back the people. Thus, the bourgeoisie-led leadership chose the limited, Western-inspired modernization rather than emancipatory transformation. It was thus forced to rely on Western capitalism, which has now become rampant with the drive towards globalization. This remains the problem with democracy. Whether it is poverty, caste oppression or gender discrimination, the disabling inequalities have not been lessened. The struggles within democracy in India are, therefore, primarily for equality.[51] Javeed Alam argues that if democracy as a value translates itself as a set of practices informed by norms and procedures within an institutional set-up, the question is, how can it get transcribed in Indian conditions? If the people, being poor, cannot acquire education and remain ill-equipped to accomplish enough in way of culture, then how do democratic practices get affected? He says India is suffering from both modernity and tradition. Indian democracy has to uphold traditional beliefs and religious sentiments and, at the same time, claim the part of a modern democracy. Hence, he argues, Indian democracy is in a dilemma. It is not possible to see Indian democracy as a success state in a short span of time. This confused notion gave the scope for people's movements once again.[52]

Indian democracy is facing four drawbacks: one, there is great pessimism among the people and disappointment with the institutions; two, leaders who occupy positions in these institutions lack principles; three, there has been a decline of morality in public life, with rampant corruption and growing of an unclean political climate; four, there has been a sharp increase in social disharmony and therefore caste conflicts and casteism have become the bane of politics.[53] Denials and affirmations form a complex amalgam in Indian society. A Dalit may be denied access to the village well or an upper caste house or even a barber's shop. Women may not be allowed to regulate their work. Nevertheless, the vote of a Dalit or a woman is not less worthy than a Brahmin's or a landlord's. This distinction between social existence and citizenship does impose on the functioning of an oppressed citizen, but does not impose on the functioning of a space for struggles.[54] A large number of people in India are living under severely disabling conditions: poverty, discrimination, and lack of facilities to realize their meagre wishes. To overcome these social problems, struggle is a means of enhancing one's capacity to function as a citizen. When people also become conscious of numerical strength, they begin to feel more able to influence things in their own favour. Indian democracy could become a reality when democracy with its struggles, agitations, mobilizations and electoral participation breaks the rigidity of the enforcement mechanisms of the social structure.[55]

Indian democracy has been witnessing both positive and negative aspects for the past two decades. India has made significant progress in fostering high levels of economic and industrial development, reducing poverty, and promoting the general well-being of the population. During the same period, however, democracy, human rights, and rule of law have been undermined in several parts of the country. Ethno-religious violence has flared up in many corners and the tentacles of transitional terrorism have spread rapidly. Rapid economic progress seems to have unleashed violent class warfare in some areas. Ethnic conflicts in various forms have become an enduring feature of the Indian political landscape.[56] Although India is a constitutional secular democracy, yet violent conflicts between majority Hindus and minority Muslims have flared up and became a part of the problem; that has been the way secularism has been defined and the level of commitment that Indian leaders have had towards religion.[57]

Indian democracy has two descriptions. One is the optimistic narrative of democracy: that Indian democracy is producing an ever-greater politicization of social relationships; the discourses of equality and the assertion of agency are spreading to more areas of social life; impressive voter turnouts amongst the poor and dispossessed suggest that democracy has a wider social basis. In particular, its character is ever greater for non-middle classes. The second is the pessimistic narrative of democracy. This narration emphasizes the enormous variability in the political structure: the high and constant rise of new social groups, the high turnover of incumbents on governments, the intensification of social struggle, and the rising consciousness of rights. All these instances not only speak of the success of the movement, but deepening of democracy. Even if democracy, as practiced today, has not allowed as spectacular an improvement of our material conditions as hoped, it has at least managed to avoid total failure such as mass starvation. Even though the progress in India's democracy might be slow, it has laid the foundation for more enduring inclusive success.[58]

On the other hand, there is the severe narrative of decline, or at least crisis. Democratic mobilization, while it has produced an intense struggle for power, the broad frameworks within which practices of popular authorization can be carried out remain intact. But politics itself has become an area where norms exist only to be breached. The very mechanism designed to secure the liberty, well-being and dignity of citizens in representative democracy – the laws, that are supposed to enshrine republican aspirations – are incapable of commanding minimal respect. India has also witnessed corruption, mediocrity, indiscipline, venality and lack of moral imagination of the political class. These negative aspects of democracy give the compass to be incapable to strengthen democracy and the political process becomes violent, because of the lack of any ideological coherence. All suggest that democracy has become a hollow shell.[59] The political mobilization has placed demands on Indian institutions to the point that they have been rendered dysfunctional, producing a crisis of governability. Too many demands make it impossible for the state to make anyone happy. This situation leads to the 'crisis of governability'. In the Indian political process, leaders continue to concentrate on power. Sometimes, state actions lead to a crisis in governance. The state itself has taken on the character of a trading company and most public offices.[60]

The strength and weakness of Indian democracy is reflected in the range of movements that India saw in the past and continues to witness. The strength lies in the fact that there is political space for the people to organize, protest and articulate their interests and aspirations. The weakness lies in the fact that the rising unrest is a result of failure of the formal structure of democracy is not being able to inspire confidence of the people in its capacity to politically resolve the endemic tensions. This failure leads to cumulative frustration, resulting in prolonged agitations. Hence, demands for separate statehood are one such problem reflecting failure of the federal political arrangement of power. This impasse in Indian democracy is being witnessed as there is a gap between the spirit in formulation of policies and implementation. The study focuses attention on this issue.

One crucial element of both the successes and failures of Indian democracy has been the civil society. In the success of Indian democracy, the role of civil society is self-evident as an element in the political framework of liberal-democratic institutions. But civil society is also a part of the narrative on the failures of Indian democracy: in the absence of political parties performing the sort of interest-aggregating functions that they do in established democracies; a large section of citizens thus remains outside the scope of organized civil society. These citizens become objects of civil society action, rather than participants in civil society. Civil society also plays the role as civil society associations (social reform), counterweight to the state (political party), the development section (volunteer sector) and uncivil society (religious fundamental groups).[61] In democracy, especially in India, people's movements play a vital role. They include Dalit, women and environmental movements. Along with these, we have the regional and sub-regional movements. Since the study concentrates on the issue of a separate Telangana, it is imperative to understand the historical, political and cultural aspects of Telangana and social and economic conditions of Dalits, tribals and minorities.[62]

The Studies on Democracy

The study attempts to review the literature from the perspective of movements: Marxist, Ambedkarite, democratic and liberal perspectives. Out of all the selected perspectives, the study emphasizes on the democratic and Ambedkarite perspectives and tries to look at the Telangana movement from the rights perspective to access the potential of substantive democracy.

In the book *Democratic Theory: Essays in Retrieval*, Macpherson has attacked the elitist-pluralist theory of democracy as espoused by Joseph Schumpeter and Robert Dahl and the entire range of scholars of modern political theory, as well as the utilitarian theory expounded by Bentham. He has pointed out that the traditional or classical theory of democracy was erected on a moral foundation. It saw democracy as a developmental process, as a matter of emancipation of humanity. The elitist-pluralist theory, on the other hand, treats democracy as a mechanism whose essential function is to maintain equilibrium. Under this theory, democracy is reduced from its humanist aspiration to a market equilibrium system. The classical theory had throughout treated democracy as the cry of the oppressed, their claims for recognition as equal human beings – a means by which all men could enjoy and develop their human capacities. The exponents of the elitist-pluralist theory have reduced democracy to a means by which men can register their wants as political consumers in the market. In contrast, Macpherson has developed a new theory of democracy, based on a humanist vision. It aims to emancipate human beings from the constraints of the prevailing competitive social order of the capitalist world and usher in a new society which will promote 'creative freedom'. In order to understand the real character of capitalism, he has pointed to the exercise of two elements: one, the principle of utility maximization and the other, the principle of power maximization. In order to explicate this theory, he has drawn a distinction between two types of powers: one is developmental power and the other, extractive power. Macpherson has pointed out the conditions under which non-owners of property are deprived of what is due to them. He has also explained the concept of possessive individualism and simple exchange economy.[63]

In the book *Social Origins of Dictatorship and Democracy*, Barrington Moore Jr. explains the varied political roles played by the landed upper classes and the peasantry in the transformation from agrarian societies to modern industrial ones. It is an attempt to discover the range of historical conditions under which either or both these rural groups have become important forces behind the emergence of Western parliamentary versions of democracy, and dictatorships; the right and the left; fascist and communist regimes. The first part of the book presents a discussion on the democratic and capitalist way to the modern age, as this transformation worked itself out in England, France, and the United States. The other part of the text focuses on Germany and Russia in order to show how the social origins of fascism and communism in Europe differed from those of parliamentary democracy. As part of this process, new social arrangements were managed in certain countries by political leaders at different points in time during the first half of the 20th century. The focus of interest is on innovation that has led to political power, not on the spread and reception of institutions that have been hammered out elsewhere, except where they have led to significant power in world politics. The analysis of the transformation of agrarian society in specific countries produces results at least as rewarding as larger generalizations. It is a necessary designation for certain violent changes that took place in English, French, and American societies on the way to becoming modern industrial democracies and the historians connect with the Puritan Revolution (the English Civil War), the French Revolution, and the American Civil War. A key feature in such revolutions is the development of a group in society with an independent economic base, which attacks obstacles to a democratic version of capitalism that has been inherited from the past.

The first way through the great revolutions and civil wars led to the combination of capitalism and Western democracy. The second route has also been capitalist, but culminated during the 20th century in fascism. Germany and Japan are the obvious cases. In these countries, the bourgeoisie impulse was much weaker. Afterwards, a relatively weak commercial and industrial class still dominated the ruling classes, mainly recruited from the land, to put through the political and economic changes required for a modern industrial society. Industrial development may proceed rapidly under such auspices. But the outcome, after a brief and unstable period of democracy, was fascism. The third route is, of course, communism, as exemplified in Russia and China. The great agrarian bureaucracies of these countries served to inhibit the commercial and later industrial impulses even more than in the preceding instances. The results were two-fold. In the first place, the urban classes were too weak to constitute even a junior partner in the form of modernization taken by Germany and Japan, though there were attempts in this direction. And in the absence of more than the feeblest steps towards modernization a huge peasantry remained. This stratum, subject to new strains and stresses as the modem world encroached upon it, provided the main destructive revolutionary force that overthrew the old order and propelled these countries into the modern era under communist leadership, that made the peasants its primary victims. The fourth part of the book focuses on India, that desires modernization. In India, so far, there has been neither a capitalist revolution from above or below, nor a peasant one leading to communism. On the other hand, at least some of the historical prerequisites of Western democracy did put in an appearance. A parliamentary regime has existed for some time that is considerably more than a mere facade. Hence, the author argues modernization has been weakest in India. It is especially useful in trying to understand peasant revolutions, since the degree of rural misery in India, where there has been no peasant revolution, is about the same as in China where rebellion and revolution have been decisive in both pre-modern and recent times.[64]

D.N. Dhanagare, in his paper on 'Civil Society, State and Democracy: Contextualizing a Discourse', held that the rise of several post-colonial states was the most striking phenomenon of the second phase of the 20th century. As new nation-states were born, the air was full of excitement, filled with more hope than despair. In the Third World countries that had succeeded in their anti-imperialist struggle, whether by insurrectionary, or guerilla or peaceful, non-violence means, there was a triumphant mood. Their right to self-determination had been conceded by history; efforts were now on to move to the proverbial democratic form of governance, holding out the promise to fulfill the aspirations of people. Competing ideologies of modernity – capitalism and free market economy, socialism, fascism and democratic socialism – were directly the reconstruction of measures in the new states. However, Dhanagare says, the ruling classes in most post-colonial states found democracy to be too slow to respond to the rising expectations of people. Civil liberties of people came under a cloud as military regimes replaced democratically-elected governments one after the other, either by peaceful means or takeovers. Dhanagare tried to comprehend democracy and civil society, the Indian experience. He explains the politics post-independence, political trauma of pre and post-1970s, analyses the crisis during the Emergency period and explains the reasons for declining Congress strength. He argues that to see an effective democracy, universities and academics in India have to play a crucial role. He feels it is high time the role of universities as a forum of civil society independent of state intervention is debated, so that ideas are crystallized for actions aimed at strengthening the institutions of civil society in India.[65]

James S. Scott's *Weapons of the Weak* is both a political and ethnography study based on research and perceptive fieldwork in Sedaka village. Its emphasis is on individual human beings in their particular situations. He looked at ordinary, everyday peasant resistance and the reasons why open revolts are so rare. Scott feels that unnecessary attention has been paid to the rare occurrences of open revolt by peasants, and too little to ordinary, everyday forms of resistance and their symbolic and ideological underpinnings. He also stresses the importance of placing individual agents, in their particular settings, at the centre of analysis. In another chapter, Scot analyses the language associated with exploitation and the ways in which the truth is distorted to serve class interests. The rich rationalize their exploitation and refuse to abide by the traditional dictates of community feeling by such devices as claiming to be poor themselves or denying the morality of the poor; they do not attack the shared norms of the village directly. Several case studies are used to illustrate this: the landowners justifying sacking tenants; a dispute over control of the village gate; and drastic bias in the distribution of funds handed out by the national government for a village improvement scheme. Scott then goes on to look at forms of resistance that go beyond words. Scott suggests that the ideological superstructure must always be seen as a product of the struggle in Sedaka village, not as something predominant. As for hegemony, he also argues that elite values do not really penetrate into the lower classes; inevitability is not seen as implying legitimacy; hegemonic ideas are always subject to conflict, and are continually being reconstructed; and resistance is rooted in everyday material goals – rather than a revolutionary consciousness. He suggests that this analysis applies to the working class as well as to peasants, and that there is a clear need to rethink concepts of hegemony and ideological domination.[66]

Marc Williams, in his paper 'Social Movements and Global Politics', envisages that changes in political, security and economic structures in the past decade have given rise to speculation concerning the current nature and future trajectories of world politics. Central to this debate has been speculation concerning the nature of agency and political behaviour in the contemporary world order. Before he explains the social movements and global politics, he mentions other scholars' argument, that the globalization of world politics has significantly transformed international relations. In the context of globalization, it has been argued that the state and governmental authority no longer fulfill the roles they once did. In this respect, authority relations are fractured, consensus is difficult and new forms of democracy become necessary. Whether the discussion is couched in terms of the death of the state, the moving away of the state, the end of sovereignty or the birth of a post-sovereignty world, recent transformation in the global system indicates that the role played by non-state actors in global politics is immense. Within this new global political space, specific attention is given to the role of social movements. With this argument, the author attempts to explore one aspect of current global politics and focus upon globalization through an analysis of the role of social movements in world politics.

The paper does not test significance of social movements in global politics through an empirical assessment of the role of various social movement actors, but rather assesses evolution of processes whereby social movements have attempted to secure participation in relevant issue-areas in international relations. As such, this paper also expresses the manner in which transformation in the world politics has created a political space for representatives of civil society to play an enhanced role in international relations. It also explores the extent to which globalization is fulfilling its promise of creating a global community of interest and influence. The book has five parts. The first part tries to briefly outline the key characteristics of social movements. The second focuses on situating the emergence of social movements in the context of the evolving global civil society. The third part explores the manner in which globalization is transforming the global political space and the implications of this development. The fourth part focuses on the activities of global social movements. It also tries to give a meaning to the term 'new politics'.[67]

Amartya Sen, in his paper on 'Democracy and its Global Roots', raised the question of democracy in Iraq, America's view of democracy, and poses the question: is it democracy? He has taken democratic movements in Myanmar, Zimbabwe and enhanced today's democracy which reflects the people's determination to fight for political participation and an effective voice. He also argues that voting is not the only way, but certainly it is an important way of making public discussion effective and to speak, to listen, without fear. But, he says that a broader view of democracy could be beyond the freedom of elections and ballots. Amartya Sen places 'democracy' in the broader perspective of public reasoning. It has to give a central place to free public discussion and deliberate interactions in political thought and practice – not just through elections, nor just for elections, but what is required, as John Rawls observed, is the safeguarding of 'diversity of doctrines'. It calls for 'pluralism', which is central to the 'public culture of modern democracy' and must be secured in a democracy by 'basic rights and liberties'. He adds, 'To ignore the centrality of public reasoning, the idea of democracy not only distorts and diminishes the history of democratic ideas, it also detracts attention from the interactive processes through which a democracy functions and on which its success depends. The neglect of the global roots of public reasoning, which is a big loss in itself, goes with the undermining of an adequate understanding of the pace and the role of democracy in the contemporary world. Even with the expansion of adult franchise and free elections, free and uncensored deliberation is important for people to be able to determine what they must demand, what they should criticize, and how they ought to vote'. When he talks about Indian democracy, he opines that although India is facing many problems, it still is a democratic country.[68]

Jean Dreze, in his article 'Dr Ambedkar and the Future of Indian Democracy', opines that the future of Indian democracy depends a great deal on the revival of Dr Ambedkar's visionary conception of democracy. He argues that Dr Ambedkar's vision of democracy was closely related to his ideal of 'global society'. Good society is based on liberty, equality and fraternity. Ambedkar, as he saw it, was both the end and means of his ideal. Another crucial feature which he discusses is that 'while Dr Ambedkar was far ahead of his time in stressing the link between political and economic democracy, perhaps he failed to anticipate the full possibilities of political democracy itself. He thought that in the absence of economic democracy, ordinary people would be powerless. Also, he thought of political democracy mainly in terms of electoral and parliamentary processes'. Jean Dreze talks about Ambedkar's understanding of rationality, rational thinking, liberation and close affinity between rationality and equality and stresses the domination of Hinduism and Brahmanism, and also on the morality and social order. He focuses on social, economic and political democracy; he saw that political democracy alone could not be expected to go very far if glaring economic and social inequalities remained. The end of the paper talks about the future of Indian democracy and Dreze maintains that Ambedkar's vision of democracy failed to materialize but a startling variety of social movements have flourished in India, creative initiatives to keep on expanding the boundaries of political democracy year to year and that Dr Ambedkar had a visionary conception of democracy, which needs to be 'rediscovered'. Going beyond that, he adds, we must also enlarge his vision in the light of recent developments and also, in practical terms, the best action may be to revive the Directive Principles of the Constitution and to reassert that these principles are fundamental in the governance of the country because governments are not respecting these principles much. He further argues that the people of the country should follow Dr Ambedkar's advice to 'educate, organize and agitate, which is more relevant than ever'.[69]

Suhas Palshikar and Rajendra Vora's *Indian Democracy: Meanings and Practices* is a collection of 16 essays. They look at Indian democracy from various perspectives and at ways to expand the meaning of democracy in order to make it more substantial. The compilation focuses on Indian politics since the beginning of the 1990s: the crisis of secularism, backward caste assertion, the volatility of party politics, and the decline of social movements. Democracy, like so many other important notions like independence, socialism, secularism, constitutionalism, equality, and liberalization, was thrust upon the Indian masses by their enlightened elites. The authors suggest that democracy is a result of the persistent failure by the ruling elites to solve economic problems which severely expose their claim to legitimacy. The authors argue that the elites in India realized that the economic problems could not be solved without endangering their own established interests and further emphasized on Indian socialism. It was a notion that was neither planned nor implemented with the required capacity. It was propagated for some time after Independence but what has happened is that India remained socialist in intention and capitalist by inertia and default. This closet capitalism instigated socio-structural changes on a large scale in an insidious manner, which has been animated and expressed by the neo-market forces. This has catalyzed the dichotomy of the existing pluralities, like Brahmin versus non-Brahmin, Hindu versus non-Hindu, Sikh versus Hindu, rich versus poor, and North versus South, and so on. This has the real potential to fragment the political system and give rise to neo-Fascist. movements and lend legitimacy that they would otherwise lack. Further, they also point out that a key cause for the crisis of secularism is the fact that those who are convinced of its benefits for each other and never for those who are not convinced.[70]

The authors suggest that substantialization of democracy can be best achieved by strengthening the formal structures of procedural democracy over a period of time, that will enable the masses to improve the quality of their role in deciding matters. However, this will not be an easy task. The exhaustion of the democratic structures to accommodate the burgeoning interests of the masses means that grassroots and local movements are required. These local movements are always marginalized over time. Nevertheless, the crisis of representation continues to be a danger to democracy. Representative institutions no longer represent voters, who have been short-circuited and corrupted by an institutionalized system of bribery that only renders them responsive to powerful interest groups like big business houses and 'extra-constitutional organizations' like the Sangh Parivar. It is argued that neither the Left, nor the opposition parties and not even the marginalized groups like tribals have been able to effectively mobilize the public against the BJP and counter its communal and cultural archaism or its neo-market hegemony. At the same time, the middle classes are kept hanging between a perpetual fear of unemployment on the one hand, and continual expectation of fantastic rewards once the new economy booms further on the other. Even though India adopted a democratic Constitution in 1950, democracy, as both a form of government and as an organizing principle of politics, continues to be a controversial concept in Indian political discourse. A significant contribution of this volume is how Indian democracy has survived the challenges posed by widespread illiteracy, poverty, secessionism and communalism.[71]

Rajni Kothari's *Rethinking Democracy* is a monograph on democracy and it revisits the core arguments that he has laid down in his varied writings in the past four decades. Kothari interrogates some of his earlier formulations on democracy, state and civil society, developing a new paradigm on the basis of his experience. Kothari makes a critique of current democratic theory and practice in the changing global, as well as Indian, context and concludes that democracy has failed to achieve its objectives of human emancipation. However, this disillusionment with democracy does not deter Kothari from searching for an alternative model for a decentralized, participatory and emancipatory democracy. Rethinking of democracy offers once again what should be termed a Kotharian framework of political theory that combines empirical observations, critical analysis and far-reaching vision. The author tries to conceptualize democracy in the 21st century. Kothari develops some interesting perspectives that seek to transform the current pessimistic questioning of the democratic way of life into 'an agenda transformative politics, and social and cultural emancipation'. Crucially, for Kothari, rethinking democracy does not mean rethinking politics or the role of politics. Rather, in response to the challenges posed by socio-economic inequalities, the working of the late capitalism, the ambiguous implications of globalization and fundamentalist communalism, democracy ought to be more than politics. He believes that it could be a tool of social and economic transformation by extending its concerns from functional institutional arrangements to a multiplicity of emancipatory drives that encompass a range of human behaviour and activities from productive capacities to moral development. Democracy is effectively seen as a function of contradictory process. On the other hand, there appears to be a resurgence in democratic faith among the poor and the hitherto victimized, as projected by grassroots movements of ecologists, feminists and tribal groups. The persuasive arguments that challenge the myth of representative democracy in the post-cold war era notwithstanding, some important points do call for closer scrutiny. Kothari's model of transformative democracy depends on notions of 'pluralism' and the 'masses' that are non-conflictual and non-confrontational. Certainly it remains to be seen how irreducible differences allow for the emergence of such a democratic system in the first place. *Rethinking Democracy* is a statement of mission, informed and informative. Despite his disillusionment and the contradictions of Indian democracy, Kothari is of the view that India has forged a truly democratic future for itself and recognized the need to think beyond the merely 'political' and tap deeper psycho-spiritual dimensions of the Indian reality.[72]

In the book *Indian Politics: Protests and Movements*, Mohammad Yasin and Srinanda Dasgupta raise the question: why the protests have been taking place in India? They trace them to the phase when the Indian political system witnessed a number of protests and agitations, expressing dissent against unjust conditions. They also hold that the roots of India's growing problems of governability are due to and resulting from numerous protests and agitations which are more political than socio-economic. They maintain that any protest could never be a sudden outburst; the root is to be found in the dynamic interaction of the socio-economic and political systems. As such, the causes of protests in India could be rooted in the major contradictions of India's social, economic, cultural, religious and political life. David Bayley, referring to the Indian context, speaks of six primary forms of protests: one, processions and public meetings; two, *hartals*, boycotts and strikes; three, fasts; four, instructional; five, courting of arrest and last, riots. Generally, forms of protests can be divided into two main groups: legal and illegal. And they have traced the breeding grounds for protests in India with different orientation and dimensions. These protests differ in nature. Sometimes they recede within an observable time and space without challenge to the unity and integrity and the existence of the system, but sometimes protests pose a substantial threat to the existence of functions of the political system.[73]

In the article 'Micro Movements in India: Towards a Politics of Participatory Democracy', D.L. Sheth envisages the relevance of micro-movements in the era of globalization. He argues that the global discourse on democracy has become undimensional, purveying the neo-liberal model of market democracy as the one and universally desirable model. When the Indian state begun to link itself to the vertical hierarchy of global economic and political power, strong countervailing political and social movements emerged in India at the local and regional levels. These micro-movements, led by grassroots groups of social activities, have been active in different parts of India for over three decades working on different issues, albeit all concerning struggles of the economically-marginalized and socially-excluded population of the poor. But actually in the decade of the 1990s, many of these micro-movements aligned together and formed larger alliances to protest against the Indian state on the issue of globalization, even as they got into direct confrontation with the institutions and organizations representing the global economic and political parties. In this process of opportunity for globalization, the micro-movements in India have begun to raise a new discourse on democracy and invent political practices, expanding the arena of politics much beyond the representational institutions of elections and political parties. Thus, the micro-movements have been fighting politically on several issues concerning the poor much before they joined the process of globalization; it is the challenge of globalization that has brought many of them together on common political forums at the provincial and national levels and making issues of participatory democracy a part of their ongoing struggles. This paper also analyses the discourse and politics of micro-movements and their role in reinventing participatory democracy as a form of social action and political practice, creating new spaces and infusing deeper meaning to democracy in the globalizing world. Sheth has taken several movements and tries to assess the relevance of politics of participation and democracy, and how it could be useful in strengthening and deepening of Indian democracy.[74] All these works reflect the theoretical underpinnings of democracy and people's movements in general at the national and international levels. Many of these studies look at democracy movements from the perspective of state, nation and territory. Thus, this study focuses on democracy and human rights from the perspective of rights and state.

Objectives, Scope, and Limitations of the Study

The study intends to have objectives like conceptualization of democracy, movements and human rights; assessing Indian democracy: formal and substantive; assessing movements and seeing the trends of strengthening or weakening of democracy; examining the Telangana statehood movement: its origins, issues and concerns; assessing the role of political and societal organizations in Telangana movement; focusing on Telangana people's movement and electoral politics in the region; and assessing the Telangana movement: territorial versus democratic.

The Indian state has been witnessing people's movements for a long time. Though there were movements in 1970s, they gradually started increasing from 1990s as the globalization and privatization process was initiated during this period. It is argued that the state is gradually moving away from its responsibilities and the private sector is taking over the public domain like industry, education and health sectors. This negative response of the rulers and state led to a spurt in Dalit, tribal, women, environment, student, farmers, regional and sub-regional movements. The Telangana separate statehood movement is one of them. All civil societal organizations and political parties have been debating, directly or indirectly, on this issue. A few studies argue that in the region of Telangana, a majority of the people want a separate state; hence, it is important to study the movement to understand the politics of participatory democracy in the perspective of rights of marginalized sections. This kind of study and research in political science and human rights will fill the gap and provide deeper meaning to the study.

The study on democracy, movements and human rights is not a new field in the academic world. Several studies have been done on those issues, but it is a fact that further studies on these areas need to be explored. As India's democracy is in a dilemma, its successes or failures depend on the nature of functioning of democracy. There is an in-depth debate going on among the scholars in the academic world. The Telangana People's Movement provides a vantage point. To assess Indian democracy and its formal and substantive notions, this study looks at many social concerns, commitments and, grassroots participation from all the sections. The demand of Telangana also includes the rights of Dalits, tribals, Adivasis and minorities, which helps in expanding the scope of the study. The Telangana movement is a fit case to understand even the nature of the state vis-à-vis people's assertion. In the process, the study also tries to understand the interrelation and interdependence among them, and tries to assess how grassroots movements can strive for deepening and substantialization of democracy and ultimately create human beings with human concerns. This study does not claim to have come up with definitive answers, but believes that research should be carried on in that direction. Activists who are a part of the movement have been interviewed as part of the study. To cross-check the views of the activists, the study also covers rural opinion-makers in three districts in Telangana region. In each district, one village has been selected. Public meetings, seminars and protests organized by the activists of Telangana region have also been taken note of.

Methodology

The study seeks to explore the various causes of the Telangana movement and the methods that it adopted, either as a part of the movement, or parallel to the movement. The study also seeks to evaluate the nature of the participation of both political parties and protesters. It attempts to explore whether people's movements in India strengthen and deepen democracy by bringing in the desired social change or are responsible for the growing systemic crises, leading to the crises of governability. The method for collecting information for the present study was essentially historical-analytical and, as such, exploratory in nature. Information was also collected from published books and articles on the protest movement. However, the study depends on Telugu writings, poems and media, both print and electronic. The study, to some extent, uses participatory observation, open-ended questionnaires and purposive samples to elicit the relevant information. Respondents from urban and rural Telangana have also been interviewed. This, it is hoped, would give a fairly representative view of public opinion and participation.

Notes

1. Eva Erman, *Human Rights and Democracy: Discourse Theory and Global Rights Institutions*, Ashgate Publishing Company, Burlington, 2005, p. 4.
2. Ibid.
3. Antony Birch, *The Concepts and Theories of Modern Democracy*, Routledge, London, 1993, pp. 45–46.
4. D.L. Sheth, 'The Crisis of Political Authority', in *Indian Democracy: Meanings and Practices*, edited by Suhas Palshikar and Rajendra Vora, Sage Publications, New Delhi, 2004, pp. 70–71.
5. Suhas Palshikar and Rajendra Vora (eds), *Indian Democracy: Meanings and Practices*, Sage Publications, New Delhi, 2004, p. 142.
6. Deepak Nayyar, 'On Exclusion and Inclusion: Democracy, Markets and People', in *Development Economics and Structuralist Macroeconomics*, edited by A.K. Dutt and J. Ros, Edward Elgar, Cheltenham, 2003, pp. 94–106.
7. Ghanshyam Shah, *Social Movements in India*, Sage Publications, New Delhi, 2004, pp. 26–27.
8. M.N. Karna, *Democracy, Pluralism and Conflict*, Rawat Publications, Jaipur, 2006, p. 11.
9. O.P. Gouba, *Introduction to Political Theory*, Macmillan Publications, New Delhi, 1981, p. 445.
10. Ibid.
11. H.P. Chattopadhyay and S.K. Sarkar, *Global Encyclopedia of Political Sciences*, Vol. 2, Global Asian Publications, Calcutta, 2006, pp. 683–84.
12. Adam Kuper and Jessica Kuper, *The Social Sciences Encyclopedia*, Routledge, London, 1985, pp. 314–15.
13. Ibid.
14. Manas Chakrabarty and Ruchita Chakrabarty, 'Human Rights and Indian Democracy', in *Democracy and Human Rights*, edited by Anil Bhuimali, Serial Publications, New Delhi, 2007, pp. 53–54.

15. Adam Kuper and Jessica Kuper, op. cit.
16. Prakash C. Sarangi, *Liberal Theories of Rights*, Post Graduation Diploma in Human Rights Material (PGDHRM), Centre for Distance Education, University of Hyderabad, 1992, pp. 106–08.
17. Kodandaram A. Reddy, *Human Rights: View of Karl Marx*, PGDHRM, Hyderabad, 1992, p. 126.
18. Ibid., p. 130.
19. Howard Davis, *Political Freedom: Associations, Political Purposes and the Law*, Continuum Publications, New York, 2000, pp. 1–2.
20. G. Haragopal and B. Jagannatham, 'Terrorism and Human Rights: Indian Experience with Repressive Laws', *Economic and Political Weekly*, Vol. XLIV, No. 28, July 2009, p. 77.
21. Ibid., p. 76.
22. G. Haragopal, *Political Economy of Human Rights: Emerging Dimensions*, Himalaya Publications, Bombay, 1992, p. 4.
23. Ibid.
24. Eric Hobsbawm, *The Age of Revolution: 1789–1848*, Vintage Books, New York, 1996.
25. John Charvet and Elisa Kaczynska-Nay, *The Liberal Project and Human Rights: The Theory and Practice of a New World Order*, Cambridge University Press, Cambridge, 2008, pp. 83–93.
26. Ibid.
27. Mahendra P. Singh, 'Human Rights in Indian Tradition: An Alternative Model', *NUJS Law Review*, Vol. 11, No. 2, 2009, pp. 148–75.
28. Ibid.
29. Amartya Sen, *Argumentative Indian: Writings on Indian Culture, History and Identity*, Penguin Books, London, 2005, p. 9.
30. Ibid., pp. 6–10.
31. Ibid., pp. 10–11.
32. Ibid., p. 15.
33. Ibid., p. 17.
34. Ibid., p. 25.
35. Ibid., p. 132.
36. Ibid., p. 26.
37. Ibid., pp. 27–30.
38. Ibid., pp. 287–88.
39. T.S.N. Sastry, *India and Human Rights: Reflections*, Concept Publications, New Delhi, 2005, pp. 41–43.

40. K. Murali, *Civil Liberties Movement during Freedom Struggle*, PGDHRM, Hyderabad, 2005, pp. 7–10.
41. T.S.N. Sastry, op. cit., pp. 41–43.
42. Ibid.
43. Ibid.
44. Rajeev Bhargava, 'Democratic Vision of a New Republic', in *Transforming India: Social and Political Dynamics of Democracy*, edited by Zoya Hasan, Oxford University Press, New Delhi, 2000, pp. 26–59.
45. Javeed Alam, *Who Wants Democracy?*, Orient Longman Publications, New Delhi, 2004, p. 8.
46. Ibid.
47. Ibid., p. x.
48. Ibid., p. 9.
49. Ibid., p. 10.
50. Ibid.
51. Francine R. Frankel, *India's Political Economy 1947–2004*, 2nd edition, Oxford University Press, New Delhi, 2005, p. 4.
52. Javeed Alam, op. cit., p. 6.
53. Ibid., p. 6–7.
54. Ibid.
55. Ibid., pp. 22–23.
56. Rajat Ganguly, 'Democracy and Ethnic Conflict', in *The State of India's Democracy*, edited by Sumit Ganguly and Marc F. Plattner, Johns Hopkins University Press, Baltimore, 2007, p. 50.
57. Ibid., p. 57.
58. Ibid.
59. Ibid.
60. Ibid., pp. 20–21.
61. Niraja Gopal Jayal, 'The Role of Civil Society', in *The State of India's Democracy*, edited by Sumit Ganguly and Larry Diamond, Oxford University Press, New York, 2009, pp. 143–44.
62. Ibid.
63. C.B. Macpherson, *Democratic Theory: Essays in Retrieval*, Clarendon Press, Oxford, 1973.
64. Barrington Moore, *Social Origins of Dictatorship and Democracy: Lord and Peasant in Making Modern World*, Penguin, Harmondsworth, 1979.
65. D.N. Dhanagare, 'Civil Society, State and Democracy: Contextualizing a Discourse', in *Civil Society: Issues and Perspectives*, edited by N. Jayaram, Sage Publications, New Delhi, 2005.

66. James C. Scott, *Weapons of the Weak*, Oxford University Press, Delhi, 1990.
67. Marc Williams, 'Contesting Global Governance: Multilateral Economic Institutions and Global Social Movements', in *Transitional Social Movements and Global Politics*, edited by J. Smith, C. Chatfield and R. Pagnucco, Syracuse University Press, Syracuse, 1997.
68. Amartya Sen, 'Democracy and its Global Roots', *The New Repubiic*, 6 October 2003.
69. Jean Dreze, 'Dr Ambedkar and the Future of Indian Democracy', *Indian Journal of Human Rights*, Vol. 9, Nos 1–2, 2005, pp. 1–9.
70. Suhas Palshikar and Rajendra Vora (eds), op. cit.
71. Ibid.
72. Rajni Kothari, *Rethinking Democracy,* Orient Longman Publications, New Delhi, 2005.
73. Mohammad Yasin and Srinanda Dasgupta, *Indian Politics: Protests and Movements*, Anmol Publications, New Delhi, 2003.
74. D.L. Sheth, 'Globalization and New Politics of Micro Movements', *Economic and Political Weekly,* Vol. 39, No. 39, January–February 2004, pp. 47–59.

2 Interrogating Democracy and Human Rights

The previous chapter tried to give an overall view of democracy, development and rights by analysing the evolution of rights from a historical perspective. To contextualize those concepts, this chapter tries to comprehend the essence of people's movements and their impact on democracy. It is intended to focus on the theoretical concepts of liberal democracy, human rights, development and their interconnection. It attempts to see the notion of democracy in a critical manner. Therefore, it focuses on Bentham's utilitarianism and Rawlsian theory of justice to assess the concept of individual and collectivity. This study further analyses several perspectives of democracies: liberal, feminist and neo-liberal. It also focuses on human rights, their evolution and the human rights movement in India, its prospects and challenges as these perspectives fit to provide a deeper meaning to the rights discourse.

Before contextualizing the concepts of democracy and human rights, it is necessary to look at their interconnection and interdependence: both have historically been regarded as distinct concerns, occupying different areas of the political sphere: one a matter of organization of government, the other, a question of individual rights and their defence. When one speaks of democracy, one has to think of institutional arrangements such as periodic elections, multi-party system, separation of powers and independent judiciary. These are essentially matters of constitutional order, the organization of public power. Human rights, on the other hand, take the individuals as their points of reference and ensure to guarantee individuals the minimum necessary conditions for freedom to pursue one's own interests. Moreover, as the term 'human rights' implies, such rights have always been defined as universal in their scope and subject to international definition and regulation, whereas the constitutional arrangements of government have traditionally been regarded as entirely an internal matter of the sovereign state. One has to explore the possibilities of stitching them together. It is often said that democracy is the system of government 'most likely' to defend human rights, while democracy needs to be 'supplemented' by human rights. The core idea of democracy is that of popular control over collective decision-making. Its starting point is with the citizen, rather than with the institutions of government. Its defining principles are that all citizens are entitled to participate in public affairs through the associations of civil society and through participation in government, and that this entitlement should be available on terms of equality to all. Control by citizens over their collective affairs and equality between citizens, in the exercise of that control, are basic to any democratic system.[1]

It is understood that civil and political rights constitute an integral part of democracy and without them no liberal democracy can be thought of. The absence of freedom of speech, association, assembly and movement would make elections a farce, rendering any political control over government impossible. Economic and social rights complete the notion of democracy. The widespread absence of economic and social rights leads to erosion of civil and political equality and the quality of life, which may endanger viability of democratic institutions themselves. Democracy, on the other hand, constitutes a necessary, if not sufficient, condition for the protection of economic and social rights. The defence of cultural rights, finally, in the context of multi-cultural societies, requires a re-evaluated conception of democracy and its procedures. Democracy in the contemporary age has to be understood not merely as political democracy, but social and pluralist democracy as well.[2]

Human rights constitute an intrinsic part of democracy, because guarantee of basic freedom is a necessary condition for people's voice to be effective in public affairs, and also to secure popular control over government. There are still deeper levels through which democracy and human rights are connected and that is in the assumptions about human nature on which their justification is founded. The philosophical justification for the human rights agenda is based on an identification of the needs and capacities common to all humans, whatever may be the differences between them; in particular, the so-called liberty rights to personal freedom, to the freedom of thought and conscience. Democratic rights presuppose the same capacity in matters affecting the common or collective life. The right to vote or to stand for public office assumes the capacity to take part in deliberations about the public, as well as one's private interests.[3] Ramashray Roy argues that the idea of democracy and its expression in certain political institutions and practices today has taken definite shape though not all at once. These institutions and practices have developed over a long historical time spanning over about 2,500 years. This long span of time has been marked, in many ways, by evolution and revolutions. They have affected rather profoundly the process of development of political ideas, institutions and practices. The changes occurring in the process of history meant succession of one historical era by another. The changes in the historical era one after another brought to the fore certain forces that, in turn, deeply influenced the core ideas of democracy as it had developed in the Greek city-states in the 5th century BC. This core idea was transformed through the process of segmentation and accretion. This means, first, that certain fundamental aspects of the democratic idea integral to Greek democracy were either dropped or modified beyond recognition. Second, certain other ideas appearing in different historical eras were added to the core idea of Greek democracy. The modern idea of democracy and its institutional expression are a result of this process of segmentation and accretion.[4] Hence, it is necessary to define democracy.

Defining democracy as a rule by the people may sound innocently straightforward, but it immediately raises a number of complex issues. Who are to be considered 'the people'? What kind of participation is envisaged for them? What conditions are assumed to be conducive to participation? How broad or narrow is the scope of rule to be construed? If rule is to cover the political, what does this mean? It readily appears that a discussion on democracy must involve not only the theory about possible ways of organizing rule by the people, but also the philosophy about what ought to be (that is, the best way of forming a government) and an understanding of the practical experiences with the ways in which government has been organized in different societies at different times.[5]

Arthur MacEwan viewed democracy as the basis for economic development, along with political democracy. Political democracy is usually understood as elections, civil liberties and the right to organize. But beyond these essential forms of democracy (formal), there is something more: substantial democracy, which enables people to participate in decisions about the effective exercise of political power over their economic lives. A democratic strategy also believes that benefits of development should go to the population generally and thereby enhance their power. As economic growth increases, goods and services increase and are available to people. It also involves something more important, like the basic standard of living of a great majority of the people, equal distribution of income, the maintenance and strengthening of social community about political, social and economic affairs.[6] To contextualize the term further, it is a prerequisite to emphasize on approaches and perspectives to the notion of democracy.

Different Approaches to Democracy

To understand democracy, the approaches to democracy need to be analysed. There are broadly three approaches. One could be external and instrumental approach or political approach. It asks: what are the properties of this kind of political regime? How does it arise and maintain itself? This approach exists in several variants and concentrates on an existing designated set of concrete institutions, mechanisms and political structures, and investigates various properties. The second approach focuses not on such relatively instrumental advantages, but on the purportedly inherent normal superiority of democratic procedures. It has become a part of the common phenomenon of adulatory self-description on the part of 'democracies'. Moral right, would make a person free and self-legislating and avoid such dependence on the will of others. The only way to avoid such dependence on a complex society is by a process in which people institute self-legislating political systems. Democracy deserves moral approval as in a democracy, the people have the political power and they form a self-legislating community by themselves. The third approach to democracy, pioneered by John Dewey, is one which comes in the modern period. This approach emphasizes the epistemological significance of democracy as a form of organization of collective action. Among these three approaches, two deal with the inherent superiority based on democratic procedure and the last approach with the institutional and mechanical aspects, with a focus on the collective action of association.[7]

Concept of Democracy: Different Perspectives

Joseph Schumpeter formulated the narrow concept of democracy. For him, democracy was simply a political method and a mechanism for choosing political leadership. The citizens are given a choice among rival political leaders competing for their votes. After the elections, those who get elected will take part in the decision-making. If people are not satisfied with the performance of their representatives, they can replace then in the next elections. This ability of choosing the leaders among the contestants in elections is characterized as democracy. In Schumpeter's words, 'the democratic method is that institutional arrangement for arriving at political decisions in which individuals acquire the power to decide by means of competitive struggles for the people's vote'. At the opposite end of the spectrum, we have a comprehensive notion of democracy suggested by David Held, who combined insights of the liberal and Marxist traditions in order to arrive at a meaning of democracy that supports a basic principle of autonomy. He called it democratic autonomy, that requires both a high degree of accountability of the state and a democratic reordering of civil society. It foresees substantial direct participation in local community institutions, as well as self-management of cooperatively-owned enterprises. It calls for a Bill of Rights that goes beyond the right to cast a vote, to include equal opportunity for participation and for discovering individual preferences, as well as citizens' final control of the political agenda. It also includes the social and economic rights to ensure adequate resources for democratic autonomy. George Sorenson argues that 'without social and economic rights, rights with respect to the state could not be fully enjoyed; and without state, new forms of inequality of power, wealth and status could systematically disrupt the implementation of social and economic liberties'. The narrow notion of political democracy suggested by Schumpeter, and the extremely comprehensive understanding, presented by David Held, lie in the debate about what democracy is and what it ought to be. In a narrow concept of democracy, it is just about political but in the comprehensive concept, it is not only political but social and economic.[8]

A contribution by Robert A. Dahl is helpful in defining democracy as a political system. He emphasized the responsiveness of the government to the preferences of its citizens, and considered them as political equals. In his view, it is a key characteristic of democracy. Such responsiveness requires that citizens must have opportunities to formulate their preferences, signify their preferences to their fellow citizens and the government by individual and collective action, and have their preferences weighed equally in the conduct of the government. These three opportunities, in turn, are dependent on the following institutional guarantees: freedom to form and join associations, freedom of expression, right to vote, eligibility for public office, and right of political leaders to compete for votes, and free and fair elections. Policy-making of government always depends on people's expression of preferences through the voting. When these conditions are met, it could be argued that we have a political democracy. Based on their argument, it is understood that Schumpeter promoted political democracy, whereas David Held emphasized not only political, but also socio-economic democracy, as well as for participatory, inclusive and creative democracy. Out of these perceptions, the study intends to take David Held's principles as the basis to understand the people's participation or people's movements in democratic culture. In formulating of policies, people's involvement is necessary.[9] Robert Dahl has stated that modern corporate capitalism tends to 'produce inequalities in social and economic resources so great as to bring about severe violations of political equality and hence, of the democratic process.' This view of the need to extend democratic decision-making beyond government, to economic and social life assumes considerable importance.[10]

Democracy can also be understood as a procedure for taking decisions in any group, association or society, whereby all members have an equal right to say and express their opinions. It encourages collective decisions at any level, from the smallest group to society as a whole. Sometimes members may disagree with each other. Hence, procedure or decisional rules are required to determine how such disagreements should be resolved, and who is allowed to take part in doing so. In most associational life, throughout human history, the vast majority of those affected by collective decisions have been excluded from any participation in them. Decisions have been preserved by a very few people like the wisest, the oldest, the wealthiest, an expert, or physically strong to coerce the rest. As forms of societal rule or government, these examples of rule by a few have carried distinctive names such as aristocracy, meritocracy, oligarchy, and so on. And where decisions have been the preserve of a single individual, the system has historically been called a monarchy. With this kind of democracy, there is no scope for individual liberty, no scope for association, and no scope for public meetings, debates and discussions. Politicians maintain silence they are involved in corruption. In contrast to these, democracy involves the principle that all members of an association should have to take part equally in the decisions that affect them. Hence, it could be the only solution that people want to choose participatory democracy, wherein a democratic culture can be brought to create an ideal society.[11]

David Beetham proposes key ideas of democracy: one, all members have interests that are affected by collective decisions; two, everyone (adults) is capable of taking a view about what the best or least bad decision would be, both for themselves and for the association as a whole; three, the best decisions over the long run will be ones where all such views have been publicly debated; four, where debate and discussion fail to produce a single agreed outcome, decisions should be taken by a vote of all participating members; five, the principle of 'one person, one vote, and one value' reflects a wider conception that all persons are of equal worth.[12] He also argues that ancient Athens and its democratic allies in cities provided two key features which have been an inspiration to democrats/democratic states ever since. The first was an effective example of a popular assembly, in which ordinary citizens debate, decide laws, enact and implement the policies for their society. Other democratic practices include the rotation of the citizens in turn, selected by a group to serve on an executive body or council and of people who control their own common affairs and survived for a century and a half. He also demonstrates that public debate and disagreement were not incompatible with effective policy or decisive collective action. A second exemplary feature of Athenian democracy was the strong defence and where every individual, including poor people, are capable as the well-to-do of deliberating and voting on issues of public policy. Supporters of direct democracy argued that a capacity for moral awareness and recognition of the public interest were common to all citizens as members of society and they shall not examine the sphere of any special experts.[13] Macpherson argues that democracy in its original sense is rule by the people or government in accordance with the will of the people. He further argues that most of the backward countries were in colonial backing to liberal democratic states, and it was assumed that before being granted independence, they were to be brought along to the point where they would run themselves on liberal democratic lines. True, one substantial part of the world had rejected the liberal democratic way as early as 1917, with the Russian Revolution and the formation of the Soviet Union.[14]

To defend his argument, Macpherson proposes three points: first, democracy is not properly to be equated with unique Western liberal democracy, but there are liberal systems which prevail in the non-liberal systems of most of the underdeveloped countries of Asia and Africa; second, liberal democracy is a system of power; third, liberal-democracy and capitalism go together but it is not such in non-liberal states. It is maintained that liberal democracy is found only in countries whose economic system is wholly or predominantly that of capitalist enterprise. He said at the beginning that until about a 100 years ago, democracy was a bad thing, that in the next 50 years it became a good thing, and that in another 50 years it has become an ambiguous thing. He also held that the current non-liberal systems have some historical title to call themselves democracies. In Western societies, the democratic franchise did not take place until after the liberal society was formed. The liberal state was firmly established and democracy came as a top dressing. It had to accommodate itself to the soil that had already been prepared by the operation of the competitive, individualist, market society, and by the operation of the liberal state, which served that society through a system of freely competing though not democratic political parties. In the process, he said democracy was liberalized. That is one change in the nature of democracy but in the rest of the world – Soviet countries and other newly independent underdeveloped states – democracy came as a revolution against the liberal capitalist society and state.[15]

Liberal democracy has conceded that civil society organizations play an important role. It is conventionally accepted that a strong civil society keeps elected representatives on their toes, and does so through organized interest groups, all of whom press their causes on government, sometimes through political parties, sometimes through independent lobbies. Sometimes certain special interest groups – most notably unions and business groups, but locally also residents or voluntary sector organizations – have been drawn into corporatist arrangements with government, gaining a special political status so that the government negotiates with them over decisions affecting their interests. This sort of deal, however, has often undermined the credibility of both groups: the non-governmental organizations are seen as both too close to government and as pursuing their own special interests; the government is seen as favouring one group or two groups against others, or organized interests against 'the people'. One of the frustrations and flaws of representative democracy is that while civil society has grown in size and developed in terms of structures and internally democratic forms, it has remained marginalized in its impact on the formal political system. In contrast, participatory democracy provides a real alternative, or complement, to elected power: a distinct and organized public sphere in which the demands of the people can be articulated, developed and negotiated between each other, and finally negotiated with the local or other relevant state institutions.[16]

Collective Action and Individual Choice

David Beetham looked at the notion of collective action and individual choice to understand the very notion of democracy. The distinction between collective and individual is central to contextualize what democracy is about. Individual choice is defined as a 'consumer demand' or 'consumer democracy'. It is certainly a form of power, but it could be that such 'democracy is a misnomer'. It is characterized by enormous inequalities in wealth and power sharing, and political equality as the power is based on individual and private, rather than collective public. Consumer decisions are self-oriented, but not collective voices. It is true that the sum of individuals' decisions may produce a collective good but certainly not collective decisions, which involve discussions, debates and democratic voices. It is argued that it is always the powerful, wealthiest and socially privileged individuals who influence public policies, whereas collective decisions could be taken by a group for a group or society as a whole. Generally, with agreement/disagreement it is quite possible to come up with a good decision/policy. It involves discussion, argument, the demands for evidence and the need for an agreed method to arriving at the decisions. All these processes are necessary to democratize the state and civil society.[17] The members who enjoy power in a democracy are either elected through electoral politics, or could be selected directly to take part in the policy-making. Both can contribute and influence the decision-making. This usually requires joining with like-minded others to make their choice and vote more effectively.[18] Based on these interpretations on collective and individual, David Beetham argues that among individual and collective notions, the notion of collective represents the democratic voice whereas the notion of individual represents the domain of private interests. He posits that because of their interests, the bourgeois class, disadvantaged classes/castes, and proletariat always face problems. It results in a spurt in people's struggles. As a domain, the notion of collective reflects the democratic notion of equality and justice as it is based on the principles of equality among the citizens. It values the vote in association; the right to contest and to hold elected representatives accountable for their decisions. This logic is even equally applicable to small local associations and to the government.[19] Consumer democracy deals with the individual choice or a few elite and wealthiest individuals and electoral politics deals with conventional participation. Hence to comprehend democracy, it needs to assess the politics of participation to deepen democracy effectively.[20]

Liberal Democracy

It is imperative to distinguish between liberalism and democracy. Friedrich von Hayek makes a sharp distinction between liberalism and democracy. He calls the former a doctrine about what the law ought to be and the latter a doctrine about what will be the law. Democracy is an old concept, whereas liberalism is of recent origin. Today, liberalism is generally thought to be inseparable from democracy. The highest political end is liberty, which can be achieved only if there are strict limits on the activities of governments. George Sorenson believes that government intervention in civil society must aim at protecting life, liberty and estate and intervention should create the best possible framework for redistributive measures as they facilitate free market. In this view, democracy is desirable as a mechanism for securing the majority support. However, the democratic majorities respect the limitations on government activity. If they do not, democracy will be in conflict. Democracy can be a means of achieving this end, but is not the end itself. If there is a democratic core in this way of thinking, it is the principle of the political equality of citizens. This is central and positive to democracy.[21]

The term 'democracy' is applied to indicate 'liberalism'. It represents a combination of free market economy with universal adult franchise. It is an attempt to resolve the conflicting claims of the capitalists and the masses by making gradual concessions under the umbrella or garb of a welfare state. Liberal democracy is distinguished from other forms of political system based on certain principles and characteristics, which essentially include procedural and institutional arrangements for the realization of principles.[22] Liberal democracy works on certain mechanisms. Broadly, it includes government by consent, public accountability, majority rule, recognition of minority rights, constitutional government and political parties getting power through elections. Rational consent of the people can be obtained by opinion and an atmosphere of free discussion, which is essential for any regime where the consent of the people is to be obtained without freedom of expression of divergent opinions. Liberal democracy is based on the consent of the people and must constantly remain answerable to the people who created it.[23] But it is argued by many Indian scholars that though Indian democracy consists of a constitutional mechanism recognizing minority rights, it has not been implemented substantially. The responsibility and accountability are also lacking in reality. Hence, many scholars criticize the liberal notion of democracy. To comprehend the notion of liberal democracy, it is crucial to figure out the thoughts of liberal philosophers.

Liberal Thinkers and Evolution of Rights

Hobbes viewed that the idea that human beings have rights was clearly articulated when the medieval mould was broken in the 17th century. During the decade of 1640s, England was not merely known for its wars between adherents of different religions and political constitutions, but it was also recognized by widespread misery because of high food prices, rents, taxes, unemployment, and landlessness. With the demise of feudalism, the property rights of the landed gentry had become absolutized. Aristotle cautioned that it is the responsibility of property holders to share property with those who are in need. The 'masterless men' of the 17th century found themselves in a situation in which others were no longer recognizing them or their needs in a very nasty world. Rights claims were at once an expression of suffering and agony and the reminder of the obligations that they have to extend to each other as a certain kind of social recognition. With the breaking up of the feudal pattern of recognition, human beings increasingly were conceived as individualists. They were free, in the sense of being released from the bonds of compulsion and recognition with a master. But since the former master continued to hold on to the property and wealth that had been built on the labour of the serfs, those freed serfs were as vulnerable as the slaves who were freed after the American Civil War.[24]

Hobbes was committed to central and absolute political power. While he would accept political power being centralized in a legislature, his primary objective was to get out of this hellish state into which the security of individuals could be guaranteed, or at least maximized. From the very nature of an individual in a state of nature who experienced pain and pleasure, Hobbes drew the lesson that the worst pain of the individual is the threat of termination, and the greatest pleasure is its preservation. From this argument, he concluded that everyone has, by virtue of his inherent nature, the right to life. As he maintained, every individual who is naturally antagonistic must come together and agree to obey his/her sovereign power.[25] Locke expanded the realm of rights. He added the rights of liberty, property and limited constitutional government with a preferably monarchical and centralized government. His theory of rights also included two other important issues. First, the extent of political rights and the second that of individualism and its economic implications. Locke advocated parliamentary supremacy. A fundamental right would be the right to participate in the election to the legislature as a voter or candidate and was given for propertied class, but not property-less class. Hence, he thought that the property-less class do not express their franchise effectively. This fundamental political right of judging legitimacy turns out not to be a human right, but rather the right of a particular section of population. While Hobbes ties rights to individual physical security, Locke ties them to both physical security and individual property rights. Rousseau ties rights to two conceptions that were to be given prominence during the French Revolution, that were equality and fraternity.[26] John Locke says the government acts as a 'trustee' of the power vested in it by the people for the protection of their natural rights like right to life, liberty and property; he also held that people must not trust the government fully and should remain constantly vigilant.[27]

Rousseau argues that there is no property in nature but there is only possession. He considered possession is a physical fact. The strongest or the fastest might possess something more than others, because of his/her qualities. He argued that these qualities are immoral and said nothing about the 'right' of possessors to whatever is possessed. So, Rousseau argues that this is one of the reasons that people of the state of nature enter into a social contract. So that people can have property rather than mere possessions, so that the state and its citizens will recognize and protect what they legitimately possess. Rousseau tries to mediate between the right of the individual to property and the rights of other individuals and the claims of the collectivity itself. Rousseau thus tries to mediate between the collectivity and the individual. He is unequivocal that 'every man has naturally a right to everything he needs for his subsistence'. On the other, he insists that right to property, as well as political rights, are civil rights in that they both must be determined and protected by the collectivity for the general interest. Thus, he argued there could be no liberty without a large measure of both political and economic equality.[28]

John Stuart Mill sees democracy as an important element in free human development. Participation in political life could lead towards the 'highest and harmonious expansion of individual capacities'. He also shared one of the basic assumptions of protective democracy: that the maximum freedom of citizens requires a limitation on the scope of the state's activity. He envisaged representative government in combination with a free-market economy. Thus, J.S. Mill is in favour of certain restrictions on the scope of government and governmental activity. With regard to enfranchisement, J.S. Mill recommends a system of plural voting in order to give the 'wiser and more talented' votes than 'the ignorant and less able' people. He does not support universal franchise. He was more democratic as he sees participation in the political process as a way to liberty and self-development and he directly confronted with a number of inequalities in mid-19th century. He severely criticizes the subjection of women and pointed to the need for complete equality between the sexes as a precondition for human development and democracy. He is also highly critical of the extreme inequalities of income, wealth and power which hindered the human development of lower classes.[29]

Jeremy Bentham envisages liberal democracy as political machinery that would ensure the accountability of the governors to govern. For Bentham, human beings want to maximize their happiness. So, he opines, to fulfil their wants, the government is responsible to make them (people) happy. He also emphasizes on the recognition of minority rights in a democratic state and for implementation of this, he considers legal safeguards as essential for the realization of their rights, because its presence helps to raise the level of awareness of both majority and minority, so that it promotes a conducive climate for democratic politics.[30] C.B. Macpherson observed that till the 19th century, liberal theory like the liberal state was not at all democratic, and much of its principles were specifically anti-democratic. Classical liberal theory was committed to the individual's right to unlimited acquisition of property and to the capitalist market economy that implies inequality not only in economic sphere, but also in the political sphere. Thus, classical liberalism of the 18th and 19th centuries insisted on property qualification for the right to vote. It also encouraged capitalism and a free-market economy that was responsible for a large working class centred in large industrialized cities and forced to live in sub-human conditions created by a cruel and competitive economy. Thus, the labour was forced to take recourse to democratic principles in order to preserve their own existence.[31]

Liberalism developed in opposition to the medieval hierarchical institutions, the despotic monarchies whose claim to powerful rule rested on the assertion that they enjoyed divine support. Liberalism attacked the old system on two fronts; first, the liberals fought for a rollback of state power and the creation of a civil society where social relations, including private business, non-state institutions, family and personal life, could evolve without state interference. Second, liberalism was the claim that state power was based not on natural or supernatural rights, but on the will of the sovereign people. Ultimately, this claim would lead to demands for democracy – that is, for the creation of mechanisms of representation that assured that those who held state power enjoyed popular support in a sense that the development of liberal democratic thinking evolved around the setting up of the complex relationship between these two elements.[32] Apart from these liberal thoughts, C.B. Macpherson saw democracy in a different way.

C.B. Macpherson has summarized liberal democracy in four different models: protective, developmental, equilibrium and participatory democracy. The earliest model of democracy, derived around 1828, builds on contributions from Jeremy Bentham and James Mill. Macpherson called it protective democracy because of the model's preoccupation with protection of citizens from government and its attempts to ensure that governments would pursue policies in accordance with the interests of citizens as a whole. The way to such protection was seen as universal franchise. The vote gave political power; 'one person, one vote' provided self-protection because the rulers could be removed. In practice, however, Bentham and Mill were willing to accept severe restrictions on the right to vote; women and large sections of the working classes did not enjoy this privilege. Their cause was more liberal than democratic: the aim was to restrict the sphere of politics, especially that of governmental activity and institutions.[33] Developmental democracy is non-extractive. It is non-extractive in that it does not depend upon the continued existence of class-based power relationships. By developmental, Macpherson means that the theory implies the expansion of a person's power to use his ability to develop his supposedly essential human capabilities. These include a person's capacity for moral judgment of action. Developmental democratic theory requires not the maximization of individual utilities, but rather the ability of each to use and develop those capabilities, the use of which does not prevent others from using theirs. Equilibrium democracy refers to political inequalities that are understandable like inequalities in purchasing power. This model lacks the ethical dimension of the previous one and offers a description and justification 'of a stable democracy' as a 'competition between elites which produces equilibrium without much popular participation'. Democracy, according to this model, is 'simply a mechanism for choosing and authorizing government', not a kind of society or a set of moral ends. Macpherson discusses the ways in which direct democracy could occur in large states. He advocates an ideal democratic model consistent with the socialist notion of property. He proposes a participatory system, with direct participation at the base, at the level of neighbourhood and workplace, constituting the ground for indirect 'pyramidal' representation at higher levels. With this framework, parties would compete, although in the future they might be replaced by 'other representative groups'. It gives scope for a sense of community that is necessary for participatory democracy. According to him, participatory democracy is a process of collective decision-making that combines elements from both direct and representative democracy. Citizens have the ultimate power to decide on policy and politicians assume the role of policy implementation.[34]

Liberal Democracy: Feministic Critique

Spike Peterson, one of the prominent feminist writers, argued that scientific developments of the 16th and 17th centuries profoundly affected liberal thought and practice, and 'human nature' as articulated in the liberal tradition as Cartesian mind and body dualism. The feminist perspective explains the notions of abstract and concrete and degradation of women in theory and practical grounds and considers women as the notion of private. Human nature, as described and discovered by philosophers such as Aristotle, Aquinas, Machiavelli, Locke, Rousseau, Hegel, and many others, is intended to refer only to male human nature. Even Emmanuel Kant's moral agents and rational beings refer to the male. Feminist scholars argued that liberal philosophy considered that women lack these humanly essential characteristics. Liberalism, Marxism and other theories and philosophies considered the domestic work of women, giving birth and rearing children as the private sphere, apolitical, devalued and ineffective and the experience of women was not considered as the experience of men. Additionally, the liberal patriarchal worldview has ensured that women's life activities continue to be primarily defined through androcentric lens. Women were considered as abstract and men's activities as concrete and the contribution of men was considered as public, valued, effective, political in the liberal philosophy. These negative approaches, in terms of theory and practice, gave the scope to feminist scholars to build the movements against both theory and practice. This approach is a reflection of feminist consciousness to participate in people's struggles and public life across the world by the women activists. Indian democracy is not exceptional to this critique.[35]

Understanding John Rawls' Theory of Justice

Rawls' philosophy has been guided by the question: 'what is the most appropriate moral conception of justice for a democratic society?' He tried to pursue this question as a part of an inquiry into the nature of social justice and its compatibility with human nature and the well-being of human beings. Rawls aimed at restoring the predominance of utilitarianism in modern moral philosophy. As an alternative to utilitarianism, Rawls developed the tradition of social contract that widens the conception of justice. According to this conception, justice requires individual liberty and distributive justice is closely associated with this principle of equal basic liberties. The first principle is that of equal basic liberties, which include conscience, freedom of thought, freedom of association, the rights and liberties that define the freedom and integrity of the person (freedom of movement, occupation and choice of careers and a right to personal property). It also includes equal political rights and liberties ensured by rule of law. They are morally more significant to the freedoms of democratic citizens. He believed that the basic liberties are necessary for pursuing a wide range of conceptions of good. These are essential to the exercise and development of the moral powers. They are liberty, opportunity, income and wealth, and the basis of self-respect to be equally distributed. To elaborate his theory, he developed two principles. The principles of justice require that certain important liberties be provided equally for all, and that these 'basic' liberties have priority over aggregate social welfare and perfectionist values. That fair (not just formal) opportunity is to be provided equally to all citizens without considering differences in income and wealth and in social positions, those benefits should reach maximally to the worst-off members of society.[36] Rawls, in his 'Theory of Distributive Justice', argues that all individuals in society should enjoy liberty or freedom equally, which means even the servant, driver and maid are equal owners of liberty. Secondly, his theory points out that inequalities in the social structure can be justified only if inequalities benefit the lowest person in society. Rawls also elucidates that no person has the right to a larger portion of the pie than another. Even if one born rich is exceptionally talented, he/she can't enjoy his/her benefits unless the lowest person in society is benefiting from the same. Entrepreneurs are given better rights than their employees only to make sure that standards of life of the labouring class are improved. In other words, everybody should be better off in the process. But what we see is the opposite of that, which means that even the system of distributive justice is not operational. What we see is the rich becoming richer and the poor becoming poorer. Governments in democratic societies are supposed to provide equal opportunities for the less privileged.[37]

Any democratic country should have a just Constitution ensuring equal liberty and equal citizenship. The government guarantees a social minimum which the government meets by family allowances and special payments in times of unemployment or a negative income tax. The government has to be divided into four branches. For instance, the allocation branch, which keeps the economy competitive, disallowing unreasonable market power, regulating prices for social benefits and costs. The second branch is the stabilization branch, which guarantees full employment, free choice of occupation and proper deployment of finance in the face of existing demand. The third branch, the transfer branch, takes care of ensuring the social minimum, establishing a certain level of well-being. The fourth branch, the distribution branch, takes care of the just distribution of income and wealth, including taxation on inheritance and for raising revenue. The inheritance of greater wealth is justified, as long as it is to the advantage of the worst-off.[38]

Rawls has sought to work out a realistic ideal of justice. His conception of ideal is designed for the ideal conditions of a 'well-ordered society' where reasonable persons are free and equal. He argues that human beings are capable of it, given their nature, under normal conditions of social life. Rawls seeks to discover the fundamental moral principles that regulate reasoning and judgments about justice and the principles that presuppose these are deeply implicit in ordinary moral awareness and is evidenced by moral judgments. He does not suppose that principles of justice are based on 'pure practical reason' alone, but human nature and the empirical conditions within which practical reason is normally exercised are relevant to discover and justify principles of justice on certain psychological tendencies of human nature and own capacities for sociability. This explains Rawls' emphasis on the 'stability', or feasibility, of a moral conception of justice.[39] He argues that basic liberties should reach maximally to the worst-off members of the societies. If these basic liberties do not reach the vulnerable sections, there is a possibility of people's struggles in the democratic society for their basic rights and liberties. Governments in equal democratic societies are supposed to provide equal opportunities for the less privileged. This means, like in America, the Indian state governments should provide cheaper education for the lower classes. Institutions and organizations are not supposed to choose better educated, talented youth, unless the least educated and most invaluable candidate is benefited.

The feminist scholarship and Rawlisian notion of justice offer a powerful critique of the classical liberal theory and their conception of democracy. The assumption that the individual is autonomous and self-seeking does not apply to a woman as her life is inter-dependent. And the notion of private in the concept of liberty is more a means to remove the family and relations within the family from public and collective scrutiny. These assumptions and arrangements are more male-centric than universal. The liberal theory also falls short on the notion of justice in terms of equitable distribution of benefits and resources. Therefore, democracy for Rawls is concern for the weakest in the society. It is on these lines that Marx would build the logic but locate the cause in the class divisions of the society. Marx holds that inequalities are intrinsic to a capitalist society and the only way humankind can eliminate inequalities is to overthrow the class 'enemies' through people's struggles.

Ambedkar's Understanding of Democracy

Ambedkar, in his writings on 'annihilation of caste', argues that, without social efficiency, no permanent progress in their fields of activity is possible. Hence, he argues that social reform should carry on political reform. In the name of customs, Dalits and other marginalized sections of the society have suffered in all fields like education, health, property, and status, etc. Ambedkar argues that the state shall take the responsibility to empower those sections as they suffered in the name of caste and customs. Ambedkar argues that 'economic' property is the source of power, but that economic source is not enough as both the social status and property are the sources of power. Hence, he argues that all the deprived communities should develop in all these spheres. Socialists ignored the problem of social order in the society, whereas Ambedkar's high priority was social order and that it has to be equalized. According to him, social order should be democratized and the structure of hierarchy in the society should be eliminated and caste system abolished. He was for economic reforms that could take place along with equalization of property, irrespective of caste and creed. It could be possible only when social reforms take place. It is the social system which embodies arrogance and selfishness of perverse section of minds who were superior enough in social status to set in fashion and who had authority to force it on their inferiors.[40] Ambedkar says, 'There is no doubt that unless you change your social order, you can achieve little by way of progress. You cannot mobilize the community either for defence or for offence. You cannot build a nation, you cannot build morality. Anything that you build on the foundation of caste will crack and will never be a whole.' There is a view that for caste reforms and social reforms, the first step is to abolish sub-castes. Revolutionary changes should take place in social, as well as economic, terms. As long as the problem of caste system continues, other social problems would remain.[41] Unless common and marginalized sections of the society get the advantage of democratic results, it cannot claim to be a true democracy.

Ambedkar argues that all human beings are equal, there should not be any discrimination based on caste and creed and strived for social, economic and political liberty. Since Ambedkar believed that all are equal, he argued for annihilation of caste to equalize the society as it curtails the freedom of the least advantaged sections in the society. To develop these sections, Ambedkar argued for reservation (preferential treatment) to develop social, economic and political equality. Ambedkar's philosophy emphasized equality, liberty, and fraternity as they strive for an egalitarian society. Ambedkar argued that social justice could be dispensed in a free social order in which an individual is the end in itself. Similarly, the terms of associated life between members of society must be regarded by considerations founded on liberty, equality and fraternity.

Karl Marx's Notion of Democracy

Marx's condemnation of liberal democracy rests upon historical materialism. Marx developed his system in opposition to idealism. Hegel upheld the concept of 'spirit', but Marx dismissed such speculation as mythical nonsense and said empirical observation alone could deliver the truths of existence. Marx argued that man's productive interchange with nature was the real subtext of history. He maintained, 'Human beings are defined not by ideal essence, but by the totality of actions whereby they reproduce their own material existence.'[42] He argued that the social structure and the state continually evolve out of the life process of definite individuals because they work, produce materially, and act under definite material limitations and conditions. The behaviour of men depends on material behaviour. Religion, morality and philosophy are not embodiments of eternal truth, but 'necessary sub-limitations of man's material life-processes'.[43] Karl Marx critically analysed capitalism and the existence of inequalities with the class division produced by it. In Marx's view, in a capitalist society, a free market and a state based on politically equal citizens are simply formalities that hide the reality of rule by the capitalist class. The only way to achieve real political and economic equality and full democratization of state and society is to abolish the capitalist system and replace it with socialism and, ultimately, communism.[44]

Marx says class relations are exploitative and imply fundamental divisions between the ruling and subordinate classes. These relations are also inherent by a conflictual situation giving rise to an overt struggle. He also argues that the modern bourgeois society is market-oriented by a dominant exploitative relationship – that is between those who own capital and those who own only their labour power. The only solution, he believes, is that capitalism must be replaced by socialism as the necessary basis for democracy. Marx replaced political democracy as the determining factor of politics with economic democracy; it is economic democracy that determines political democracy.[45] Marx argued that 'the rights of the man' and its proponents confuse the bourgeois man with the man-in-general. The so-called rights of man (life, liberty, property and security) are only the rights of an egoistic man, man separated from other men and from the community. In idealism, Marx said, the idea of inviolable rights presupposes an atomistic conception where society appears to be an external framework for the individual. The limitation inherent in the concept of natural rights is the assumption that within certain spheres, collective needs must be subordinated to individual claims. This he was not prepared to accept. Hence, his objection to the statement, contained in the French Declaration of the Rights of Man, that liberty is the power of man viewed as an isolated man; liberty in this sense is based not on the association of man with man, but rather on the separation of man from man.[46]

The political and juridical institutions systematically serve the interests of the dominant economic classes as a surface plausibility.[47] Hence, he condemned bourgeois civil society based on unrestrained individualism, as a violation of man's social being. Marx thus struggled to create a society that overcomes the horrors of social problems. He referred to this noble vision as 'true democracy'. For him, true democracy would abolish the alienation between the individual and the political community by resolving the split between the 'egoistic' interests of individuals in civil society. In democracy, the formal principle could go along with the material principle. Hence, he argued, extending the franchise to the masses is the way to unify the ideal and the real. He also argued that what made democracy 'true' is not the equal opportunity to the citizen to devote himself to public life as something special, but the immediate participation in all deliberations and decisions on political matters. There should be no professional bureaucrats, no professional politicians, no political office, but he said true democracy is participation of all-representative principle with self-determination of the people.[48]

All the perspectives are different in their own way: liberal perspective advocates individualism, consisting of fundamental ideas as constitutions, human rights, capitalism, free trade, and the separation of church and state. These ideas are widely accepted, even by political groups that do not openly profess a liberal ideological orientation. Liberalism believes strongly in the constitutional guarantees of individual liberty. It also believes that all individuals are created equal and are endowed with certain inalienable rights and all individuals can do whatever they want, as long they believe in a free capitalist market place. Marx's philosophy is based on class. He argues that society is divided on the basis of rich and poor (capitalists and proletariats). Capitalists always dominate proletariats, which leads to conflicts in the society and gives scope for people's agitations for a classless society. Ambedkar argues that caste is the main obstacle to the development of society. He argues that it divides the society into high castes and lower castes, which leads to antagonism between these two groups and gives rise to people's agitations. John Rawls argues that justice should be fair and benefits should reach the bottom level of the society and to the least advantaged sections. All the above thinkers have emphasized self-respect, decent and dignified life. All the basic rights, liberties should reach the least advantaged sections. Their philosophical points of view support, in essence, substantive democracy and lead to creative and meaningful democracy. They believed in the development of all the people, irrespective of class and caste; low and high status, not merely economical but also social and political. If these conditions are not fulfilled, it is not a real democracy.

Neo-liberalism is different from liberalism as it believes that every individual is personally responsible for own actions, own successes and own failures. Liberalism has undergone a process of initial growth, intermediary decline and finally a recent rejuvenation. Alternatively, neo-liberalism might be perceived as a distinct ideology, descending from, but not identical to, liberalism 'proper'. Under this interpretation, neo-liberalism would share some historical roots. In other words, it is a modified or revived form of traditional liberalism based on the belief in free-market capital and the rights of individuals. Neo-liberalism is a market-driven approach to economic and social policy based on neoclassical theories of economics that maximize the role of the private business sector in determining the political and economic priorities of the state. It emphasizes markets, efficiency, consumer choice, and individual autonomy, shift from governments and corporations to individuals and to extend this kind of market logic into the realm of social relationships. It believes that citizenry mandates a collective effort to create economic equality. It believes that big government is better to decide what should be done with the fruits of each individual's labours, rather than the individual himself/herself.[49]

Neo-liberal Political Reforms and its Impact on Political Economy

No state in the world is exempt from the neo-liberal policies. Whether they accept it or not, directly or indirectly, it impacts on their country. It is argued by a web of scholars that no state is in a position to reject the policy of the neo-liberal model of development. According to neo-liberalism, the state should gradually withdraw its responsibilities and transfer its responsibilities to the individualistic market forces or global forces. India is no exception to this global scenario. Obviously, it argues that the state need not think of welfare of the people and further argues that it is indispensable. There is a need to analyse neo-liberalism. Arthur MacEwan defined neo-liberalism as the economic policy that became dominant during the final decades of the 19th century. During the 1980s, Ronald Reagan and Margaret Thatcher established an international political climate that allowed the spread of neo-liberalism in an extreme form. The demise of Soviet Union gave further impetus to extreme arguments about the limits of state action in economic affairs and the miracles that could be performed by markets. Behind the rhetoric of neo-liberalism, large firms and wealthy individuals have often enriched themselves through various favours from the government. The policy calls for reducing the economic role of government in providing social welfare, in managing economic activity at the aggregate and sectorial levels, and in regulating international commerce. The ideas at the base of this policy are not new: they come directly from the classical liberalism that emerged in the 19th century and proclaimed the market as the proper guiding instrument through which people should organize their economic lives. Neo-liberalism pushed the government to play a minimalist role in economic affairs; it generally depends upon a very strong, repressive government. It is proved that the state denies the gains to the majority in the name of long-run economic growth and it argues that implementation of the neo-liberal policy faces stiff popular opposition and can only be contained with police action.[50] Macpherson has argued that because of neo-liberal agendas of present governments, political movements, especially in postcolonial countries, became inevitable. Neo-liberalism, impersonal market, allocation of work and rewards in response to individual choice took shape. Everyone was swept into the free market and all his/her relations with others were increasingly converted to market relations.[51]

The World Development Report (1997), in its 'The State in a Changing World Order', emphasizes on the neo-liberal approach. It maintains that the state 'will not be able to adapt to the demands of a globalizing world economy'. It pleads for an effective state and the effective state in their view is the one that 'allow markets to flourish and people to lead healthier and happier lives'. They hold that the 'state is central to economic and social development not as a direct provider of growth, but as a partner, catalyst and facilitator'. The report observes that in many countries, 'private initiative is held hostage to a legacy of antagonistic state-market relations' and adds that 'poorly-performing state enterprises are often a big drain and privatization provides an obvious solution'. While developing a framework on 'Rethinking the State', the report states, 'The central difficulty in redefining the state's role is that the ground beneath the government's feet is always changing.' It adds, 'Many of the most successful examples of development, recent and historical, entail states working in partnership with markets to correct their failures, not replacing them.' The rest of the framework discusses more of matching role to capability, re-innovating the state's capability, and suggests that the state evolves rules and restraints, competitive pressure, voice and partnership. This only indicates that the discussion on the state shifted from its role and purpose to that of process.[52]

The purpose of defining the process is something logical, but the process becoming the purpose cannot answer any question emanating from the concerns for equity, justice, freedom and transformation. The problem with the neo-liberal approach to the state is its attack on the institution of the state. It does maintain that its working has become obsolete, and therefore incapable of coping with the new global challenges. While it is true that the states have not done well as allocator of values, so is the case with the market. Once there is an argument for partnership, the question is: partnership for what? A profit-seeking market, driven by self-interest of the individual, has its own laws. What is that the state does as a partner? The more crucial question is one of growing inequalities, inaccessibility to basic resources and non-availability of minimum provisions for the very survival. The retreating minimalist state in terms of reducing regulations on the market forces is one side of the story, but the other side is the shattering of hopes of ordinary masses, resulting in delegitimisation of the state. It is in this backdrop that the Indian state needs to be assessed.[53]

Sarah Joseph argues that the wide influence and legitimacy of neo-liberal theories and its political agenda today is attributed to growing problems which beset the welfare state and capitalist economy in the West after the 1960s. The slowing down of the high rate of economic growth had characterized Western economies in the post-war decades and generated rising inflation and unemployment. Coupled with the expansion of the public sector and increasing public expenditure on social services, the welfare state seemed to be in a crisis by 1970s and 1980s. As a result, criticisms of the developmental state and of modernization theories also gained momentum at that time. This situation provided the ideological space in which neo-liberal theories gained legitimacy.[54] She observes that there is a distinction between the non-state sector and civil society, global and national corporate associations. They are all considered as natural partners and come under the neo-liberal model. The liberal concepts of sovereignty and autonomy are therefore being replaced by terms like 'embedded autonomy'. With reference to the state, the focus now is on networking across the public-private divide, and on state-society synergy.[55] The political reforms being undertaken today have a more radical aspect in that they represent an attempt to incorporate market rationality into the structures and practices of the state. Moreover, the implications of these changes for the understanding and practice of liberal democracy such as the distinction between public and private and between state and its citizens are being reinterpreted in terms of political values which neo-liberalism embodies.[56]

It is paradoxical that, along with the pride in Indian democracy, a growing cynicism about politics and politicians is also evident. Politicians are widely perceived as self-seeking individuals, motivated by a ruthless drive for power and personal gains and politics is associated with dubious deals and corruption. This negative impact led to a spurt in people's movements. Although the primary objective of political reforms has been to improve efficiency and productivity of governance, yet states are now expected to share with corporate interests and the responsibility of civil society in promoting the public interest itself may be reinterpreted in market terms. Neo-liberal theories reject the democratic notion of public welfare, social justice and responsibility. It envisages the state to promote interests of the business and other elite class. It also rejects the social democratic view that citizens are entitled to all political, social and economic rights to enable them to live with dignity and self-respect. As against this view, neo-liberal theories define citizens as consumers of services which the state provides, and as active participants in the market, capable of promoting their own interest. The emancipatory notion of freedom that was also present in the liberal tradition has been marginalized in the process.[57]

In fact, the defence of humanist values and democratic norms is to a great extent now left to social movements and the more radical civil society groups. So, Joseph argues that there is a need for a rethink on the existing development models and work towards more creative solutions which would make not only business, but also the poor, partners in the development projects, which is more democratic, inclusive, creative and participative. In a vibrant democracy, political parties and elected bodies would be expected to play a central role in safeguarding the rights and interests of all members of the population. Hence, she believes that liberal democracy is under stress today.[58] As the world is being increasingly drawn into the neo-liberal model of development, the inequalities between the individuals, groups, nations, classes and regions are bound to widen and the attributes of liberal democracy do not any more hold good. This approach will subvert democracy and the rights associated with it. It leads to assertion of rights and the demand for new rights. An analysis of the rights position and the nature of new social and political movements is called for.

Understanding of Political Rights

Manoranjan Mohanty argues that the historical anti-colonial struggles, people's revolutionary movements and a variety of ongoing social struggles present a perspective of rights which was missing in the Western discourse on rights. He maintains that rights are political affirmations of a desirable human condition and in course of a struggle, a prevailing human condition is considered as wrong by a sufficient number of people, making its alteration a demand at a new point of development of human civilization. He also argues that rights are posited against wrongs but rulers have always linked rights with duties, conceding rights at an advanced stage of a political struggle while enforcing duties for those who exercise rights. But, he says that duties are important in themselves – and not in exchange for rights. Duties of the individuals to each other and to society and the state and the duties of the state to individuals and many other such relationships have justifications for the human good.[59]

The political theorists argue that democracy is not just in terms of spread of liberal democratic institutions, but also deepening of the democratic qualities of all societies. Democracy is not just universal adult citizenship rights, but more substantial, so as to include a variety of disadvantaged categories like ethnic, religious, indigenous people, women, the old, youth and unemployed, etc. They argue that the notion of 'inclusion' is possible by influencing the state or entering the state through organizations and participating in policy-making and implementation. This sort of inclusion therefore involves more than attainment of basic citizenship rights, such as the right to vote and associate as the right to participate in people's movements.[60] Political freedom includes not only speeches, but also other forms of action.[61] These forms of action sometimes may go beyond what is conventionally defended in the justification for freedom of speech. Political freedom, on the other hand, includes actions that go beyond the democratic methods in order to get the desired results. These methods, of course, involve generally accepted criminal actions such as deliberate damage to property or violence. But this form of action, other than extremism, is acceptable in a democratic state.[62] Howard Davis also says that 'individuals can conduct their own personal campaigns, but it has less personal control over the political causes in democratic states'. Hence, resistance has to be in an organized manner and unorganized activity would not be helpful in getting the problems solved.

Richard Norman tries to understand the difference between various conflicting interpretations of freedom and equality combined. He argues that these two political philosophies, one dealing with equality and the other with justice, are fundamentally contrary to each other. Both are identified with two long-standing traditions of political thought of action. Both argue 'why people protest against the oppression of one section of society by another'. Richard Norman argues that both are violation of freedom and equality. The freedom which they seek is a shared freedom, the freedom of the oppressed from the domination under which they suffer. Hence, the oppressed classes believe that it could be achieved only when that domination is replaced by the relationships of equality. A central feature of the equality for which they aim is the shared ownership of property. It is, therefore, implied that the ownership of these things is at present monopolized by a limited class of people.[63]

Self-determination

The principle of self-determination for peoples has been recognized since 1919, when the League of Nations was established. At the time of the League of Nations, the focus was on a 'principle' of self-determination and not a 'right' to self-determination. Following the creation of the United Nations in 1945, the 'principle' of people's self-determination evolved into a 'right' under international law and even *jus cogens* a peremptory norm.[64]

Self-determination embodies the right for all peoples to determine their own economic, social and cultural development. Self-determination has thus been defined by the International Court of Justice (in the West-Saharan case) as: the need to pay regard to the freely expressed will of peoples. It is important to stress that for indigenous people, the term 'self-determination' does most often imply secession from the state. The right to self-determination is a fundamental principle in international law. It is embodied in the Charter of the United Nations and the International Covenant on Civil and Political Rights and the International Covenant on Economic, Social and Cultural Rights. The Covenants provide that: 'All peoples have the rights of self-determination. By virtue of that right, they freely determine their political status and freely pursue their economic, social and cultural development'. The right to self-determination has also been recognized in other international and regional human rights instruments such as Part VII of the Helsinki Final Act, 1975 and Article 20 of the African Charter of Human and Peoples' Rights, as well as the Declaration on the Granting of Independence to Colonial Territories and Peoples. It has been endorsed by the International Court of Justice. Furthermore, the scope and content of the right to self-determination has been elaborated upon by the United Nations Human Rights Committee and Committee on the Elimination of Racial Discrimination, as well as international jurists and human rights experts.[65]

A non-self-governing territory, listed under Chapter XI of the UN charter, can exercise the right to self-determination through the creation of an independent state, or through the establishment of an association with an independent state. Furthermore, the right to self-determination must also be regarded as establishing the right to separate from the existing state, of which the group concerned is a part, and to set up a new independent state. If the state concerned gravely violates its obligations towards a distinct people or community within its boundaries, it loses the legitimacy to rule over those people. Thus, if the state and its successive governments have repeatedly oppressed a people over a long period, violated their human rights and fundamental freedoms, and if their means of achieving a sufficient degree of self-government have been tried and have failed, then the question of secession can arise as a means for the restoration of the well-being of the people.[66] The World Summit for Social Development, held in Copenhagen in 1995, expressed the view 'that social development and social justice are indispensable for the achievement and maintenance of peace and security within and among the nations. In turn, social development and social justice cannot be attained in the absence of peace and security, or in the absence of peace and fundamental freedoms'.[67] Though the right to self-determination embodies the right for all peoples to determine their own economic, social and cultural development, in case of Telangana, people are not free to develop economically and politically. As per the right to self-determination, the people of Telangana can exercise that right through the creation of an independent state. Furthermore, the right also gave the right to separate from the existing state, if the existing state gravely violates its obligations towards a distinct people. That means, the Central and state governments are not respecting the international norms and rights, though they are signatories to the UN and other international pacts.

Right to Development

The discussion over the UN Declaration on Right to Development demands a basic understanding of the term 'development'. There are other terms like underdevelopment and inequalities, which also need to be clarified in the process of understanding the concept of development in the traditional way of analysing development where per capita income and GDP are taken as yardsticks; there is thus a need for redefinition. The concept of development is generally understood as the 'availability of high quality of physical life to all the people of that particular society without any differentiation on any lines'. A high and equally accessible level of material well-being is a pre-requisite for many other dimensions of development such as political rights, freedom, intellectual, cultural and social. Development is all about equity in distribution through efficient allocation of resources. The interconnection among the terms development, underdevelopment, allocation of resources and the capacity to utilize the human resources in a scientific manner at international, national, regional and sub-regional levels leads to economic inequalities, which further breed socio, political and cultural inequalities. The existing inequalities force certain nations, regions or sub-regions into underdevelopment. Inequality in income and wealth reduces the possibilities of overall growth. Economic inequality allows certain individuals certain material choices, whereas it denies certain societies the right to development.

Evolution of the Concept of Right to Development

The right to development is an inalienable human right by virtue of which every human person and all peoples are entitled to participate in, contribute to and enjoy economic, social, cultural and political development and fundamental freedoms of all human beings. The 1986 Right to Development Declaration defines 'development' as a comprehensive economic, social, cultural and political process, which aims at the constant improvement of the well-being of the entire population and of all individuals, on the basis of their active, free and meaningful participation in development and in the fair distribution of benefits therefrom. Sengupta asserts if these outcomes are not accompanied with an improvement of the well-being of all people and people do not meaningfully participate in the process of the distribution of benefits and they are iniquitous and unfair, it would not be called 'development'. Among different processes of development, only one in which human rights and fundamental freedoms are capable of being realized can qualify as an object of claim as a human right.[68]

In the development discourse, it is economic growth that is of central concern, with human rights remaining largely marginal. While the development discourse evolved through various phases, focusing on Gross National Product (GNP), basic needs and so on, a focus on 'rights' was missing. The definition of 'development' has a primary focus on economic growth and material prosperity, to the exclusion of the freedom, dignity and overall 'well-being' of the people, and development was not linked to human rights standards.[69] These notions are very important in understanding the notion of democracy. The consciousness that evolved in developmental studies in due course of time forced the United Nations to adopt a Declaration on Right to Development. Though the concept of right to development was introduced in 1986, the common consensus was arrived at only in the 1993 Vienna conference. Earlier, it was the nature and content of the concept of the right to development which was subjected to dialogue, discussions and controversies. Later, the attention shifted to the procedure and implementation of the Right to Development. An enquiry into the historical evolution of the Declaration reveals the obstacles faced in achieving universal acceptance. The need for the creation of awareness of human rights, the establishment of an egalitarian society and the necessity of equity in distribution of resources had come to be realized by the world community during the Second World War.[70] Later, the consequent changes in the international political scenario resulted in the codification of rights in two International Covenants: Covenants on Economic, Social and Cultural Rights and the International Covenant on Civil and Political Rights, which were given legal status according to international law. Right to Development has thus become a major concern for the member governments since the adoption of the Declaration. Now the member states are assigned the responsibility of ensuring Right to Development of all its members without any discretion on any grounds, of race, language or religion.

Article 1 refers to the Declaration recognizing the people's right to self-determination by virtue of which the people of the soil are free to determine their political status and to pursue their economic, social and cultural development. Article 2 of the Declaration refers to the human person as the central subject of development and as the beneficiary of development. Article 3 refers to the state government's responsibility to promote the new international economic order based on sovereignty, equality, interdependence, mutual interest and cooperation among all the states. It also stresses on removing the obstacles to development. Article 4 refers to the duties of the state government to promote development and facilitate fuller realization of the Right to Development. Sustained action is recommended to promote rapid development. Article 5 deals with the necessity of the state mechanism to react towards discrimination on any ground. Article 6 stresses on the state's responsibility to eliminate the obstacles to development. Article 8 constitutes the equality of opportunity for all in their access to basic resources, education, health services, food, housing, employment and the fair distribution of income. Article 9 refers to the indivisibility and interdependence of the Right to Development and it stresses on the necessity of viewing the Declaration in a holistic perspective. Article 10 includes the required steps to be taken to ensure the realization of the objectives of Declaration on the Right to Development.[71]

Amartya Sen has developed the notion of 'development' as a process of expanding the real freedom that people enjoy, instead of expanding the per capita income or the aggregate utilities enjoyed by the people. Development should be seen as expanding freedoms. Sen appreciates the instrumental value of income or utilities in expanding the freedoms and capabilities of people. Amartya Sen describes five freedoms that enhance true development.[72] They are: political freedom, economic facilities, social opportunities, transparency and protective security. He also argues that enhancement of human freedom is both the object and the primary means of development. The objective of development relates to the valuation of the actual freedoms enjoyed by the people involved. Individual capabilities crucially depend on economic, social and political arrangements. Further, he argues that the state and society have extensive roles in strengthening and safeguarding human capabilities.[73]

Application of Declaration on Right to Development to Telangana Sub-region

The right to development and self-determination comes under the purview of international domain. Both are interrelated and interconnected. Since all the nation-states are signatories of UDHR, they are bound by the rights and values of these documents. If they do not respect them, they are responsible for their ineffectiveness in implementation. India is not insulated from the same responsibility. The concept of development is understood as equal development in terms of political rights, freedom, intellectual, cultural and social development. equity in distribution of resources, the capacity to utilize the human resources in a scientific manner at international, national, regional and sub-regional levels, create awareness about human rights, and the establishment of an egalitarian society. Thus, it is intended to establish a fair and just world. At the international scenario, the United Nations, and at the regional and sub-regional levels, it is the responsibility of central and state mechanisms to see that the objectives of right to development are implemented. The right to development approach to Telangana sub-region highlights the way the implementation of these rights is done. In this context, it is argued that the people of Telangana region possess the rights for their full-scale development, as part of the larger world community which has agreed upon the right to development. The right to development approach to Telangana sub-region highlights the way the implementation of these rights is done. An analysis of the existing social, political, economic and cultural scenario of Telangana sub-region through the perspective of Declaration on Right to Development or Right to Self-determination reveals the variance between the objectives of declaration and the injustice done to the Telangana region for many years. The principle of self-determination for peoples has been recognized since 1919, when the League of Nations was established. At the time of the League of Nations, the focus was on a 'principle' of self-determination and not a 'right' of self-determination.[74]

In other words, this paper tries to emphasize that rights are very important in the development of individuals. All the liberal thinkers have emphasized on how rights of individuals and several perspectives which I discussed give a scope for people's participation. Robert Dahl and David Held laid stress on the participation of the majority but this perspective, it seems, has not been realized in real terms. Hence, Karl Marx and feminist scholars are critical of liberal theories. It resulted in revolutions, wars and agreements and so on and ultimately this confrontation or crisis gave scope for rights to the humanity like emergence of UNO and UDHR (Universal Declaration of Human Rights). These developments further led to other international rights. Based on this theoretical background, it maintains that people want not merely conventional rights or participation, but democratic participation from all sections in the state and society. Hence, to contextualize the notion of substantial participation, the next unit emphasizes on that domain critically.

Notes

1. J. Norman, 'Human Rights and Democracy: Conceptualization and Application in Palestine', Palestinian Human Rights Monitoring Group (PHRMG), July 2005, p. 5.
2. Eva Erman, *Human Rights and Democracy: Discourse Theory and Global Rights Institutions*, Ashgate Publishing Company, Burlington, 2005, p. 4.
3. Ramashray Roy, *Democracy in India: Form and Substance*, Shipra Publications, New Delhi, 2005, p. 4.
4. Ibid., p. 26.
5. David Beetham, *Democracy: A Beginner's Guide*, Oneworld Publications, Oxford, 2006, pp. 2–3.

6. Arthur MacEwan, *Neo Liberalism or Democracy: Economic Strategy, Markets and Alternatives for the 21st Century*, Zed Books, London, 1999, pp. 2–3.
7. Adam Przeworski, Susan C. Stokes and Bernard Manin, *Democracy, Accountability and Representation*, Cambridge University Press, Cambridge, 1999, pp. 280–81.
8. George Sorenson, *Democracy and Democratization*, Westview Press, Oxford, 1998, pp. 9–11.
9. Ibid., pp. 3–5.
10. Ibid., pp. 9–11.
11. David Beetham, op. cit., p. 2.
12. Ibid., p. 3.
13. David Held and Christopher Pollitt, *New Forms of Democracy*, Sage Publications, London, 1986, p. 7.
14. C.B. Macpherson, *The Real World of Democracy*, Oxford University Press, New York, 1978, pp. 1–2.
15. Ibid.
16. Hilary Wainwright, 'Why Participatory Democracy Matters – And Movements Matter to Participatory Democracy', June 2005, source: *http://www.tni.org/es/archives/act/2351*
17. David Beetham, op. cit., p. 3.
18. Ibid., p. 8.
19. Ibid.
20. Ibid.
21. George Sorenson, op. cit., p. 6.
22. C.B. Macpherson, *Democratic Theory: Essays in Retrieval*, Clarendon Press, Oxford, 1973, pp. 5–15.
23. O.P. Gouba, *An Introduction to Political Theory*, Macmillan India Limited, New Delhi, 1981, pp. 425–27.
24. A. Belden Fields, *Rethinking of Human Rights for the New Millennium*, Palgrave Macmillan Publications, New York, 2003, pp. 10–18.
25. Ibid.
26. Ibid.
27. Ibid.
28. Tony Evans, 'If Democracy, then Human Rights?', *The Third World Quarterly*, Vol. 22, No. 4, 2001, pp. 624–27.
29. George Sorenson, op. cit., p. 8.
30. Ibid.
31. C.B. Macpherson, op. cit.

32. Goran Therborn, 'The Rule of Capital and the Rise of Democracy', *New Left Review*, Vol. 103, May–June 1977, pp. 3–41.
33. C.B. Macpherson, op. cit.
34. Ibid.
35. Spike Peterson, 'Whose Rights? A Critique of the "Givens" in Human Rights Discourse', *Indian Journal of Human Rights*, Vol. 3, Nos 1–2, 1999, pp. 4–28.
36. John Rawls, *Theory of Justice*, Oxford University Press, Oxford, 1971, pp. 11–12.
37. Neha Singh, Professor John Rawls, source: *http://blogs.mybandra.com/2009/06/27/professor-john-rawls-theory-of-distributive-justice/*
38. Ibid.
39. Joseph V. Femia, *Marxism and Democracy*, Clarendon Press, Oxford, 1993, p. 10.
40. Jean Dreze, 'Dr Ambedkar and the Future of Indian Democracy', *Indian Journal of Human Rights*, Vol. 9, Nos 1–2, 2005, p. 138.
41. B.R. Ambedkar, *Annihilation of Caste: Ambedkar's Writings and Speeches*, Vol. 1, Education Department, Maharashtra Government, Bombay, 1979, pp. 38–67.
42. Joseph V. Femia, op. cit., p. 11.
43. Ibid., p. 12.
44. Ibid.
45. Ibid.
46. Ibid., p. 25.
47. Ibid., p. 66.
48. Ibid., p. 70.
49. Arthur MacEwan, op. cit., pp. 3–4.
50. Ibid.
51. C.B. Macpherson, op. cit.
52. World Development Report, *The State in a Changed World*, Oxford University Press, New York, 1997, pp. 24–26.
53. Ibid.
54. Sarah Joseph, 'Neoliberal Reforms and Democracy in India', *Economic and Political Weekly*, Vol. 42, No. 31, August 2007, p. 3213.
55. Ibid., p. 3214.
56. Ibid., p. 3215.
57. Ibid., p. 3217.
58. Ibid.

59. Delivered an Inaugural Lecture on 'Globalization and Democracy' in the International Conference on 'Challenges of Globalization: Indian and Australian Perspectives', Department of Political Science, University of Hyderabad, Hyderabad, 7–9 December 2006.
60. John S. Dryzek, 'Political Inclusion and Dynamics of Democratization', *American Political Science Review,* Vol. 90, No. 1, September 1996, pp. 475–76.
61. Howard Davis, *Political Freedom: Associations, Political Purposes and the Law,* Continuum Publications, New York, 2000, pp. 1–2.
62. Ibid.
63. Richard Norman, *Equality, Priority and Social Justice,* Blackwell Publishers, Oxford, 2009, p. 126.
64. Christian Erni and Marianne Jensen, *Indigenous Affairs,* IWGIA Publications, Copenhagen, 1999, p. 7.
65. Source: *http://en.wikipedia.org/wiki/Self-determination*
66. Christian Erni and Marianne Jensen, op. cit., p. 10.
67. Ibid., p. 11.
68. Arjun Sengupta, *The Right to Development: A Primer,* Centre for Development and Human Rights, Sage Publications, New Delhi, 2004, p. 48.
69. Ibid., p. 44.
70. Rob Buitenweg, 'The Right to Development as a Human Right', *Peace and Change*, Vol. 22, No. 4, October 1997, p. 414.
71. Suneeta Eluri, 'Political Responses to Right to Development: A Case Study of Telangana', Unpublished M.Phil Dissertation, Department of Political Science, University of Hyderabad, Hyderabad, 2001, pp. 11–16.
72. Amartya Sen, *Development as Freedom*, Oxford University Press, Oxford, 1999, p. 10.
73. Ibid., p. 53.
74. Suneeta Eluri, op. cit.

3 Politics of Participation
Deepening of Democracy

The study reveals the evolution of movements from historical and theoretical perspectives. There were several revolutions and wars that laid the foundation for the rights discourse at the international level. There were several reformist and resistance movements in pre- and post-independence India which had a major impact on the freedom movement and ongoing movements, as well as deepened, and are deepening, democracy. This study tries to analyse critically and comprehend the term 'politics'. It further tries to analyse contemporary politics critically and assess the participation in conventional and unconventional politics which strive for deepening democracy. With this backdrop, it tries to explore the possibilities of seeing Indian democracy succeed and points our limitations of Indian politics and what can be one done to substantialize Indian democracy. Through this, it tries to study the relevance of people's movements.

Relevance of People's Movements

The disciplines of Political Science and Sociology have largely focused attention on moral political philosophy, normative concepts and working of political institutions such as the executive, the legislature, parties and elections, but the dynamics of these institutions and political processes are not sufficiently studied. The study of politics of masses, their aspirations and demands, articulation of their problems, the modus operandi in asserting their demands outside the institutional framework and their occasional efforts at overthrowing the existing state power are, by and large, ignored by political science scholars. Scholars argue that earlier, under the influence of the British tradition, political science in India was confined to political philosophy, formal governmental institutions and legal framework. Second, the concept adopted by political scientists was influenced by the American and British traditions, confined to a political system whose functions were rule making, rule application and rule adjudication. Many political scientists define 'politics' as who gets what, when and how? For some, the definition of politics is 'the authoritative allocation of values'. In the discipline of Political Science, politics is confined to the conventional politics rather.[1]

The contemporary world is passing through unusual movements emanating from the worldwide unrest. There is an intense debate on these eruptions and ways and means to deal with this rapidly changing alarming global context. The state, being responsible for governance, derives its power from the laws of the land. Every law confers powers on the state, but also limits the powers so that power does not become tyrannical. The laws also define the rights and freedoms of citizenry through which their relation with the state is determined. It has been a worldwide experience that it is in the very nature of the state to transgress the limits of the law. In case of citizens, at least in some sections of the citizenry, there is a tendency to use freedoms to the extent of challenging the very legitimacy of the state. It is, therefore, a civilizational question that how a balance is struck between these two powerful tendencies without abandoning the project of transformation of the human society into a more equitable, peaceful, fair, just and humane global order. Movement is one part of societal experience. The tragedy of governance has been that, instead of bringing in higher values into a terror-stricken society, the state and, more particularly, the law-enforcing agencies are ending up imitating and imbibing fanatic methods and culture. This is an inevitable fallout of a mechanistic confrontationist approach to the national turmoil which, in essence, is political. That is the crux of the crisis of civilized governance.[2] The people's struggles in India and abroad represent varied and much complex issues: they are described as movements in literature variously as grassroots movements, micro-movements, protest movements, community-based or mass-based movements, etc. This chapter intends to use the term 'politics of participation' interchangeably but reference to a particular genre of social movements and have since been active on a variety of issues which, in their own perception, are directly or indirectly related to what they see as their long-term goal of democratizing development and transforming the society.[3]

The relevance of social movements, coupled with democracy, has become almost evident at a global level. Popular movements contributed to the collapse of authoritarianism and have undergone a transition to democracy in the Philippines, Korea, and much of Eastern

Europe and Latin America. The social movements have been credited with ushering in democratization and with raising new issues and prompting state institutions to respond to newly articulated needs. The importance of social movements in challenging authoritarianism and in sustaining democratic transitions is well demonstrated. The significance of social movements under conditions of authoritarianism is broadly captured in the thought that they serve as a venue for sustaining and ultimately expressing popular civic sentiments and interests under circumstances where the prevailing authoritarian political climate does not allow for such forms of expression.[4]

Today, the world is in great turmoil and upsurge everywhere. One notices that all the sections in the society are protesting against widespread hunger, disease, unemployment, rapes, murders, violation of human rights and civil liberties, pollution of water and environment, etc. Literally all sections of the society are at war. Local is transforming into global and the global into local very fast. Every nation-state is losing its democratic character by resorting to violence against its sovereign people.[5] The international situation has changed qualitatively during the past two decades, from what it was during the 20th century. The socialist bloc does not exist anymore. The world is no longer bipolar. The pole is situated in USA. Market has become an absolute dictator. It has assumed the right to unrestrained exploitation of natural and human resources. The transnational corporations have become more powerful than most of the nation-states. The older forms of resistance movements like political parties, trade unions, class and mass organizations, social reform movements, etc., have become almost ineffective due to a number of limitations. They are (a) unable to respond to the new and more complex political situations and to new and emergent problems; (b) address, normally, only local or national issues, seldom international and global issues; (c) have only generalized concepts and understanding with little specialized knowledge and skills; (d) view from a mechanical class angle issues related to race, caste, culture and identity; and (e) are concerned more with central political power than with building from bottom upwards. Hence, the relevance of new resistance movements became necessary in response to the emergent global and local situations, in the context of the weaknesses of older movements, and also of new possibilities – new technologies, Internet, communication revolution, new organizational patterns like networking and chain formation, cyber guerillas, free software, etc. – and they sprang up in the form of movements based on environment, gender, justice, human rights, peace, food security, consumer rights, anti-war peace movements, anti-free trade, anti-globalization, etc.[6]

Social Movements: Concept and Context

Movements are considered the backbone of human rights movement. There are several types of struggles that have been taking place in the society. They are related to class, gender, caste, religion, language, culture, region, etc. Organizations of toiling people not only struggle on specific class or sectional demands, but the movements are also considered as a training ground for raising consciousness of its members. Most of the struggles are won or lost depending on the strength of mobilization within the organization, supplemented by outside support that becomes critical at some point of time.[7] Sidney Tarrow argues that social movements enhance democratic processes by providing unrepresented sectors of the population with alternative channels for political participation. They also comprise organizations whose mobilization targets state institutions as well as those that engage with the state. Some movements utilize violence as well as adhere to methods of civil disobedience, explicitly identifying the state as a dominant agent of oppression and oppressive policies.[8]

Social movements are one form of group action. They are informal groups of individuals focusing on specific political or social issues and resisting for a social change itself defined as social movement. Modern Western social movements became possible through education (the wider dissemination of literature), and increased mobility of labour due to the industrialization and urbanization of 19th century societies. It is argued that the freedom of expression, education and relative economic independence prevalent in the modern Western culture is responsible for the unprecedented number and scope of various contemporary social movements. Sidney Tarrow defined a social movement as a collective challenge against the dominance of elites, political authorities and cultural groups. The term 'social movements' was introduced in 1850 by the German sociologist, Lorenz Von Stein, while referring to developments in England and North America during the first decades of the 19th century. Tilly Charles argues that the early growth of social movements was connected to broad economic and political changes, including parliament, market capitalization, and proletarian. In the 1970s, women's rights, peace, civil rights and environmental movements emerged, often described as new social movements. Some find in the end of the 1990s the emergence of a new global social movement, the anti-globalization movement.[9]

Barnes and Kaase define protest as an 'unconventional form of political action that earns the label unconventional because protesters seek to influence social and political outcomes not through traditional channels of political participation such as voting and campaign contributions, but by exerting pressure and demands outside the traditional channels and institutions'. Gamson asserts that protest is 'simply politics by other means'. Dalton and Sickle state that protest is a 'continuum of unconventional political action which seeks to influence the course of social and political change from outside traditional institutions'. Protest is difficult to measure 'because it is an unconventional activity' as protest activity is not readily available in conventional politics. Dalton and Sickle stress that 'people protest not because they are frustrated and excluded from politics, but because they expect governments to respond'. Gurr defined protest in economic terms: 'protest is viewed as a product of societal problems and unmet grievances'. Gurr further provides more details of the grievances model that 'changing social conditions cause people to experience relative deprivation that increases a sense of grievance or dissatisfaction, which is a prime cause of political action. When people have slightly less than what they think that they are entitled to, that leads to relative deprivation, which leads to general spur to action'.[10]

Charles Tilly defines social movements as a series of contentious performances, displays and campaigns by which ordinary people make collective claims on others. For Tilly, social movements are a major vehicle for ordinary people's participation in politics. He argues that there are three major elements of social movements. One, campaigns – a sustained, organized public effort making collective claims on target authorities. Second, repertoire – employment of combinations from among the following forms of political action and three – creation of special-purpose associations and coalitions, public meetings, solemn processions, vigils, rallies, demonstrations, petition drives, statements to and in public media, and pamphleteering.[11] Protests are not strictly social movements, but more often a social movement developed in the course of time. They may begin with an agitation without any organization or ideology but consider it as a movement. It depends upon the way of analysis and the perspective of scholars. Agitations, protests, strikes and even riots are quite often, but not always, a part of social movements of a particular stratum of society.[12]

Partha Mukherjee classifies movements based on the criterion of equality of change these intend to bring about or the kind of change that has been effected. According to him, the nature of movements could be accumulative, alternative and transformative. If social mobilization demands changes 'within' the system, the changes that are likely to happen would be accumulative. If the social mobilization is aimed at creating new structures which would qualitatively affect the entire system, the change, in case attained, will be alternative. But in transformative movements, social mobilization seeks to replace one structure and substitute it by another.[13] M.S.A. Rao calls the accumulative movements as quasi-movements in the full sense. Rao himself talks about three types of social movements which aim at bringing about 'reform' in some area of life or the other, involving new relationships, activities, norms and values. In contrast, 'transformative' movements are oriented towards effecting changes in power relations, i.e., the super-ordinate and subordinate relationships. And, there are movements which aim at 'revolutionary' changes in all domains of life of all basic values.[14] Thus, there are different types of social movements which are talked about. Essentially, they could be put into two categories – one referring to changes 'within' the system, and the other implying changes 'of' the system. In the first category, could be placed the reformist and alternative/transformative movements, and in the second, the revolutionary movements. This is in terms of their ideological orientations and consequences. Reformist movements would refer to changes of 'minor' nature within the system. Transformative movements would involve 'major' changes within the system. And replacement of one system by another would be the trait of revolutionary movements.[15]

Components of Movements

The important components of social movements include objectives, ideology, programme, leadership and organization. They are inter-dependent and influence each other. Objectives of the movements start from narrow local issues to broad aims for social transformation. The ideology provides direction for evolving strategies. The programme keeps participants together by developing a feeling of 'we' ness. Various strategies and programmes are evolved to mobilize the masses and make them play a crucial role in articulating ideology and objectives. Ranajit Guha points out that though these components are found in all types of movements, including the spontaneous and rebellious movements, but their forms vary from structure to organizations.[16]

Typologies

Andre Gunder Frank and Marta Fuentes have explained about nine facets of social movements. They are: (1) movements responding to circumstances, through which change will occur as a result of political economy and ideological fluctuations; (2) social movements, which tend to have lifestyles of their own; (3) social movements which are composed of region, religion, race, ethnicity, language, caste, etc.; (4) most of the social movements do not speak about power but influence the state institutions; (5) those which lead to social transformation; (6) social movements delink and transition to socialism; (7) coalitions and conflicts among social movements; (8) the lack the behaviour of 'goodness'; and (9) those which differ with the state but share moral motivation.[17]

Paul Wilkinson pointed out two basic elements such as a minimum degree of organization and commitment for the existence of a social movement. He gave the following definitions of social movement: (a) a social movement is a collective attempt to promote change in any direction and by any means but not including violence, illegality and revolution, and (b) a social movement's commitment depends upon the conscious violation, normative commitment to the movements, aims or beliefs, and fuller participation of the followers or members.[18] Given different dimensions of protest movements, the structural conditions and motivational forces that give rise to these movements can be explained. Viewed in a broad historical perspective, we may identify four major phases in transformation of political authority structures and associated variations in the nature of social movements.[19] Protest is an important form of social movement. It is a non-institutionalized mode that brings the desired goal of either change in the existing social, economic and political order or resists that change. There are a large number of techniques of protests. These include small meetings, distributing leaflets, pasting posters, submitting memorandum, press conference, press statements, long marches on foot, holding meetings at public places, mass rallies, processions, observing protest days, political drama, mass deputation, torchlight processions, demonstrations, *hartals*, strikes, picketing, *satyagraha*, *dharna*, fasting unto death, destruction of public property, holding up of transport, uprooting of railway tracks, wires, localized attempts to throw off state authority and run a parallel administration, declared or undeclared warfare in a region, etc.[20]

David Bayley speaks about six primary forms of protests in the Indian context such as processions and public meetings, *hartals* (work stoppage), boycotts, strikes, obstructions, and courting of arrest and riots. These general forms of protests can be divided into two main groups: legal and illegal. Again, the illegal protests are sub-divided into violent and non-violent. The nature of protest depends on the causes that it espouses. Since the society has been hierarchically organized on the basis of caste and characterized by oppression, a number of protest movements sprang up around the causes of caste in India. Opposition, conflict and protest mark the relationship of the lower castes with the upper castes.[21] Srivastava has said that there has been growing resentment and protests of the people belonging to the Scheduled Castes towards atrocities perpetrated and various types of discriminations practised against them. They adopted such course of action more in self-defence, or to gain self-respect and assert their dignity in pursuing their socio-economic development through the constitutional measures. Sometimes, such protest movements appear to be well organized, and get quickly dissipated depending upon the degree of social and political consciousness and mobilization of the groups involved in organizing and carrying out protests and movements.[22]

A Model of Protest Bargaining and the Size of Demonstrations and Change

As Michael Lipsky convincingly showed, publicity about the protests can serve to recruit ideological allies who already have bargained for resources with decision-makers. Lipsky provided two important models of bargaining protest. They saw protest as a bargaining resource which enabled the politically powerless to mobilize resources and apply negative sanctions to decision-makers. The powerless relied on unusual measures to create disorder and thereby applying pressure on their opponents. The active groups have manoeuverability, which would occur if the issues were populated by a wider collection of organized interests. But when real or imagined threats to widely-shared values are perceived by a large proportion of the public who believe that public officials can eliminate the threat, the demand get under stress, swamped by new participants and the earlier manoeuverability of the organized groups gets greatly constricted.[23] Lipsky holds that the power of direct action is partially a derivative of the order it threatens or the disruption it causes. Lipsky further says that authority does not respond to demonstrations by non-assertive activists, but two decades earlier, the authority used to respond immediately. Due to these reasons, organizations try to enter into a coalition with other sister organizations and try to make it a success. The small protests possibly cause more disorder than protests with thousands of participants. Usually, the authority customarily equates size with the strength of the movement. Surprisingly, large demonstrations were followed by some change in government policies significantly more often than smaller demonstrations.[24]

Understanding the Notion of Politics

Politics is seen as associated with governmental activities. Politics means 'the science of government of states'. Robert A. Heywood has defined politics as 'the art and practice of government of human societies'. Today, however, the government of states is related to that of other human societies. The term 'government' means organized power, the institutions of command and control. Politics also means competition between the individuals for political power. The situation roughly corresponds to the elementary distinction between its rulers and ruled and between leaders and members.[25] This could be easily illustrated by analysing classical Greece politics. In Greek politics, the term 'participation' refers to decision-making and exercise of authority. In the 1960s, David Easton conceptualized politics as the 'authoritative allocation of values'. Bernard Crick illustrates that politics refers not so much to authoritative decision-making, but the processes by which decisions could be reached warmly. Politics is also understood as referring to the public domain through the use of covert and/or overt coercive power. Public domain emphasizes that politics refers not merely to decision-making, but pertains to the manner in which power, wealth and resources are distributed in society. Politics is also not seen as confined to the public domain, but as something which permeates all institutions and unfolds at every level of social existence.[26]

It is essential to understand politics in two directions: (1) politics is conflict, a struggle in which power allows those who possess it to ensure their hold on society and profit by it; and (2) politics is an effort to bring the rule of law, order and justice in which power guarantees general interests and common good against the pressures of private interests. Another way to understand the polity is that politics serves to maintain the privileges of a minority against the majority. It is also a means to realize the integration of all citizens into the community and create a just state. The acceptance of one or the other of these notions is in part determined by the social situation. The oppressed, the unsatisfied, the poor, the wretched, whether as individuals or a class, cannot see power as assuring a real order, but only a caricature of it behind which is hidden the domination of privilege; for them politics means conflict. Those who are rich, well provided for, satisfied, find the society harmonious and see power as maintaining an authentic order; for them, politics means integration. The two attitudes express only a part of the truth.[27]

Rajni Kothari argues that politics of India moved from 'from politics of trust to politics of suspicion' two decades after independence. He characterized it as 'decades of trust'. Politics in these decades was determined by a sense of trust between people, marked by a mutual concern and understanding about what constituted the 'common good'. Politics was seen as an 'ethical space' where conflicts were resolved agreeably and honourably. He argues that in the seventies, the trust got shifted to the end of politics. The 'ethical space' of politics was dominated by violence, crime, corruption and repression, marking, what Kothari calls, the 'virtual elimination of politics'. What people confront today is not the crisis of politics, but its virtual elimination. The last decade has marked the beginning of the Indian state that has not only deprived society of a basic consensus, but avoided any scope of a dialogue on it. The violence, the fear, the repression, the rhetoric of deceit and doublespeak, are symptoms not merely of crises, but the end of politics.[28]

Indian politics no longer provides the democratic space where, through dialogue and interaction, the aspirations and needs of the people could be affirmed and resolved. The 'end of politics' is seen as the period in which the relationship of dialogue among people, as well as the people and the state, is ruptured by crime, repression and terror as the means of conflict resolution.[29] The Telangana movement of the last six decades for separate statehood stands as a testimony. All the sections are taking part in the movement, including Dalits, tribals and other backward classes for not merely a territorial Telangana but also for a democratic Telangana in which, they believe, their rights could be secured and self-respect could be upheld. Almost 350 students and youth died in the 1960s and many youth were arrested, irrespective of their socio-economic background. The state considers it as a law and order problem and uses the police and Army battalions to put down the movement. Both the state and central governments tried to delay the issue rather than solve it quickly. Though the government formally constituted several committees, enacted laws and formulated pacts and agreements, these were never taken seriously. Thus, this negative attitude of the state led to a spurt in agitations again and again. The same experience was once again witnessed in 2009–10, though the movement has been on the edge since a decade. In this background, Kothari's argument of a shift 'from the trust of politics to end of politics' gets reflected in the Telangana movement. It is argued that when the state delays the issue or uses the police force to repress a movement, there is a scope for violence in the movement. The Telangana movement witnessed it as well. Either it is state violence or private violence in terms of self-immolation by the agitators, it leads to a crisis in governability, as argued by Atul Kohli. This poses a danger to the very notion of democracy and weakens it. Hence, the state has to deal with the demands in a democratic way with substantive deliberations. This positive approach seems to be lacking in governance.

Participatory Democracy

A new generation of young scholars rejected the elitist theory of democracy because of its conservative ideology, and sought to reconceptualize democracy based on the ideas of 'power to the people'. Traditional democracy rests on the assumption that all citizens should become essentially equal in both their concern with public issues and their competence to make decisions concerning the issues. Consequently, all citizens should participate equally in public decision-making and should exercise relatively equal amounts of influence in the political system. 'One man, one vote' became the rallying cry of this political movement in the 18th century, and its principal goal was the election of all governmental leaders through popular voting. The best interest of the total political community is served when all citizens participate in the political process and the majority rules. Democratic theory offered a radically different conception of how power should be distributed and used in society. The democratic ideal of political power rests collectively in the hands of all citizens, who entrust it periodically through mass elections of those empowered and trusted to act on behalf of the people.[30]

Participatory politics goes beyond voting. An individual either joins in non-political organization or one political in nature which attempts to influence the conventional political system.[31] Carole Pateman argues that the intellectual roots of participatory democracy lie in the classical writings of Jean Jacques Rousseau and John Stuart

Mill. This is not a new idea. Both Rousseau and Mill believed fervently in the necessity of citizen participation for political democracy. Rousseau sought to justify this assumption on the grounds that participation performs a vital educational effect, for educated people to be informed, interested and involve citizens who have a sense of control over their lives and concern for the broader community. As these qualities develop throughout the population, they will, in turn, strengthen the democratic processes and institutions that promote citizen participation, in a continual cycle of self-reinforcement. Mill added the observation that the major educational effect of participation in collective decision-making occurs in local government and in the workplace, where the individual can have a direct influence on these decisions, practice participatory skills on a regular basis, and perhaps even serve on a governing body of some kind. Pateman's principal reason for examining these two political theorists at considerable length is to make clear that democratic theory has always stressed citizen participation in public decision-making.[32]

The participatory democracy which emerged in the 1960s was basically just a rediscovery of traditional democratic philosophy. Nevertheless, the 1960s did contribute in at least three important ways to the re-emergence of the ideal of participatory democracy. The social and political turmoil of that decade, swirling around the twin themes of racism and poverty, awakened in many people a concern for public issues outside their own immediate lives, and demonstrated that through collective action, ordinary citizens can influence governmental policy and programmes. The organized social movements also developed during the same decade from community organization programmes to environmental protection campaigns. They were primarily grassroots efforts that drew most of their support from ordinary citizens, and, in the process, introduced them to political action.[33]

The features of participatory democracy are that all individuals must have full opportunities to participate as extensively as they wish in all collective decision-making pertaining to them; participation in collective decision-making must not be limited to voting, but should include a wide variety of activities requiring varying degrees of commitment and involvement; the responsibility for collective decision-making is to be widely dispersed, so that it is not limited to officials and/or experts, but includes all persons who will be affected by those decisions; participation in collective decision-making must not be limited to the political system, but should extend throughout all realms of social life; and that participation in collective decision-making within non-political spheres of life will teach individuals political skills and norms and will motivate them to become involved in larger political issues.[34]

For the past 200 years, Western nations have been struggling with the questions of what roles citizens should play in political processes and who should be entitled to enact these roles. As T.H. Marshall pointed out, this pervasive movement to extend and expand the rights of citizenship has been fraught with conflict and is presently nowhere near resolution. The central tenet of political democracy is that all qualified citizens should enjoy full rights and opportunities for meaningful political participation. The concept of participatory democracy repudiates the elitist model of democracy, as it believes that people's participation is the basic principle of democracy. Political participation denotes the active involvement of individuals and groups in the governmental processes affecting their lives. Even passive resistance, civil disobedience and satyagraha are included in the concept of political participation. They are the manifestation of a strong awareness of public interest.[35] Participation refers to actions through which ordinary members of a political system influence, or attempt to influence, outcomes. Ordinary members of a political system can be any persons except those who perform the activities in question as a requirement of their principal jobs. According to Jack H. Nagel, participation has to do with influence from the bottom-up, not from the top-down. He also says that participation can be determined through participating in elections as voters and contestants. By pressurizing officials directly through referendums and meetings, common people can influence decisions. Politics includes not only governments, but also other organizations that control the behaviour or resources of their members through sanctions or legitimacy.[36]

Partha Chatterjee refers to participatory democracy as a deliberative dialogue and decision-making process which hears all voices and diverse perspectives to enact meaningful change. Ideally, it would be an equitable process embarked upon by a group empowered with decision-making authority, a deeper understanding of issues, and is consolidated around a common purpose, forging a collective decision out of individual interests. Participatory democracy is inclusive, requires practice and reflection, accepts and absorbs conflict, actively addresses dissent, and pays attention to those who speak softly or who are on the margins. He argues that the growth of democracy does not depend primarily on the strengthening of civil society but on something else; for instance, increasing entry of the rural population and urban poor into the political society. This is the space of governmentality, in which population groups are able to compel the post-colonial state to negotiate their entitlements.[37] It is argued that this positive type of inclusion is missing in India's political process.

The origins of participatory democracy came to the fore in the movements that emerged in the late 1960s and 1970s in the North. These included the women, students and radical trade union movements – in response to the weak, ineffective nature of electoral democracy. These radical social movements were the product of a very specific historical experience. Although the movements themselves were defeated in many ways, some of their ideas have lasted and now get connected closely with participatory developments in the South, especially Latin America, and particularly Brazil.[38] Traditional representative democracies tend to limit citizen participation to voting, leaving the actual governance to politicians. Participatory democracy strives to create opportunities for all members of a political group to make meaningful contributions to decision-making, and seeks to broaden the range of people who have access to such opportunities. Some define the term 'participatory democracy' based on community-based activity within the domain of civil society and non-governmental public sphere as it is considered as the precondition for the emergence of a strong liberal democracy. Participatory democracy is usually not considered as representative democracy, but as an alternative term to representative democracy. Participatory politics is a long-range political theory that incorporates many characteristics of representative politics. It strives to create a political system that will allow people to participate in politics as much as possible in a face-to-face manner.[39]

Huntington and Nelson made an instrumental, or utilitarian, argument to elucidate the concept of participation. If participants want to influence policy-making, they cannot achieve it through purely private effort or individually, but can achieve it collectively. They are more powerful when they are collectively strong. The idea that participation is a source of influence seems self-evident to most of the people. By participating in politics, people possibly will get or gain their desired goals. If the objectives of participation do not seem worthwhile, the cost can be secured by other means, and then from the instrumental perspective, people need not participate at all. They consider participation as developmental or educative, as it changes participants by developing in them new values, attitudes, skills, knowledge and beliefs. Because the individual is thus transformed by the participatory experience, advocates of the educative effects of participation rarely invoke the individual's present preferences to justify political involvement. Indeed, they usually hope that people will change by adopting more worthy values. First, they believe that people who participate will gain in political efficacy. They will learn how the system works and develop skills that enable them to affect its decisions. Second, by interacting with others with diverse views, participants will become better democratic citizens. They would learn to accept people who differ from themselves. Third, involvement in making decisions will elicit greater commitment to the system as a whole. Obviously, the various educative effects of participation can greatly facilitate the smooth functioning of a polity or organization.[40]

No human rights perspective can be complete without a comprehensive vision and also an action strategy against all structures and forms of dominance. He called it participatory politics. The civil liberties and democratic right movements have been able to grasp this essence through not only a very excruciating experience, but also sacrificing of its own members. The movements have also realized that the gains of democracy or people's movements should not only be consolidated, but also further extended as a part of the overall transformative process. In other words, commitment, sacrifice and creativity are the main tenets of participatory democracy. This leads to a creative society. He also holds that there are two perspectives on protest movements in India. One, the protest movements are to be viewed as potential instruments for bringing about the desired change in the society. The protests are viewed as instruments or avenues reflecting the aspirations of the people, thus preventing the system from deviating. People's struggles also help the system in refining, designing and reorienting priorities in politics. In contrast to this, other scholars argue that the protest movements are antithetical to the smooth governance of politics and, as such, halt economic growth and social change. This could be debated in understanding substantive democracy. The rise in productive forces may take faster than the change in the structure of consciousness. There is also a possibility of consciousness undergoing change even on an underdeveloped material base. This depends on the groups and parties that take up the task of change and the levels of consciousness.[41]

Participatory Democracy and its Responsibility

The first view of participation draws attention to the power that the mass of people, conventionally defined as 'powerless', possess by virtue of the need that the existing social order has for their complicity. This gives them a power of refusal; refusal to reproduce the status quo and with it the power collectively to transform social relationships. This approach emphasizes people's creative power to make alternatives within the present society, alternatives that illustrate or exemplify the values that they are struggling to realize in the future. The struggles raise many issues of popular autonomy and the creation of alternatives which would involve democratic control over public resources and therefore imply a transformation of the state – both its internal hierarchies and its relation to struggles within society.[42] A few politicians and public administrators argue that the institutions/organizations are in danger of losing credibility with the people. Their solution is to open up institutions to representatives of local organizations, but without sharing of power, this would be futile. Another section of politicians and administrators argues people join a struggle to participate in the decisions of the state. Participatory democracy gives an opportunity for activist groups to change the rhetoric ideas/policies to reality/concrete.[43] Participatory democracy challenges and balances the existing representative arrangements. The legitimacy of participatory democracy lies in the high degree of participation with transparent, open discussion and is based on mutually agreed rules.[44] It is also a radical form that is rooted in an autonomous public sphere. It can monitor the work of the executive and state apparatus. It is able to do what politicians never do. Its legitimacy comes from the intensity of the activity and the transparency and openness of the process. It generates self-confident expectations and pressure in the form of lobbying or campaigning on the representative elected bodies who participate in the decision-making process.[45]

Evolution and History of Movements

The evolution of movements can be understood from two directions: philosophical or natural and historical movement. Initially, the protest movements started when human beings started struggling with nature. The deeper process that governs this phenomenon is (a) the struggle of human beings with nature, and (b) the struggle of human beings, to be more specific struggles of the oppressed classes, against stifling and strangulating structures of domination. The struggle that human beings carry against nature is more to meet their physical and material needs; whereas the class struggles aim at realizing 'spiritual' urges. Since human beings have an inner craving for love, friendship and solidarity, they oppose the constraints on freedom and creativity through different forms, ranging from mild protests to violent revolt. All the structures that impose these constraints are fought till they are demolished. It is in this process of demolition of the old that there spring up new human values with fragrancy. In the process, human life is pushed to unknown, but higher, material and spiritual heights.[46]

Barrington Moore argues that industrialization was the major determinant of totalitarianism in the 20th century. Moore argues that the process of modernization led to different paths depending on the degree to which capitalism penetrates rural life, where the landed classes have turned to production for market in a way that enables commercial influence to permeate rural life, and peasant revolutions have been weak. In such circumstances, there is a spectrum of bourgeois revolutions, ranging from France to the semi-capitalist transformation in Germany and Japan, where traditional elements survived to arrest the political excesses (democracy) of capitalism. Moore argues that the development of modernization can be reached through three different paths. One road is the capitalist democracy. Moore calls it the 'bourgeois revolution', which was the road that England took through the Puritan Revolution, the French through the French Revolution, and the United States, through the Civil War. Second, the development that took place in Japan and Germany. Moore points out that 'in the absence of a strong revolutionary surge, it passed through reactionary political forms to culminate in Fascism'.[47]

Protest movements can be understood as a complex set of many actions done by different collective actors oriented towards either some broad issues and goals or specific objectives. A protest activity can be defined as a form of political action involving resistance to one or more policies or conditions created by favouritism or display of an unconventional power. Protests in terms of mass actions are used exclusively for negative inducements, which are not preferred in an absolute sense but preferred over alternative possibilities. In fact, it was during the 16th century, which was considered pre-political or a stateless phase in history, that most of the movements were identified as unorganized or spontaneous mobilizations. During this phase, protest movements were invoked through notions such as primitive rebellions, tribal outbursts, slave riots, etc. The 18th century witnessed anti-imperialist and anti-colonial mobilizations, which led to collective activities and larger movements, and the 19th century witnessed the emergence of people's movements across the world. They challenged centralized economic and political power in both industrial nations and the Third World countries. The protest movements are rooted in the global political economy, in general, and third world countries, in particular. India is one of the striking examples of this. Even this century witnessed the spread of science and technology, followed by industrial revolution and development of modern capitalism. The antagonism between classes or occupational categories got accentrated and resulted in movements.[48]

Barrington Moore argues that the 20th century has been a century of democratic upsurge. Classical forms of democratic imperialism and colonialism were overthrown in Asia and Africa in the course of struggles for liberation. Right to independence of national and self-determination of people acquired the status of basic human rights. The great social revolutionary in Russia, China, Cuba, Vietnam and elsewhere challenged the foundations of class oppression by landlords and capitalists, and created visions of equality and freedom as cherished values for social reconstruction. Despite the reversals of some of those revolutions, their legacies have an abiding significance. Therefore, the struggles for liberation are multidimensional.[49] The phenomenon of Fascism and Nazism, military dictatorship, authoritarianism, eternal intervention and new forces of domination, through transfer of technology and capital and modern communication, are some of the indicators of the process of domination. Such trends have been visible not only at the international level, but also at national and local levels.[50]

Reform (Protest) Movements in India

Pre-independence India witnessed many reformist protest movements. These reformist movements were under the leadership of Brahmo Samaj of 1825, Prarthana Samaj of 1867, Arya Samaj of 1875, the Theosophical Society of 1875, Wahabi Movement and Aligarh Movement. All these early protest movements were basically reformist in character, aiming at bringing certain incremental changes in the socio-religious life of the people. These movements were directed against the conservative and irrational elements practised in India. These were reformative movements that influenced the society and contributed significantly to the growth of nationalism among the

Indian people.[51] In south India, there were many social reformers who worked for reforms in the social system like Mahatma Jyotirao Phule's Satya Shodak Samaj movement and Ambedkar's anti-caste, anti-untouchability struggle in Maharashtra, Periyar Ramaswamy Naicker's non-Brahmin movement in Tamil Nadu and Sri Narayana Guru and Sri Ayyan Kali's social reform struggles in Kerala. Thus, the multi-directional lower caste struggles were in essence not only against the Brahminical and feudal social order, but also against the colonial collusion power structure. They questioned the authority of the Vedas and other Hindu sacred texts, which endorsed the colonial administration that was dominated by the upper castes, and their maintenance of deceptive land accounts, which prevented the Dalits from owning land.[52]

In Andhra Pradesh, several reform movements took place and they influenced people enormously. Kandukuri Veereshalingam attacked official high-handedness as well as prostitution and concubines systems prevailing in society. He created awareness and social consciousness among the youth and strived for spread of education, in general, and women, in particular. He also strived to spread knowledge to liberate people from their deep-rooted superstitions and social evils. He also strived for scientific education in the local language and growth of rationalist thinking. Apart from Veereshalingam, there were others like Desaraju Pedabapaiah, Ragupathi Venkataratnam and Unnava Laxminarayana who worked for social and educational reforms in Andhra society. Basaweshwara, who was the founder of Veerasaivism, denounced the caste system, the Vedic rites of animal sacrifices, the inferior status of women compared to men and the ritual concepts of purity and pollution. He opposed child marriages, advocated widow remarriage and pleaded for individual freedom in matrimonial matters. Vemana attacked social inequalities and distinction based on birth and every external aspect of Hindu ascetic devotees, who set their hopes of salvation upon formal ceremonies. He condemned caste and emphatically stated 'that it is worth, not birth, that should determine a man's position'.

Brahma Naidu of Palnadu was a Vaishnavite by faith and introduced certain reforms in social matters. He appears to have discarded caste and custom and encouraged the heterodox practice of interdining among people belonging to different castes. Potuluri Veerabrahmam propagated his ideas of reform through poems written in a simple style, called Kalagnana Tatvalu. He condemned the hierarchical system of caste and believed that Vedic knowledge could be gained by one and all and pleaded for the discontinuance of idolatry, while strongly criticizing superstitions. He advocated marriage reform and stated that girls should be married only after they passed the age of puberty. He admitted women into his order and made them eligible for sainthood. His philosophy was his trenchant criticism of untouchability and pollution. Narsaiah preached mostly among the Madigas. He argued for a moral code of good conduct and exhorted them not to worship idols and preached unity of Godhead.[53] Dalits in Telangana started the autonomous 'Adi Andhra' Self Respect movement under the leadership of Madari Bhagaiah, popularly known as Bhagya Reddy Varma. Ariga Rama Swamy and B.S. Venkat Rao endlessly engaged themselves in conscientizing Dalits on their identities and plight. There were Dalit organizations called Manya Sangam, Adi Hindu Social Service League, Sawstik Dala Yuvagana Sangam, Adi-Hindu Jatiyonnati Sabha, Sabhari Sangam, Arunodaya Yuvajana Sangam, etc. These worked for the emancipation of Dalits before formation of Andhra Pradesh.[54]

Several Forms of Resistance

Sri Aurobindo, in his theory of passive resistance, has emphasized on three methods of political resistance in India, which include petition and prayer, revolt, and self-development. He discussed the policy of self-development in the form of *swadeshi* and boycott, national education and establishment of arbitration courts on its own and also achievement of political freedom for the country. The bureaucrats and colonial forces definitely opposed the policy of self-development, resulting in boycott and *hartals* by common masses. It put great pressure on the British government to keep up certain promises that they made to the Indian people. He maintained that if the British opposed the concept of self-development or followed any kind of oppressive methods against the common people, people would organize active resistance, instead of passive or defensive methods. He held that prayers, petitions in protests were not always possible and might not produce any result. He also said that passive resistance and boycott were perfectly ethical as they were aimed at the realization of higher goals. He did not favour revolutionary terrorism and instead, always advocated a political protest movement by which political development could be achieved.[55]

Ambedkar, in his theory of social and political resistance, advocated and built the Dalit movement. Though Ambedkar did not completely approve of Gandhi's satyagraha, he used the term 'satyagraha' as a part of Dalit movement. He opined that the struggle against injustice had begun by those who suffered the evils of Hindu religion, and also said that 'satyagragha' was the means to fight against injustice. He further stressed that 'if our cause is based on truth, we need not worry about its success, as truth always leads to success'. The spirit of resistance originated out of his moral conviction that was based on truth. He said that violence and non-violence do change the moral character of the cause. Sometimes one has to take recourse to violence for sheer self-preservation and this type of violence is admissible. The main objects of Ambedkar's social movement include: (i) create awakening in the minds of people, (ii) educate depressed classes, organize themselves to agitate against the social evils of Hindu religion, and (iii) pressurize the government through confrontation and conciliation and plead for politicization of the issue.[56] Mahatma Gandhi's theory of political disobedience strongly believed that untruth and falsehood could only be defeated by truth. He fought for attaining pure ends over means through non-violence. He further held that ends and means were equally important and unity between the two was needed. His freedom movement (struggle), was based on truth, non-violence, 'satyagraha', civil disobedience and non-cooperation, brought freedom to India.[57]

As long as the notion of discrimination, deprivation and denial of fair treatment continues, the phenomenon of protests leading to outbursts in one form or the other, violent or non-violent, will continue to operate. As such, past experience shows that these protest movements have been able to affect the entire process of nation building, national integration and the process of socio-economic development in a multilingual, regional, ethnic society and polity. A highly interventionist state dealing with a poor economy became an object of intense political competition, leading to frustration for some in the game of politics, and thereby resulting in the mobilization of common masses for growing access to and control over political competition. Past experience shows that the protest movements have influenced the working of the Indian social, economic and political system, in general, and federal government, in particular. Given these contradictions, which are thought to be the breeding grounds for protest movements in India, one observes a large number of protest movements of different types and natures sometimes recede within observable time and scale without much challenge to the unity, integrity and existence of the system. But some protests, in course of time, assume a much higher scale and operational area, posing a substantial threat to the existence and functioning of the political system.[58]

Public Opinion: Media and Internet

Social movement-oriented organizations, seeking to influence public opinion and political agenda, depend in part upon mass media to communicate their messages to a more general audience. Michael Lipsky identifies the objectives of mass media, such as (i) protest group constituent, (ii) communicate the message, (iii) refer to public, and (iv) government or political target. In this analysis, protests serve as both internal solidarity building functions, as well as broader functions of communicating movement in a critical manner. Protest constituents have the means of direct communication with protest organizers through participation in demonstrations themselves and interpersonal ties. By organizing the protest events, activists hope to attract the attention of the media through which they influence the policy-makers.[59] It is widely believed that mass media has an important role to play in achieving national goals. The UNESCO report provides the following functions of communication: dissemination of information, socialization, motivation, promoting discussions on public issues, education, culture promotion and entertainment and integration based on the political, cultural and social motivations that influence the people who select information. Theodore Peterson criticized mass media as it has wielded enormous power to its own ends and propagated its own opinions at the expense of opposing points of view. He says that the media have been subordinated to big business and sometimes allowed the advertisers to control the editorial policy and content. Further, the mass media often pays more attention to the superficial and sensational issues in their reports on human events than to the critical issues. The mass media does not emphasize much on public issues but focuses on private interests as it controls the rich socio-economic class or 'the entrepreneurial class'.[60]

Role of Technology in Contemporary Era for the Success of Protest Movements

Technology serves multiple functions that are both positive, as well as negative, for organizations which are fighting against the violation of human rights. It is understood that protest movements were traditionally based on activities such as street theatre, public demonstrations and direct action to challenge the authorities. In modern times, technology has provided new dynamism by electronically promoting the spread of protest ideals and tactics quickly and efficiently across national boundaries. The Internet may serve multiple functions for all these organizations by means of e-mail lobbying with elected representatives, public officials and policy-makers; networking with the related associations and organizations; mobilizing organizations, activists, and members using action alerts, newsletters and e-mails; raising funds and recruiting supporters and sending communication to the public along with the traditional news media.[61] The global reach and real-time speed of the Internet make it particularly useful for transnational support networks, as exemplified by various campaigns. Through the Internet, people can subscribe to advocacy and lobbying groups affiliated with the organization, receive e-mailed policy newsletters and action alerts, sent faxes and e-mails to decision-makers, circulate electronic petitions, learn about forthcoming street demonstrations, protest events as well as share effective strategies for activism.[62] It is understood that, after the manifestation of science and technology, many NGO groups, through the use of websites and e-mail, convey their uncensored messages to the world in order to activate and motivate groups. For example, the success of many international grassroots campaigns has been contingent upon usage of the web and the collaboration of a variety of international citizens' groups as they coordinate their positions, exchange information, and alert politicians.[63] Both identity and interest-based social movements in India have made use of the opportunity the global network affords.

Identity movements, no less than interest-based movements, have become immersed in global networks. Movement-based organizations have used global networks, including the Internet and web pages, to secure visibility abroad, to establish themselves as legitimate actors and to promote their interpretation of controversial issues and events. Movements have made use of technology to exert pressure on policy-makers at home. The Narmada Bachao Andolan is a case in point. Movement-based agitations receive global publicity and are able to exert pressure on policy-makers abroad with the support of international networks.[64] Against this backdrop, it argues, that the Telangana movement also exerted pressure on policy-makers with support of technology as there is an organization called Telangana Development Forum consisting of NRIs supporting the Telangana movement, assisting financially and campaigning internationally in support of a separate statehood for their region. They conduct seminars, conferences and workshops. They have invited speakers, singers and artists to the countries where they are settled to create awareness and explain the necessity of statehood to the NRIs.

People's Movements: Indian Experience

The politics of resistance or mobilizational politics has always occupied a legitimate space in India's democratic framework. It is both due to India's constitutional commitment towards establishment of a welfarist social democracy as well as because of the legacies developed by anti-colonial politics and the national movement. The essence of the nationalist movement was enriched by its reddressal of socio-economic issues. Similarly, the post-independence social movements in India have contributed to the development of a transformative agenda in the mobilizational arena. Their ideological and political interventions have helped in expanding the scope of the formal democratic exercise. Political parties and leading agencies of mainstream politics, have also remained associated with these movements at various levels.[65]

There is an argument that mass movements or protests are inevitable in the Indian context due to its diverse culture. The oppressed classes, who remained submissive, obedient and pessimist, are awakening. Some maintain that protests and agitations have taken place in independent India more due to the accentuation of the conflict between tradition and modernity. The scholars who adhere to the theory of political development consider that rising aspirations of the people are not adequately met by the existing political institutions as they are rigid and incompetent. So, Rajni Kothari argues that direct action is inevitable in the context of India's present-day parliamentary democracy. The general climate of frustration, the ineffectiveness of known channels of communication, the alienation and atomization of the individual, the tendency towards regimentation and the continued state of conflict between the rulers and the ruled make the ideal of self-government more and more remote and render parliamentary government an unstable form of political organization.[66] In India, there are many types and levels of non-party formations. These include typical voluntary organizations involved in constructive activities that started during the national movement. Later, they started to work for the rural poor, artisans and the tribes. On the whole, they happen to be non-political. These types of organizations receive funds from the government and international agencies and provide linkage points between the seats of government and the rural power structure.[67] Another important type of non-party organizations are struggle-oriented groups that take up cudgels against the government on behalf of the deprived and dispossessed. The civil liberties groups also encompass the struggle for a variety of entitlements – shelter, housing, food and nutrition, protection against exploitation of children and women, and bonded labour – in the so-called informal section, apart from the excesses committed by the state itself.[68] Social movements in the Indian point of view are classified on the basis of issues such as forests, civil rights, anti-untouchability, linguistic and nationalist and others are classified on the basis of groups such as peasants, tribals, students, women and Dalits. In some movements, all sections of people participate. In some, only a few sections of people participate. For instance, Indian politics in 1970s saw student movements that raised issues varying from corruption, rise in prices, and rights of the sons of the soil in employment to total revolution. There are several such examples all through the last two to three decades.

A galaxy of scholars discussed the place of protest movements in the Indian political context, notable among them being David Bayley and Rajni Kothari. Y.B. Chawan divides public protests into two categories: peaceful protest movement and direct action. According to him, large-scale demonstrations for the redressal of grievances in a peaceful manner are permissible in a parliamentary democracy. But direct action organized in defiance of law on a mass scale has no place in parliamentary democracy since it means the end of it. According to him, there are different types of direct action.[69] In the former, a group of persons takes law into their hands and administers direct punishment to the supposed wrongdoer without going through the due processes of law. In the second type of direct action, a particular group of people (religious, economic or caste) perceives that injustice was done by the state and wants to take revenge against the other group by the methods not permitted by law. Third, when a group of persons feels disappointed by the policies of the government in power, it launches an organized defiance of law as a technique to get the problem solved.[70]

David Bayley argues that public protests have a certain functional utility even in a parliamentary form of government. A.R. Desai asserts that the parliamentary form of government as a political institutional device has proved to be inadequate to continue or expand concrete democratic rights of the people. Therefore, there is the rise of protest movements. They would continue till adequate political institutional forms for the realization and exercise of concrete democratic rights are found. The liberal polity is in a state of crisis. The institutions of government and political parties, ideas of welfare and distribution, based on Keynesian economics, and the whole model of development to be pursued are out of gear under the impact of powerful global forces with which domestic vested interests have got aligned. Rajni Kothari has talked about the dilemmas of development that led to the growing divide between governments and people.[71]

When the global discourse on democracy has become unidimensional, purveying the neo-liberal model of democracy as the one and universally desirable model, and when the Indian state has begun to link itself to the vertical hierarchy of global economic and political power, strong countervailing political and social movements have emerged in India at the local and regional levels. These micro-movements, led by grassroots groups of social activists, have been active in different parts of India for over three decades, working on disparate issues, especially by economically marginalized and socially excluded sections. Especially in the 1990s, many of these micro-movements aligned together and formed larger alliances to protest against the Indian state on the issue of globalization, even as they get in direct confrontation with the institutions and organizations representing the global economic and political power. In this process of opposition to globalization, the micro-movements in India have begun inventing political practices, expanding the arena of politics much beyond the representational institutions of elections and political parties. It is the challenge of globalization that has brought many of them together on common political platforms at provincial and national levels, making issues a part of their ongoing struggles. In this context, the micro-movements are reinventing participatory democracy as a form of social action and political practice, creating new spaces and infusing deeper meaning to democracy in the globalized world.[72]

Especially in the era of globalization, civil society organizations, activists, intellectuals and academicians are critical about globalization and its implications, that make the majority of the sections helpless. They argue that these developmental trends did lead to resistance both at the global and local levels. At the global level, forces of civil society have been active in organizing demonstrations at the meeting of multi-lateral institutions. Their voices have been drowning their official deliberations at each meeting. They also observe that 'the problem, however, is in creating a critical mass of support and awareness amongst the larger public for the issues that affect them at local, regional, national, and global levels'. It also understood that, in a globalizing world, civil society movements present perhaps the best method of guarding against disproportionate burdens being placed on the poor. The struggles of the subaltern classes in India and their highly specific daily experiences of oppression of resistance remain isolated. Their specific memories of past struggles, many of which have been encapsulated in local rituals and myths, have been transformed and homogenized by previous hegemonic projects into Brahmanic traditions, extolling religious divinities and their heroic deeds. While these have been used to mobilize subaltern support for chauvinistic campaigns, the daily struggle against oppression continues to be isolated and divided along the boundaries of caste, language, region or religion. In the absence of new and reinterpreted shareable spaces and arenas from which they could become part of a mass struggle for societal transformation, they are in danger of being easily suppressed. Metanarratives of religious fundamentalism and chauvinistic regionalism or nationalism will continue to exploit them, either by submerging and homogenizing their distinctiveness, or by turning it into a hostile self-protectionalism. Crude class analysis as a counter-discourse is also a futile option and a source of failure of many initiatives taken on behalf of the unprivileged classes.[73] With this understanding, it is argued that implications of globalization have a major impact on the development model of India, in general, and identity and gender movements, in particular.

Identity and Gender Movements in India

Jean Dreze and Amartya Sen argue that inequality between men and women is one of the most crucial disparities in many societies, and this is particularly so in India. Differences in male and female literacy are one aspect of this broader phenomenon of gender-based inequality in India. It is argued that women face the problem in private and public life as well, compared to men. This is reflected not only in such matters as education and opportunity to develop talents, but also in the more elementary fields of nutrition, health and survival. The discrimination reflects even in her family itself.[74] Ilina Sen argues that the last two decades have seen a conscious articulation of women's issues among many urban and educated middle class women. Many women from educated backgrounds have come together in groups in realization of their strength and potential and have lobbied and protested against the blatant forms of discrimination they face in society.[75] Kancha Ilaiah argues that Dalits organized themselves into the independent Ambedkaraite movement and it slowly created a consciousness of community, as well as sub-community, identity.[76]

Reasons for the People's Movements in India

Mungekar argues that the people of India witness that the contemporary human society is grossly inegalitarian and unequal, where a small number of people in every country and region enjoy a substantially large amount of privileges of all kinds, while a vast majority of them are unable to have adequate access to food, clothing, shelter, elementary education and primary health. They, therefore, wage daily battles for sustaining their bare existence. But history has also recorded such struggles and movements of fundamental nature, since their objective was to abolish the endemic inequalities and establish a better social order. He traces the people's movements to income inequalities, scale of poverty, incidence of hunger, unequal distribution of means of production, gender inequalities, caste inequalities and discrimination, lack of education entitlements, poor access to health, lack of civil facilities, unemployment, globalization and commercialization of social services, the challenge of agrarian crisis, displacement and challenge of communalism, fundamentalism and terrorism. The movements by the oppressed and of the oppressed have enormous inherent potential to stimulate creative intervention. It is necessary to analyse protest movements in philosophical and operational terms. It is in this process that they not only develop a new vision and wider horizon, but also direct a large number of humanistic and democratic groups in building a better social order where dignity, freedom and decency – the philosophical base of human rights – would become human concerns.[77] Given this changing context, social protest movements seek to draw the attention of the ruling elite and public at large to the problems and issues that they consider are important by organizing demonstrations.[78]

K. Balagopal argues about the protest movements and the response of the Indian state. In the 60 years of independence, India has achieved the reputation of being a functioning democracy. That is no doubt true and it is not a small achievement considering that there are not many functioning democracies in the Third World, but nevertheless stock must be taken of how it is functioning. For that, the definition of democracy cannot be restricted to more or less free elections, freedom of expression and an independent judiciary. These are the attributes on the touchstone of which India has been classified as a viable democracy. An equally important element of democracy is the availability of the right to protest by peaceful means. This right is very important since a democracy is measured by the extent to which its government is responsive to the needs of the people. Right to vote, right to move courts and the right to expression merely allow the people an entry into the portals of sovereignty on occasions. They only make India an occasional democracy. The right to agitate to put pressure upon the rulers to listen to people is an important complement. This right, which in India is exercised by means of mass action as processions on public roads, public demonstrations, strike, *dharna* and *bandhs*, find no place in the law and are viewed not as expressions of democracy but as a nuisance and an obstacle to democracy. Excepting occasionally when the Supreme Court held in 1973 that to take out a procession on a public highway is a fundamental right of Indians that can only be subjected to reasonable restrictions, the courts too have taken a negative view of the democratic right to agitate.[79]

These protest movements were so evolved that people from all sections participated in the protest movements. This involves those who thought that they and their causes were neglected by governments or its institutions. This trend was buttressed by the anti-colonial struggles and freedom movements.[80] This legacy continued even during the post-independence period. While the 1950s and 1960s were relatively peaceful, it was during the 1970s that there was a spurt in people's movements. In fact, they reached unmanageable limits by the mid-1970s. The incidence and frequency of the movements reached a point that every city witnessed a protest a day, if not more. The protest movements have challenged economic and political power in all the countries. India is one of the striking examples of this. Those who think they are undermined and neglected by the government or its institutions participate in the process of protest movements which eventually turn either into general strikes, or violent outbursts.[81]

Judith M. Brown argues that given the important role of the parties and their functions in a democratic system, they function/act effectively as mediators between the government and citizens. Sometimes there can be issues and occasions that provoke dissent that is too difficult for party mechanisms. Very often based on the response of political parties, citizens feel they have to express their aspirations and need direct dissent/demonstrations. For instance, in India during the phase of Congress dominance, some groups/parties felt ignored and took to street demonstrations, protests, and acts of civil disobedience and even to violence. Government has responded to these direct expressions of dissent in varied ways. Their responsiveness has always been hampered by the need to adjust between conflicting demands and possibly governments managed dissent by organizing potentially vocal interest groups within party structures. A third alternative in the face of overt dissent coercion is employed to suppress the opinion by the state's monopoly of organized force.[82] Protest is the failure of democratic consensus and the polity's democratic goals. The fraternity of India's democratic order and its ineffectiveness in providing a link between citizens and government is abundantly clear from the accumulating evidence of citizens' violence and government's deliberate and persistent use of the authoritarian potential in its possession.[83] The courts and the administration are negative towards agitations and the government suppresses the agitations with repressive laws. Over a period of time, the administration is intolerant towards the protesters and has reached a point where police firing on protesters is considered as the solution. This negative attitude of the state gives the scope for the people to think that the state violates the right to protest, if the people oppose the state.[84] The negative attitude becomes an obstacle to the realization of the people's basic rights to shelter, food, work and dignified existence. The government on its own cares least for these rights, and without the right to protest, none of them can be realized.[85]

Separate Statehood Agitations in Post-Independent India

During the 65 years of independent India, several movements sprung up because of social complexities, caste conflicts, religious fundamentalism, negative attitude of political leadership, economic disparities, uneven distribution of resources and intra and interregional disparities. These constraints led to a spurt in people's movements across the country. In this context, it is argued that many separate statehood agitations have been taking place in post-independent India. A few of them have succeeded, a few of them did not and some are still fighting for fulfilment of aspirations of their people. A separate Telangana state movement is one among them, fighting for the last six decades with ups and downs. Let's try to understand the relevance of separate movements that strive for substantive democracy or, as Manoranjan Mohanty characterized it, strive for a creative society.

Crisis of Social Movements in India

Post-independence, social movements have, on the whole, played a peripheral role in Indian politics. In spite of strong ideological interventions of social movements, the political practice of the movements has been very limited in its scope. The movements have never been able to successfully put pressure on mainstream politics vis-à-vis their own agenda of social transformation. Especially during the last two decades, Indian politics has witnessed a complete marginalization of the transformative agenda. Social movements are on a decline. They appear to be localized, weak and fragmented. With the welfarist state withdrawing itself from the social sphere and the rightist forces dominating the electoral arena, the democratic framework has gradually become vacuous. With the onslaught of the global market forces, the expressions of domination have become complex and dispersed. The composition and character of civil society are changing rapidly. Under these circumstances, the mobilizational space available to the social movements is shrinking. On the other hand, the circumstances demand a strong intervention on the part of the social movements, not only to enhance the essence of the formal democratic framework, but also to save the framework itself.[86] The failure of the Left-led trade union movement is manifold in agrarian movements as Left forces proved completely unable to expand the dimensions of class politics. On the contrary, the movement depended on the state to a large extent in fulfilling its agenda. It remained engulfed with the ideology of trade unions, rather than developing an overall political agenda. In struggling against state monopoly and its anti-people politics, the Naxalite movement and its strategies not only alienated them from large sections of society, but also made these groups an easy target of state repression. On the other hand, when the movement was compelled to enter the electoral arena, it had to negotiate with the bourgeois parties and its success was limited. Similarly, the movement could not deal with the caste question, though it mobilized Dalits and tribals but it hardly got support from the backward classes. Farmers' movements in India never emphasized rewards like the redistribution of land or an increase in wages of agricultural labourers and there was no long-term political programme. Initially, the movement adopted a neutral political stance where all political parties were seen as equally responsible for injustice to farmers. Later, the organizations started bargaining with various political parties at the time of elections. The women's movement remained confined to urban centres and failed to communicate the injustice to women in rural areas.[87]

Though there are a few drawbacks in movements, in a broader context, movements strive to deepen the notion of democracy. Starting from World Wars, movements have come up against wrongs, feudalism, capitalism, dictatorship and negative attitude of leadership and injustice. While participating in the movements, people give themselves the opportunity to assess their nature, behaviour, inter personal relations and ultimately protest against the anti-people policies and rulers. Protest movements further strive for substantive democracy and struggle to implement the spirit of the Constitution and fundamental rights and directive principles. That is how one has to see the movements for autonomy, regional identities, women rights, tribal, Dalit rights and separate statehood agitations. These are all striving for self-rule, dignity, self-respect and development. Hence, movements do deepen the very spirit of democracy.

To sum up, the study reveals that the evolution of movements can be understood from historical and theoretical perspectives. There were several revolutions and wars that laid the foundation for the rights discourse. Evolution of movements can also be found in natural rights theories, liberalism, individualism and so on. There were several reformist and resistance movements in pre- and post-independence India which had a major impact on the freedom movement and ongoing movements, and which also deepened and have been deepening democracy. It maintains that contemporary politics has been dominated by a few elite sections. The politics of India moved from its democratic spirit to politics of suspicion and the role of media and technology is under a few elite dominant classes and does not really represent the voices of people. With this backdrop, it can be argued that the people's movements in India have been pressurizing the state to see that formal democracy should move to substantive democracy. Hence, the next chapter deals with Indian Democracy: Vitalities and Vulnerabilities.

Notes

1. Ghanshyam Shah, *Social Movements and the State*, Sage Publications, New Delhi, 2002, p. 1.
2. G. Haragopal and B. Jagannatham, 'Terrorism and Human Rights: Indian Experience with Repressive Laws', *Economic and Political Weekly*, Vol. XLIV, No. 28, July 2009, pp. 77–78.

3. D.L. Sheth, 'Globalization in India and New Politics of Micro-Movements', *Economic and Political Weekly,* Vol. 39, No. 39, 2004, p. 1.
4. Barrington Moore, *Social Origins of Dictatorship and Democracy,* Beacon Press, Boston, 1966, pp. 162–72.
5. N.P. Chaubey, 'People's Struggles and Movements for Equitable Society', *Bharatiya Samajik Chintan,* Vol. VI, No. 3, October–December 2007, p. 147.
6. Ibid., p. 151.
7. D.L. Sheth, op. cit., pp. 45–56.
8. Mary Katzenstein, Smitu Kothari and Uday Mehta, 'Social Movement Politics in India: Institutions, Interests and Identities', in *The Success of Indian Democracy,* edited by Atul Kohli, Cambridge University Press, Cambridge, 2001, pp. 243–47.
9. S.H. Barnes and M. Kaase, *Political Action: Mass Participation in Five Western Democracies,* Sage Publications, Beverly Hills, 1979, pp. 12–13.
10. Ibid.
11. Charles Tilly, *Social Movements, 1768–2004,* Paradigm Publishers, Colorado, 2004, p. 3.
12. B. Jagannatham, 'Politics of Participation and Human Rights: A Case Study of Protests in Hyderabad City', *Indian Journal of Human Rights,* Vol. 5, No. 2, January–December 2005, pp. 144–45.
13. Kameshwar Chowdhary, 'Historical Overview of Social Movements in India and Water Management', 8th Biennial Conference of the IASCP, Indiana University, Bloomington, May 31–June 4, 2000, p. 3.
14. M.S.A. Rao, *Social Movements in India,* Manohar Publications, New Delhi, 1979, p. xiv.
15. Ibid., p. 3.
16. Andrew Gunder Frank and Marta Fuentes, 'Nine Theses on Social Movements', in *Social Movements and State: Readings in Indian Government and Politics,* edited by Ghanshyam Shah, Sage Publications, New Delhi, 2000, pp. 202–33.
17. Ibid.
18. Ghanshyam Shah, op. cit., pp. 15–31.
19. Charles Tilly, 'Rural Collective Action in Modern Europe', Working Paper, Centre for Research Social Organization, Michigan, April, 1974, p. 3.
20. Mohammad Yasin and Srinanda Dasgupta, *Indian Politics: Protests and Movements,* Anmol Publications, New Delhi, 2003, p. 8.
21. Ibid.

22. S.K. Srivastava, *Social Movements for Social Development*, Chugh Publications, Allahabad, 1998, pp. 17–25.
23. Michael Lipsky, 'Protest as Political Resource', *American Political Science Review,* Vol. 62, No. 4, December, 1968, p. 1148.
24. Ibid., pp. 1144–58.
25. Robert A. Heywood, 'The Theory of Political Coalitions', *American Political Science Review,* Los Angeles, 2003, p. 54.
26. K. Balagopal, 'Crime, Repression and Terror in Indian Politics: Chapter on Indian Politics', IGNOU, New Delhi, source: *http://www.egyankosh.ac.in/bitstream/123456789/25711/1/Unit-32.pdf*
27. Maurice Duverger, *The Idea of Politics: The Use of Power in Society,* Methuen & Co. Limited, London, 1964.
28. K. Balagopal, op. cit.
29. Ibid.
30. Marvin E. Olsen, *Participatory Pluralism: Political Participation and Influence in the United States and Sweden*, Nelson Hall, Chicago, 1982, p. 18.
31. Ibid., p. 59.
32. Ibid.
33. Ibid., pp. 22–23.
34. Ibid.
35. O.P. Gouba, *An Introduction to Political Theory,* Macmillan India Limited, Delhi, 1981, p. 76.
36. Jack H. Nagel, *Participation*, Prentice Hall International, London, 1987, pp. 1–5.
37. Partha Chatterjee, *The Politics of the Governed Reflections on Popular Politics in Most of the World*, Columbia University Press, New York, 2004, pp. 33–39.
38. Ibid.
39. Ibid.
40. Hilary Wainwright, 'Why Participatory Democracy Matters – And Movements Matter to Participatory Democracy', June, 2005, source: *http://www.tni.org/detail_page.phtml?page=archives_wainwright_matter*
41. G. Haragopal, *Political Economy of Human Rights: Emerging Dimensions*, Himalaya Publications, Bombay, 1992, p. 27.
42. Ibid.
43. Ibid.
44. Hilary Wainwright, op. cit.
45. Ibid.

46. G. Haragopal's lecture on 'The Relevance of People's Movements in the Era of Globalization', at XXXI Indian Social Science Congress, Mumbai, 27–31 December 2007.
47. Barrington Moore, op. cit., pp. 427–29.
48. Ibid., pp. 441–51.
49. Ibid.
50. Ibid., p. 441.
51. Ashok S. Choulaskar, *Indian Idea of Political Resistance*, Ajanta Publications, New Delhi, 1990, pp. 5–8.
52. K.Y. Ratnam, 'The Dalit Movement and Democratization in Andhra Pradesh', Working Paper No. 13, East West Center, Washington, December, 2008, p. 3.
53. V. Ramakrishna, *Social Reforms in Andhra*, Vikas Publishing House, New Delhi, 1983, pp. 37–40.
54. Ibid., p. 4.
55. Ashok S. Choulaskar, op. cit., pp. 32–38.
56. Ibid., pp. 89–93.
57. Ibid., pp. 76–82.
58. Mohammad Yasin and Srinanda Dasgupta, op. cit., pp. 6–7.
59. Michael Lipsky, op. cit., pp. 1144–58.
60. Ibid., p. 1144.
61. G. Sudarshanam and B. Jagannatham, 'Politics of Participation: Role of Science and Technology', paper presented in the National Seminar organized by the Academic Staff College, University of Hyderabad, Hyderabad, 23–24 November 2006.
62. Ibid.
63. B. Jagannatham, *Forms of Protests: A Case Study of Hyderabad*, University of Hyderabad, Hyderabad, 2005, p. 156.
64. Mary Katzenstein, Smitu Kothari and Uday Mehta, op. cit., pp. 163–64.
65. Rajeshwari Deshpande, 'Social Movements in Crisis?', in *Indian Democracy: Meanings and Practices*, edited by Rajendra Vora and Suhas Palshikar, Sage Publications, New Delhi, 2004, p. 379.
66. Mohammad Yasin and Srinanda Dasgupta, op. cit., p. 165.
67. Ibid., p. 69.
68. Ibid.
69. Ibid., p. 157.
70. Ibid., p. 158.
71. Ibid., p. 168.
72. D.L. Sheth, op. cit., pp. 45–56.

73. Jayant Lele, 'Understanding Indian Politics', in *Indian Democracy: Meanings and Practices*, edited by Rajendra Vora and Suhas Palshikar, Sage Publications, New Delhi, 2004, p. 211.
74. Jean Dreze and Amartya Sen, 'Gender, Inequality and Women's Agitations', in *Indian Government and Politics: Caste, Class and Gender,* edited by Manoranjan Mohanty, Sage Publications, New Delhi, 2004, p. 362.
75. Ilina Sen, 'Women and People's Movement: A Space within the Struggle', in *Indian Government and Politics: Caste, Class and Gender,* edited by Manoranjan Mohanty, Sage Publications, New Delhi, 2004, p. 320.
76. Kancha Ilaiah, 'Caste or Class or Class or Caste', in *Indian Government and Politics: Caste, Class and Gender,* edited by Manoranjan Mohanty, Sage Publications, New Delhi, 2004, p. 232.
77. B.L. Mungekar, Presidential Address 'People's Movements', XXXI Indian Social Science Congress, Mumbai, 27–31 December 2007.
78. Ibid.
79. K. Balagopal, 'Protest Movements in India', *Indian Express,* 15 August 2008, p. 4.
80. T.K. Oommen, *Nation, Civil Society and Social Movements: Essays in Political Sociology,* Sage Publications, New Delhi, 2000, pp. 179–85.
81. Pippa Norris, *Democratic Phoenix: Re-inventing Political Activism*, Harvard Press, London, 2004, pp. 5–6.
82. Judith M. Brown, *Modern India: The Origin of an Asian Democracy,* Oxford University Press, New York, 1995, pp. 372–74.
83. Ibid.
84. Ibid.
85. Ibid.
86. Ibid., p. 379.
87. Rajeshwari Deshpande, op. cit., pp. 383–94.

4 Indian Democracy

Vitalities and Vulnerabilities

The modern democracy, mostly formal, has been derived from the liberal worldview that rose from the ashes of the traditional worldview. Thus, it is clear that factors and forces that emerged became active and played their part in influencing ideas, institutions and practices. Some of these ideas, institutions and practices did make their appearance from time to time, but in different forms and substantive contents. This sequence was immensely influenced by certain ideas and ideological preferences that appeared in different phases of human history.[1] The modern democracy also creates a division in the ranks of those who rule and command and those who submit themselves to the rule and command of the rulers. This division of the demos into two categories proves significant for the nature of democracy, especially formal democracy. The reason for this lies in the fact that those who submit themselves to the rule and command of the rulers are allowed only a very limited participation in public affairs; their participation is limited only to periodical elections of the rulers, who then rule in the name of the people. This limited participation on the part of demos poses certain threats to the democratic process, like the elite perpetuating their power. It is because of this fact that popular participation is considered crucial for the successful functioning of democracy in the real sense of the term and must, therefore, be embedded in the democratic process. But what formal democracy does is to rule this completely out.[2] The same experience of modern democracy reflects India's democracy. The people of India are divided into two sections like the rulers and ruled, elite and mass. Elite always dominates polity, economy and social life. Mass participation submits itself to elite sections and is confined merely to voters.

Formal and Substantive Democracy: Concept and Context

In contemporary times, the universal acceptance and acclamation of the term 'democracy' has made confusion worst confounded. The state of affairs has not only created a situation to talk for or against democracy, but it has also made democracy an object of excessive adulation and severe condemnation.[3] Niraja Gopal Jayal argues that the experience of democratic government is not merely confined to India. She argues that deeper reasons must be explored as that flows from the nature of the concept of democracy as it has evolved in the course of several centuries.[4] Democratic preconditions and democratic procedures allow goodness, truth and social justice. In the democratic states, people provide a cultural and institutional framework, within which they can articulate such values. Democratic spirit and practice is a means to promote justice and it calls for deepening of democracy beyond the superficial trappings that many societies endorse and take some steps to achieve such values. India is an exception among the Third World countries to opt for and maintain a parliamentary system. It is a political instrument intended to build a participatory, egalitarian and just social order in which popular sovereignty rests with the people and by which common men and women participate in the decision-making process to improve their socio-economic condition and enhance their living standards. The parliamentary system aims at eradicating all kinds of oppression and exploitation.[5] It is in this connection that Indian democracy needs to be assessed.

Indian Democracy: Formal and Substantive

Formal democracy and substantive democracy stand at two different poles of a continuum. The formal system of democracy carries some philosophical and theoretical framework, but it has to be carried substantially. This is so for the simple reason that two forms of democracy belong to two different streams of thinking. Both are a contrast to each other.[6] Formal democracy continues its periodic elections based on adult franchise, and party and governmental structures that are meant to institutionalize these and thereby act upon traditional institutions and affiliations. New representative levers are provided by reservation of seats and jobs for the underprivileged communities. Freedom of speech and association were all meant to usher in a revolution in social relations and provide the bases of a new nationwide integration.[7]

India, in its first 50 years, as an independent state, abundantly illustrated the expanding meaning of freedom and democracy. A dialectical process of India's political struggle is not merely involved in procedural, but also in substantial dimensions of democracy. The functioning of political institutions, elements of socio-economic change, and the politics within the state and politics in civil society fit in India's experience. On issues like weaker sections, Dalits, women, federalism, secularism, minority rights, welfare state and nature and quality of development, a certain consensus has begun to emerge in the country in the course of a protracted struggle on many fronts.[8] Indian society carves itself into ethnic, religious and caste groupings against their percentage representation in the institutions: the legislatures, the civil service, and the judiciary. Exclusion is a denial of democracy and disadvantaged groups must be represented through reserved quotas as representation is a mechanism that can facilitate participation and hopefully trigger policy impact.[9] Over the past half a century, the Constitution has evolved in response to democratic struggles in India through amendments, judicial interpretations and political rights.[10]

The Indian Constitution was written in the background of widespread hopes and expectations. It was believed that the opportunity to 'rule ourselves' would open up extensive, if not unlimited, possibilities of bettering our lives across the board. 'From the beginning of the freedom struggle, the basic purpose had been a government of the people, by the people and for the people.' Ideas of what was a better life had been thrown up by social struggles and reform movements of many kinds that dominated Indian public life for more than a century preceding Independence. The exposure to ideas emanating from the liberal West, as well as the socialist East, had their impact too. The Indian Constitution is not totally hostile to this notion, but there is no explicit recognition of it, nor any provision for it. And there is much that works against it.[11]

The Preamble of the Universal Declaration of Human Rights has emphasized on the principles of freedom, respect, dignity, peace, equality and tolerance, the rights of life, liberty and security of the person. Everyone has the right to freedom of movement within the state and everyone has the right to peaceful assembly and association, everyone has the right to work, free choice of employment, just and favourable conditions of work and protection against unemployment, right to equal pay for equal work and right to form and join associations for the protection of his interests. Similar to UDHR, the Indian Constitution is a product of the freedom movement and also the global context of the late forties which was infused with liberalism, socialism and democracy. It is not merely a mechanical arrangement of power and institutions for governance. Unlike several constitutions of the world, it has attempted to set a goal, and provide a vision and direction in building a new social order which is not only democratic, but equal and just. It envisages a very positive role for the Indian state in reconstruction of the social order, protecting political freedom and contributing to the gradual transformation of the social and economic order. In other words, it was expected to strive to build a democratic society, which would include political, social, and economic democracy. In the late 1940s, there was no option except incorporating ideology of social justice as a part of the constitutional scheme. It emphasized on fundamental rights, human rights and dignity of the individuals. It provided for equality, freedom, and equality before law.[12]

In addition to these rights, Indian citizens have several laws to protect and uphold the rights of Dalits.[13] Political and civil rights became central concepts in India's Constitution with the rule of law and an independent judiciary occupying important positions in the polity, which combined political democracy with ideas of social justice. The Directive Principles of the Indian Constitution reflect on social and economic justice. Based on these provisions, the urgent need for economic and social justice was recognized through a number of public policy responses and a series of social legislations that had a direct impact on the condition of the masses in relation to the distribution of property and means of livelihood. A variety of institutions and administrative setup were also put in place for the protection and promotion of values to enable enhancement of human rights. One of the crucial objectives of the Indian Constitution is to promote social revolution, but it found that it is difficult to struggle against the prevailing social order in Indian society substantially.[14] In this regard, it is necessary to assess the Indian Constitution and the problems in implementation.

The agrarian crisis was not only unable to sustain industrial development, particularly in terms of demand generation, but also entered into a more serious conflict with the urban, industrial, market development syndrome. In this process of managing this conflict, dependency on foreign technology increased further. This was the period which witnessed regional and sub-regional agitations, secessionist trends, food riots, collapse of one-party dominance and rise of united fronts. All these gave birth to several movements. In every stage of development, while there was some emphasis on certain agrarian changes, soon there was a compromise. While there was abolition of zamindari and intermediary institutions, there was no attempt to radicalize land reforms. A radical land reforms programme ought to have been the first step to reform the goals of Part IV of the Constitution. The ownership structure underwent some changes, more on account of market intervention, and not the state. The tensions intrinsic to the unequal and unjust rural structure were evident in their symptomatic form by the mid-1960s. Instead of attempting structural changes, the policy-makers opted for technological substitutes. Thus, the Green Revolution became a substitute for structural changes. The Green Revolution, being biased towards capital and water, reinforced uneven development across the regions and widened the disparities between different classes and also between regions. This led to considerable tensions, resulting in a political crisis.

The deep economic crisis confronting India in the decades of the 1980s and 1990s was a fallout. The liberalization, privatization, marketization and globalization process have been thrust on the economy as a part of the effort to overcome the crisis. They, however, are not policy measures emanating from either the Indian economic elite or much less the political elite. They emerged as a part of the structural adjustment.[15] Concrete experience and evidence suggests that, during the last six decades, the nation drifted so violently that the social justice vision got completely blurred. After the transfer of power, the drift began in the very early stage and there was not enough popular or democratic pressure to prevent it.

Balagopal argues that the reason is that unlike laws made for benefit of the rich, which find their way into implementation without any difficulty, laws made for the benefit of poor and the underprivileged encounter difficulties at every step as the Constitution does not recognize the socio-legal reality, and does not make a provision for it. Hence, Balgopal argues that the right to vote is not by itself sufficient. It must be adequately supplemented by the right to agitate, along with the right to assemble, associate, to hold beliefs and to speak out. It must be made clear that the right to agitate is required not only to achieve the equality that the Constitution promises in the future, but also to protect the rights that the Constitution and the laws made under it have already given. He further argues that a wide spectrum of political opinion, political sympathy and political activity is dragged into the perimeter of crime by extraordinary laws enacted in the name of tackling seditious activity, terrorist activity, and activity 'prejudicial to the nation's territorial integrity and unity'. A large area of political expression is rendered illegal under the Constitution. If the opinion is itself illegal, obviously no agitation for its dissemination or realization can be tolerated by the law. This is the sad reflection of India's democracy.[16]

India also witnessed several laws which are repressive in nature. These include: the Preventive Detention Act, at the advent of Independence, followed by Punjab Security Act, 1955, the Assam Disturbed Areas Act, 1955, and the Armed Forces (Assam and Manipur) Special Powers Act, 1958. In the 1960s and 1970s, there were two major Acts passed in each decade. In the eighties, there were five Acts and in the nineties there were two Acts. There are 20–30 repressive Acts passed either at the Central or the state level, which include Armed Forces Special Powers Act, TADA, POTA and the Unlawful Activities (Prevention) Amendment Act.[17] India has been witnessing the problem of caste since time immemorial. There were movements against untouchability, caste system and atrocities. With the result, successive Indian governments enacted several laws reforms like labour laws, land reforms, Untouchability (Offences) Act, 1955 and the Scheduled Castes and Scheduled Tribes (Prevention of Atrocities Act), 1989 to eradicate the caste system and prevent atrocities on Dalits. Other reforms followed. These included: judicial reforms, electoral reforms, economic reforms, new development policies to eradicate poverty and reduce the gap between poor and rich, urban and rural; backward and forward regions.

Indian Democracy and its Positive Measures

The accomplishments of Indian democracy include the constitutional initiative in the sphere of local democracy and the national legislation guaranteeing the right to information. There is no doubt that the new panchayats have created public spaces where citizens, including and especially women, Dalits and Adivasis, can meet with those who have traditionally oppressed and exploited them, on relatively equal terms. In the last two decades, in relation to the way communitarianism has taken shape in India, there has been pronounced expansion of democracy, seen in the enfranchisement of Dalits, the empowerment of oppressed castes, the assertion of women and the deepening of popular commitments for the ideas and potentialities of democracy.[18] Likewise, the achievement of the Right to Information is a measure of the success of Indian democracy in creating radical possibilities for civil society. Revolutionary legislations that hopefully enable citizens to recover a core component of the democratic ideal, namely, accountability, and the National Rural Employment Guarantee Act provide the right to livelihood. From decentralization to the right to information, from the right to education to the campaign for the right to food, it is these initiatives that are the more substantive ways of deepening democracy.[19] The establishment of a popular democratic government, based on universal adult suffrage, free and fair elections, guaranteed fundamental rights and an independent judiciary, provides strong foundations on which the democratic system rests in India. The effective participation of the people in a political process is ensured by the regular conduct of elections at scheduled intervals with increasing voter turnout. It has not only reinforced the system, but also helped in further consolidating the democratic institutions.[20] The wider involvement of people in political activities is further discernible in an increasing number of people coming forward to contest elections, irrespective of caste, gender and religion.[21] But the question arises: are the fruits of local democracy really enjoyed by Dalits and women? The Right to Information, is it really substantially being extended? The answers are 'no'. It results in raising the question of implementation and giving rise to people's assertions. People's struggles to keep this public space free from hierarchy and inequality are even now being mounted daily across the country.

Indian State and Anti-People Policies

The social and political erosion is bringing a sharp decline in the legitimacy and authority of the modern state. There are many reasons for the erosion of authority and legitimacy of the state. First, the erstwhile vision of making the state a condition for civilized existence has been under attack from antagonistic forces. A marked change has taken place in the growth of both Left wing and Right wing ideologies, which has had a direct bearing on the role of the state. The state is caught between globalist and localist pressures, a completely new set of interests that have emerged in the public arena. There are global corporate interests arising from the latest phase of capitalism with transnational corporations as key factors and political leadership becoming increasingly uncertain and depending on money and muscle power.[22] It has resulted in the growth in the high-tech variety of industrial institutions which are likely to further widen the class and caste divide, increase unemployment and growing exclusion of millions of people-producing growing unrest and violence on the part of many of them. The switch to the new hi-tech models of development is bringing about a division within the middle class as the basis of an expanding market, despite growing poverty, unemployment, and social disparities.[23]

Jayant Lele argues that in the era of information technology, people are way ahead of the normal run of the organized sector. The organized sector is getting increasingly disorganized. Meanwhile, the agricultural economy is showing signs of weakening. Jayant Lele further argues that the decade of 1990s was being celebrated not merely for the fair amount of reform of the economy, but it was also a decade in which poverty increased. The unorganized sector, including child labour and migration of women, has grown and a new model of mafia rule is in the forefront in polity and urban slums across the country. Globalization needs to be countered not just by building new initiatives within local, national and regional frameworks, but also by doing the same at the level of the international political economy in restructuring of the world order.[24] The study argues that though they are positive measures to strengthen the Indian democracy, there are also drawbacks in implementation.

The paradox from a human rights point of view with our Constitution is that it places the highest goals – taken equally from the liberal West, the socialist East and India's own rebel traditions – before the nation, but does not provide the people with instruments of requisite strength to realize the goals. And it puts the kind of power in the hands of the administration that would certainly militate against it.[25] The strongest instrument would be the freedom needed to agitate and struggle against the inequalities that are in the way of the goals of the Constitution. It must be made clear that the right to agitate is required not only to achieve the equality that the Constitution promises in future, but even to protect the rights that the Constitution and the laws have already given.[26]

Indian Democracy and Protests: Deepening of Democracy

The last decade of the 20th century and the early years of the new century saw momentous developments in India, signalling intensification of political struggles involving class, caste, gender and ethnicity. The launching of economic reforms in 1991 heralded a new stage of capitalist development in India. Because of global, as well as domestic, reasons, the growing capitalist class acquired new privileges and it continued to exist but in a much reduced strength. Several kinds of social conflicts got accentuated for electoral purposes. The upsurge of the backward classes was sought to be neutralized by Hindu communal mobilization. All social issues got enmeshed with the Hindu nationalist challenge. While the economic reforms went ahead under all regimes, the occurrence of violence in various parts of society and, other socio-cultural problems arose. Thus, in the early years of the 21st century, these trends – globalization, authoritarianism and communalism – had become powerful currents affecting the entire gamut of social issues in India.[27]

The combination of these problems has led to create several lines of separation among different groups in Indian society. These problems led to people's assertion. In the mid-1970s, the Emergency triggered the birth of a strong civil liberties movement that later went on to pioneer the cause of social and economic rights as well. The post-Emergency election of 1977 provided reassuring evidence of the resilience of Indian democracy and the maturity of even the unlettered voter. The second was the political mobilization and assertion of the backward castes and Dalits, processes that had been set in motion in the 1970s and 1980s, but which acquired an accelerated pace, post-Mandal. A few regional parties gave impetus to caste-based mobilization, that resulted in an increase in backward caste representation in both state legislatures and Parliament and was, therefore, hailed as a qualitative departure from the polity of the past, a signifier of the deepening of democracy. Low-caste status is often accompanied by deprivation, and traditional and historical forms of social inequality thus co-exist with, and are reinforced by inequalities arising out of the sphere of production and economic activity. If we look at NCAER data regarding human development indicators and poverty amongst various social groups, we find that levels of deprivation are highest for the Scheduled Castes, followed by the Scheduled Tribes and the Muslims. They started organizing for political power.[28]

Hence, post-independence politics in India can be celebrated as a struggle for democratic transformation. The greatest gain in the struggle has been the rise of democratic consciousness among the people and a comprehensive understanding of the meaning of democratic evolution. The oppressed people, such as Dalits, Adivasis, poor peasants, unorganized workers and women, have acquired an unprecedented level of awareness of democratic rights and their creative potentiality. Various identity groups seek autonomy and self-determination, and demand social, cultural, economic and political guarantees to fulfil their aspirations. The intensity of the challenge has shaken the ruling forces to such an extent that the rulers have resorted to many measures, such as liberalization, globalization, religious mobilization and authoritarian repression, to meet the situation. The struggle characterizes the contemporary stage of the Indian democratic revolution. In contemporary India, there's the emergence of a creative society in which the hitherto subdued contradictions have become articulate and active. Together with this, various infirmities and negative aspects have also crept into it, like the denial of rights to individuals who disregarded community injections, retaliatory politics in relation to those below them in ritual status, the humiliation of Dalits and women who defy community norms, lack of decorum, and so on. These developments have gone together and made a package of contradictory features. We can say that the widespread changes in Indian democracy are taking place in a pronouncedly untidy manner; this is so in the sense that there is a pronounced rule-deficit in the structuring of the political process.

This contradictory nature of Indian democracy is a conundrum. While it is glorified as the largest democracy in the world by some, others condemn it as fake and likely to falter soon. Such extremely contradictory representations are witnessed because the Indian democracy does not fit into any given model of democracy. Most of the stable democracies, today, are industrialized and grew into capitalist economies unlike India, which continues to be essentially agrarian with a highly hierarchical social order. Survival of constitutional government, regular elections, freedom of expression, free press and an independent judiciary existing within a hierarchical social structural setting seem incredible and unheard of in the history of democracy. While many countries may claim to be democratic, their political institutions obviously display the fragility and vulnerability of democratic arrangements. Indian democracy is situated in its republican Constitution. The newly-independent country with perplexing religious, linguistic, regional and caste diversities amidst problems of illiteracy, poverty and all-round economic and social backwardness called for development and modernization within a reasonable period of time.[29]

The electoral process is losing out on its credibility since the mid-1980s because of the ominous trends emerging in the conduct of free and fair elections. Unprecedented cases of booth capturing, the increasing number of election-related killings, the incidence of malpractices, and the uncontrolled use of money and mafia power witnessed during the last few general elections are eating into the vitals of the electoral system. The entry of 'confirmed criminals' into state legislatures, representing various political parties, seems to spoil some of the grandeur and dignity inherent in the democratic image of India. The criminalization of politics continues to gain political legitimacy, its unlawfulness notwithstanding. The menacing trends in the electoral practices are, however, not a threat to the very survival of parliamentary democracy because it is still localized and manageable. In reality, these drifts are an expression of the expanding nature of democratic participation.[30]

The experience of Indian democracy advocates that in the name of democracy, a few elite and propertied classes participate in policy-making and implement the policies in the name of globalization. They have neglected the agrarian development and farmers and marginalized communities as the governments have gradually withdrawn, or are still withdrawing, from welfare policies.[31] The democratic upsurge since 1977 dramatically transformed the political landscape. India became perhaps 'the only large democracy in the world today where the turnout of the lower orders of society is well above that of the most privileged groups'. In 1980s and 1990s, tribals and Dalits closed the gap between vote levels in reserved and general constituencies, while the odd ratio for voting of the Hindu upper castes showed a relative decline. All of this changed the social composition of voters and those who took part in political activities. The expanded participatory base of India's politics reached downward to involve nearly all groups suffering from some form of social deprivation and backwardness. In spite of several people's struggles against the globalization process during this phase, India failed to make a significant impact on the problems of mass poverty. In terms of growth in GDP and attracting investments, these achievements seem to have increased dualism between the modern industrial sector and the vast rural hinterland. Within the countryside, growing numbers of marginal cultivators swamp a minority of prosperous commercial farmers and landless labourers who have the greatest difficulty in meeting even their minimum consumption needs. This hostile development of technology and inability of the state to achieve the overall economic transformation led to a spurt in people's struggles.[32]

Post-1990s Political Economy of India

Francine R. Frankel argues that though Vision 2020 has a few positive aspects, it also has a negative impact on development projects. It may project a level of development in 20 years that will provide a comfortable life, including opportunities for education and employment; it paints the picture of a society in which current inequalities would have disappeared, poverty will have been eradicated, and disadvantaged groups will be empowered with opportunities to reach their full potential. At the same time, no part of the plan for achieving these goals directly addresses the structural inequalities in the state, especially in the rural areas.[33] Though there are positive aspects in Vision 2020, it also has the scope for regional imbalances, and widening the gap between the poor and rich, rural and urban. This negative approach led to a spurt in people's agitations and gave scope to the crisis in the polity and economy of India. The same experience reflects in Andhra Pradesh too.[34]

The rise of Hindu communalism is an important aspect in Indian democracy. During the 1990s, in the initial phases of globalization, the BJP as the ruling party at the national level showed a further stage of intensification of contradictions in India's democratic struggle. Minorities, especially Muslims and Christians, came under increasing attacks across various parts of the country. A number of political parties – some with the social justice plank and some others with a strong regional social base – rose to safeguard secularism and minority rights. During the same period, people's movements acquired a new momentum in defence of the rights of displaced people, tribal people's rights on forestland and water, workers' struggles against retrenchment and numerous other movements by Dalits, peasants and women. The dead-end in agrarian structure and overemphasis on modernization of industry eliminated the poor even from the political rhetoric. This strategy of development involved politics which had to de-emphasize social justice. Social justice concerns got marginalized; the poor, particularly the restless and conscious, had to be managed through greater coercion. In the process, the Indian state started becoming more and more brutal at the grassroots level and assumed greater sophistication and modern postures at the technological level.[35]

The question now is how to understand those challenges with reference to formal and substantive democracy. And how to relate and join the deeper inner drives of citizens and communities to the broader challenge of emancipation; how to engage in the preservation of freedom and autonomy in the face of external confrontations found within the nation-state, such as the economic divide and fundamental drives that are overtaking a vast variety of religious constellations, castes and communities and emergence of communal forces.[36] There has also been a wide-ranging upsurge of the marginalized strata, which resulted in a set of progressive measures like reservations for the Scheduled Castes and Scheduled Tribes to the more recent adoption of the recommendations of the Mandal Commission benefiting the OBCs

– all of this seeking to broaden the political base. It, in fact, led to a dampening of the attempt to have more direct forms of democracy that were once sought to be introduced through various struggles like 'direct action', the politics of self-determination fuelled by region, class and caste-based identities; and growth of political competition in various local arenas. There is a need of grassroots politics to challenge the representative model of democracy operating at the state and national levels.[37]

Rajni Kothari argues that the obstacles to development in India are religion, cultural attitudes deprecating manual labour, styles of living and working accepted as immutable on the strength of these beliefs, all of which are inimical to development. The 'inefficiency, inequality, rigidity and negative attitude of the established institutions and the unhealthy socio-economic relations are considered primary reasons for the inability to get economic plans effectively implemented'. To overcome these problems, Kothari says old religious attitudes, cultural patterns and social structures have to be destroyed before development can take place. The possibility of achieving such a complete social transformation through democratic processes of government is, of course, remote. These arguments gave scope for a rethink on traditional attitudes and modes of economic and social stratification. The first generation of political leadership did not seriously concentrate on the elimination of traditional attitudes and beliefs in the country that hampered the overall development of the country. He argued that India's poverty cannot be overcome solely through evolutionary growth models and also in the absence of prior institutional change, no matter how sophisticated the investment plans for 'inducing' other investments, but through the elimination of traditional beliefs and stop going for the globalization process.[38]

Hence, the whole design was the process of democratization which went against the norms of status hierarchy in which caste affiliations, based on birth that determined the economic and political relationships but not on individual choice. There was also a focus on shifting the basis of rights from inherited status to numerical preponderance, by mobilizing the large and hitherto subject caste against the small and traditionally entrenched upper caste, by enabling the people to decide who their rulers should be and what policies the rulers should give primacy to. The secular element in caste and community relations as against ritualistic and segmental divisions has also been noted. Thus, by dissolving the antecedent structures of local tutelage and power, the democratic principle sought to demolish a social structure which, over the centuries, had become rigid and ossified and lost inner vitality.[39] Otherwise, it is argued that there is no place for a democratic and egalitarian society, despite having a high GDP rate.[40]

The crisis seems to have overtaken the Indian society during the past several years. Short periods of heightened expectations on the basis of new promises have alternated with long periods of drift and inaction, producing a growth hiatus between promise and performance, and consequently between the government and the people. It resulted in massive discontent and unrest, an atmosphere of violence and growing confrontation. Such a state of affairs, if allowed to continue, will lead the spirit of democracy in great crisis. It is engaged in meaningless rhetoric of 'left' versus 'right', 'progressive' versus 'reactionary', and it possesses a deep sense of loss of power and authority.[41] At the same time, it is difficult to endorse the opposite view that revolutionary social transformation is necessary, or perhaps more important, is a realistic precondition for breaking down the social barriers to development. They trace the relationship between the economic and political development strategies devised by the nationalist leaders on the premise that the advent of political democracy offered an alternative to revolutionary class struggle in equalizing society. The solution, according to Nehru, was to be sought in using the vote to build up mass consciousness. Political democracy could bring to bear the strength of numbers of the poor in such powerful pressures on the ruling classes that they would be compelled to move in the direction of economic democracy.[42]

The stability of the Congress system and the legitimacy of the formally democratic state have rested on something like hegemony. The leaders from the urban and bourgeoisie articulate community and dominant castes of rural elite became the core group for the Congress party. Through its directive control over the productive processes and its moral-cultural hegemony, the rural elite took control of the local and provincial state. While providing a politically stable environment for national-state initiative in support of capitalist developments, these elites also acquired effective political leverage at the Centre and used it to their own economic, political and social advantage. A consequence of the moral-cultural dimension of its hegemony was the introduction of a few welfare features going under the name of socialism or socialistic pattern. That said, the accomplishments of the welfare state were very limited and have become counter-productive for the most deprived sections of the population. They gave the Indian polity a degree of beingness unparalleled in comparable Third World regimes of the same and later periods.[43]

The development process was considered in broader terms than economic growth to include ideological preferences for the establishment of an egalitarian, decentralized, and cooperative pattern in agriculture and the rapid expansion of public ownership in the basic industrial sector. These social goals offered a painful contrast to social realities. On the eve of independence, India was still stamped with the sharp disparities of the most deeply stratified society in human history. Second, the impoverished peasantry was hardly equipped to take advantage of new growth opportunities in the agricultural sector provided by greater incentives for private investment through improved production practices. They owned either no land or small fragments of land. Capitalist-approach rapid spread of commercial agriculture would necessarily undermine old caste-based social obligations. There was a huge gap between modernity and tradition in the development process of technology in the agriculture sector. An attempt to carry out agrarian reforms failed to be implemented.[44]

The rich class farmers effectively aborted any initiatives for land reforms. A graduated structure of patronage was established through which political power and electoral support were linked to access to welfare and developmental services, as well as production services. The use of coercive police power was much more restricted during this period, the alertness of its availability being an adequate deterrent to subaltern challenges.[45] The legitimacy of such class-coalitional politics in India has rested on popular acceptance of a formally democratic system of governance. That acceptance can hardly be traced to effective fulfillment of specific, immediate interests of the large masses of the people.[46]

Globalization: The Experience of Andhra Pradesh

The information technology sector in Andhra Pradesh did grow at a much faster rate than did the economy as a whole, but annual growth rates of SGDP still lagged behind the national average at about 5 per cent in 2000–01. In practice, the state economy would have to grow at higher levels than 10 per cent annually to meet the goals projected in Vision 2020. Yet, as the fiscal deficit continued its upward spiral, the ability of the state to increase productive investment in infrastructure and the social sectors was actually declining. Political resistance to government policies aimed at recovering higher user fees for power, irrigation, roads, and transport brought the state to the brink of a debt trap. Even after the state government 'corporatized' the power sector, the decision to moderately raise power rates provoked street riots in 2001.[47]

It became clear in the state that information technology could not be a substitute for growth in other sectors. It also anticipated that 'anything (foreign companies) is doing or making is not having any benefit to the domestic economy,' and the usage of the products they are making is 'marginal'. Rather, hi-tech products were being exported to advanced Western countries to make their industries and services more efficient. The lack of spread effects also led to an uneven distribution of the surpluses that were created. 'A few people got very good employment' while many others settled for low-paying unskilled work.[48] Suicides by poor farmers have occurred in Andhra Pradesh over the last five years. These acts of desperation have always been linked to the inability of cultivators to repay loans, some of which were incurred for reasons of social obligations; for example, to meet the cost of marriages, or to construct a house or to dig a well. Yet, it is difficult to account for the growing inability of marginal and small farmers to repay loans without taking into account the deteriorating asset base from which they operate. This kind of precarious existence traditionally was cautioned in bad crop years or in cases where cultivators had to incur loans by using their land as security for credit and, in the worst case, selling a hectare to pay off a large debt.[49] This had a major impact on Telangana particularly, which led to assertion of the people from all sections. The demand of a separate state has to be seen as a part of this development syndrome.

It is argued that two economies emerged in Andhra Pradesh, and the division can also be seen across the social and regional landscape. There is a smaller, yet sizeable, affluent economy growing up in larger cities and spreading to self-contained islands of export-oriented, high-technology parks. The increasing employment from proximity to knowledge sectors servicing global industries holds out hope to those at the margins of opportunities to join the growing lower middle classes and middle classes. By contrast, the larger predominately agricultural economy of landless, marginal and small farmers – many belonging to historically disadvantaged lower castes, minority religions, tribal groups and women – are, on the other side, suffering a lot. Poor people are suffering around the capital city of Andhra Pradesh, some have committed suicide. They have little hope of a better future, remain preoccupied with a daily struggle to secure a livelihood, and are the breeding ground of young men attracted to take part in people's agitations.[50]

Indian Democracy and Rights: Vitalities and Vulnerabilities

Though there were negative aspects in Indian democracy, but still Kothari argues that compared to the other forms of governments, the democratic form of government is the best to prevent the rulers from their inevitable temptations to abuse state power. For no individual will have a right to participate against the legitimate institution in an authoritarian form of government against its anti-people policies, but in a democratic political system, all members of a society have the opportunity to influence public policy of government and protect their own interests through different means and forms. He adds that individuals and social movements frequently appeal to government and try to articulate the grievances of their fellow citizens, who have failed to challenge or appeal to the government by their own capacity. He stresses the gap between the way state policies are formulated and the way the policies are received by individuals or groups. This contestation may arise from failure to grasp the difference between saying and doing.[51]

Transfer of power made most of the people think that democracy would provide opportunities to enjoy rights and freedoms but one commentator observed that 'the chances are likely to be wholly against the survival of freedom'. Fifty years of Indian experiences show that democratic rule has not been properly safeguarded. The contemporary institutional arrangements of the political system theoretically provide scope for expression of popular demands and grievances. These arrangements are not adequate and popular aspirations and demands have been undermined. The failure of economic policies, policy ineffectiveness and incapacity to accommodate political conflicts without violence and even which grew out of the erosion of democratic institutions or the nature of class configurations has led to a crisis of legitimacy in India. Thus, the social scenario is marked by increased violent protests and agitations. So, people are resorting to oppression of dissent through peaceful means through the constitutional, as well as extra-constitutional, methods of protest.[52]

Rudolph argues that Nehru was committed to a model of state-directed industrialization for a mass consumption society, but the obstacle in his path was the intransigence of an entrenched traditional rural elite. The tradition and modernity dichotomy in the old state – the analysis of Weiner, Pye and Manor – still runs deep in the new but equally imitative state-centrist analysis.[53] Niraja Gopal Jayal argues that free and fair elections, freedom of speech and expression, and the rule of law and its protection all are necessary for strengthening democracy and the democratic project is incomplete until the exercise of equal rights of citizenship has been guaranteed to all. She argues that political equality gets severely restricted by inequalities that deny many people from having a true opportunity to influence government decision. She argues that there is a clash between the procedural and substantial aspects of Indian democracy. The project of secularism has been in a wider threat from the ultra-communal ideology that has been seeking to redefine democracy. The welfare character of the state also increasingly has been undermined due to the shifts in the economic policies in the wake of the economic reforms, as well as the ideological struggle between the state and market.[54]

Deepak Nayyar argues that the greatest signifier of the Indian democracy has been the lack of the essential prerequisites of a democracy and argues that class-based struggles against hegemonies of upper castes and classes, emergence of women's movement struggle for their rights, tribal uprisings for safeguarding their lifestyles to defence of their culture and regional identity and nationality constitute a broad range of popular awakening that led to protests and social movements. In large parts of rural India, the role of government became that of a facilitator. The role of government was replaced with direct rule of local landlords and hegemonic castes. This led to greater penetration of commercial interests into rural areas.[55] Justice Jeeven Reddy argues that governance is becoming complex, the political executive is not able to respond, and the judiciary is stepping in. In a democracy, the faith in the impartiality of the institutions is important. The legislature and executive have a credibility crisis, if the faith in judiciary gets a setback the crisis of democracy will be far deeper and in the long run, counterproductive. He also argues that it is time that Indian democracy learns to respond to the macro and micro movements in time and in favour of the people.[56] Jayant Lele argues that India's capitalists as an outcome of historically evolved class relations have placed the Indian state in a contradictory role of mediating between the interests of accumulation and legitimation. Significant changes in the formal composition of the ruling elites and their relationships to each other, as well as to the rest of the population, have occurred in the past 45 years, often as unanticipated consequences of state policies undertaken on their behalf. An important element of these changes is the dramatic decline in the hegemony of the dominant agricultural classes.[57]

Atul Kohli argues that ineffectiveness of the state results in its growing incapacity to deal with the pressing problems of law and order, corruption and poverty. Long established inequalities are thus increasingly under challenge. The lower socio-economic classes have begun to challenge what they perceive to be unjust domination, exploitation, discrimination and inequality in the socio-political and cultural spheres and, at the same time, privileged groups have also begun to counter-organize against lower castes. He cites the crises in governability as the reasons but also the absence of enduring coalition, policy ineffectiveness and incapacity of political accommodation of political conflicts. Today, we have a government whose power rests on fluctuating coalitions and whose leaders repeatedly fail to fulfil their stated goals and to control politically directed violence and also low capacity of government to reduce the protest movements.[58] State institutions are unable to deal with the protests. In Indian democracy, due to positive discrimination, SCs, STs and backward classes perhaps are enjoying political rights at some level, but they are not certainly enjoying social and economic rights. They might have claimed that formally democracy works, but operationally democracy is not that effective as in Western countries. Unless people question the failures of government or practices of democracy, it would not function well. Unless there is freedom of association and a conducive civic culture that encourages people to meet in small groups to discuss the issues which they are facing and put up the problems in front of government through collective effort, democracy cannot be substantial.[59]

Democracy is not merely conceived in constitutional-cum political terms, but involves wider dimensions – achievement of justice, assertion of freedom, high degree of tolerance and acceptance of diversity. Second, the wider the distance between the elites and the peoples, between those who govern and the governed, the less will be the extent of democracy and less emancipated the structure of governance. Therefore, less emancipation with regard to development, culture, ecology and ethnicity leads to confusion among the people. Third, built in the framework of functioning democracies are self-imposed distances from constitutional to political, socio-economic to administrative – which engineer growing dissensions, ever-widening divisions and yawning top-down gaps. These produce alienation, widening disparities and cultures of impairment between the centres and the peripheries, and quite often along the way, regional sub-structures and cultures.[60]

Civil Society and its Role in Promoting Democratic Voices

One could conceptualize democracy as propelling a movement that produces diverse strands of transformative politics or simply as a framework of governance which then, failing to deliver the goods, leads to a variety of problems and frustrations, dilemmas and contradictions. These problems call for a more comprehensive and socially widespread movement. The movement should work towards transforming society and the state as well. Through the normative perspective of 'emancipation of the society, the emanicipatory thrust of democracy calls for a change in its very definition and the diverse contents – social and cultural, local, national, and global – through which it finds expression. Emancipation should be a deeply rooted process of change, mobilization and transformation'.[61] The objective of an egalitarian society is uplifting the poor people and thereby moving towards a comprehensive model of equity, justice and emancipation. Only a minority in the country is privileged and the majority of the people are deprived and a large population has minimum standards of living – health, shelter, education, access to a clean and safe environment and other such basics. Larger and larger number of people are excluded from the mainstream of society and driven into ghettos. There cannot be genuine emancipation without a just and egalitarian state of existence. It is not only the basic social order that should exist in an egalitarian state, but also the vast diversity in its ethnic, biological and ecological components. There can be no real democracy without an emancipated social order and a free and fulsome diversity of natural resources.[62]

Ajay Gudavarthy argues that modern society consists of three sub-systems: economic, the politico-administration and the socio-cultural. He argues that the crisis in one sub-system is simulated into other sub-systems and thereby dissipating it into the system as a whole, and it manifests in varied new forms. Economic crisis can take either a political form or even a cultural form. The new social movements that have been raising a whole range of cultural issues from body politic to sexuality can all be read as protest politics against the distortion introduced into the society as a consequence of managing or averting a fundamental crisis in the system. State intervention, in the course of mitigating the economic crisis, displaces the contradictions in the political realm. It transforms them into political problems. Economic crisis initiated by the new development model in this case is substantially transformed into a political crisis. The state began to rely more on 'experts', where 'the appeal to a "committee of experts" is itself an important instrument in resolving a "political debate", and it also progressively reduced political problems into technical problems'. The state takes recourse to more insular techniques and strategies that are less open to public argumentation and accountability. As a consequence, the distance between expert cultures and the broader public grows greater. Democratic processes were sought to be bypassed for an efficient administrative intervention.[63] That's what the people of India have been experiencing for the last four decades.

The people have lost the confidence in traditional forms of representation such as political parties and have turned towards relatively newer forms of interest aggregation and representation to help them solve their problems. The Congress party has lost its ability to inspire confidence that as a political party, it could represent the interests of the people and as a party that controlled the government it could satisfy the needs of the people. Political parties have failed to discharge their responsibility towards people. They have rapidly degenerated into corrupt, unrepresentative and power hungry machines. Moreover, the rulers of the new generation have come out from the rhetoric of Nehruvian socialism and the idea of planning for development had generated both enormous hopes on the government and sense of entitlements. The country has also failed to overcome the problems like poverty, illiteracy and unemployment. This led to restlessness in major parts of the country and discontent came to pervade large parts of the country as grassroots mobilized to target the unrepresentative state and an unresponsive party system.[64]

The overall Indian experience indicates that human rights' realization is fraught with innumerable problems and impediments. This is sharply evident in its complex experience in the domain of human rights. The system witnessed several progressive laws raising human rights standards but simultaneously saw enactment of laws after laws which are repressive, indicating dilemmas of the Indian state, which has been acting as protector and promoter of human rights at one level, but remained a major violator at another level.[65] The challenges are very large and cannot be handled by merely relying on a representative style of democracy based on elections and a party system on which people have placed their faith for around 60 years. The country should go beyond the representative style that is perhaps the participatory democracy. After six decades of promulgamation of the Indian Constitution, most of the citizens of our country still live below the poverty line, do not get two square meals a day and have no access to sufficient clothing to cover their bodies, with no permanent housing. They are compelled to lead a life of semi-nakedness, malnutrition, disease and worse still is the fact that they are in no position to make any effort to improve their lifestyle. The deep institutional crisis and the erosion of rule of law, on the one hand, and the poverty, unemployment, inequalities, uneven development and injustice to the weak and vulnerable, on the other, contributed to the growth of the protest movements, as well as civil liberties movement, in India.[66]

In Third World countries, social and economic conditions have conspired to limit the capacity of subordinate groups to effectively exercise their rights to secure substantive gains. India is no exception. This has often produced a vicious cycle in which the ineffectiveness of formal democracy produces increased social tensions, which, in turn, trigger autocratic political responses and movements of range. In India, the increasing incidence of caste and communal violence, the criminalization of politics and the spread of corruption gave rise to ethnic chauvinist and communitarian parties. Thus, we must look beyond the macro-institutional level of parliament, Constitution and elections. And we must investigate instead the intermediate and local-level institutions and consultative arenas located in the interests of state and society where 'everyday' forms of democracy flourish. The rise of rights movement demonstrates this point. The movements for human rights are partly a failure of the system, but also an assertion of democracy. Unless every individual has human rights, one would not have an opportunity to question the evils of the social system and anti-people policies.[67]

Thus, social movements in India have contributed to the development of a transformative agenda; their ideological and political interventions have helped in expanding the scope of the formal democratic exercise. It is also believed that civil society is critical to democratic performance because it extends the scope and style of claim-making beyond the formal interest represent that defines political society. Social movements, associations and unions raise new issues and mobilize new actors. In doing so, they not only provide a counter-balance to more bureaucratic and aggregated forms of interest representation, but also create new solidarities, which, in many instances, specifically challenge existing inequalities and hence help democratic society itself.[68] The emergence of micro struggles or people's movements is understood and can be explained in various ways. In the background of the failure of established political institutions, people's movements are considered as powerful autonomous expressions of popular dissent. These movements are seen as more flexible and open in nature that makes it possible for them to address multi-dimensional injustices. Strong organizational network of the people's movements show their potential. Thus, these movements are seen as helpful in further democratization of the polity and enriching the agenda of social transformation. Social movements appear to have shifted from the most disadvantaged groups to the middle sections of the society, so that the anti-caste movements started mobilizing the backward classes into activism to a large extent. The politics of resistance or mobilization politics has always occupied a legitimate space in India's democratic framework. It is both due to India's constitutional contribution or commitment towards establishment of a welfare social democracy, as well as the legacies developed by anti-colonial politics and the nationalist movement.[69] To evaluate the discourse of protest movements, the next unit accentuates the forms of protests in Hyderabad city to assess the contradictions between the executive, legislature and judiciary. This unsolicited development in democracy is going to be discussed in the next part of the study.

Notes

1. David Beetham, *Liberal Democracy and the Limits of Democratization*, Wheatsheaf Books, Brighton, 1986, p. 8.
2. Ibid., pp. 5–6.
3. Ramashray Roy, *Democracy in India: Form and Substance*, Shipra Publications, New Delhi, 2005, p. 3.
4. Niraja Gopal Jayal, 'Introduction: Situating Indian Democracy', in *Democracy in India*, edited by Jayal, Oxford University Press, New Delhi, 2000, p. 3.
5. Marian Young, *Inclusion and Democracy,* Oxford University Press, New York, 2000, pp. 22–23.
6. Niraja Gopal Jayal, *Democracy in India*, Oxford University Press, New Delhi, 2001, p. 3.
7. Ramashray Roy, op. cit., p. 19.

8. Francine R. Frankel, *India's Political Economy 1947–2004*, 2nd edition, Oxford University Press, New Delhi, 2005, pp. 99–100.
9. Niraja Gopal Jayal, 'Democratic Dogmas and Disquiets', presented as the First Pradeep Kumar Memorial Lecture at Panjab University, Chandigarh on 30 November 2005, p. 3, source: *http://www.india-seminar.com/2006/ 557/557%20niraja%20gopal%20jayal.htm*
10. Francine R. Frankel, op. cit.
11. Ibid., p. 5.
12. G. Haragopal, 'Rights of Dalits: Values and Realities', *National Journal of Human Rights Commission*, NHRC, New Delhi, 1992, pp. 137–38.
13. Ibid.
14. B. Chandrasekar Rao, *Indian Constitution*, Post Graduation Diploma in Human Rights Material (PGDHRM), Centre for Distance Education, University of Hyderabad, Hyderabad. 1992, pp. 27–30.
15. Ibid., pp. 71–73.
16. K. Balagopal, 'The Constitution and Social Movements', *Indian Journal of Human Rights*, Vols 12–13, Nos 1–2, 2008–2009, p. 3.
17. G. Haragopal and B. Jagannatham, 'Terrorism and Human Rights: Indian Experience with Repressive Laws', *Economic and Political Weekly*, Vol. XLIV, No. 28, July 2009, p. 79.
18. Deepak Nayyar, 'Economic Development and Political Democracy: Interaction of Economics and Politics in Independent India', in *Democracy in India*, edited by Niraja Gopal Jayal, Oxford University Press, New Delhi, 2001, p. 369.
19. Ibid.
20. M.N. Karna, *Democracy, Pluralism and Conflict*, Rawat Publications, Jaipur, 2006, pp. 9–10.
21. Ibid., p. 10.
22. Ibid.
23. Jayant Lele, 'Understanding Indian Politics', in *Indian Democracy: Meanings and Practices*, edited by Rajendra Vora and Suhas Palshikar, Sage Publications, New Delhi, 2004, pp. 207–10.
24. Ibid.
25. K. Balagopal, 'The Constitution and Social Movements', *Indian Journal of Human Rights*, Vols 9–10, Nos 1–2, January–December 2006–2007, p. 1.
26. B. Chandrasekhar Rao, op. cit, p. 1.
27. Manoranjan Mohanty, 'Introduction: Dimensions of Power and Social Transformation: Class, Caste and Gender', in *Indian Government and Politics: Caste, Class and Gender*, edited by Mohanty, Sage Publications, New Delhi, 2004, p. 14.

28. Niraja Gopal Jayal, op. cit., 2005.
29. M.N. Karna, op. cit., pp. 8–9.
30. Ibid., p. 11.
31. Ibid., p. 12.
32. Partha Ghosh, 'Positive Discrimination in India: A Political Analysis', *Ethnic Studies Report*, Vol. XV, No. 2, July 1997, p. 135.
33. Francine R. Frankel, op. cit., pp. 620–21.
34. Ibid., pp. 616–17.
35. Ibid., pp. 695–700.
36. Kuldeep Mathur, 'The State and the Use of Coercive Power in India', *Asian Survey*, Vol. 32, No. 4, April 1992, pp. 337–49.
37. Javeed Alam, *Who Wants Democracy?*, Orient Longman Publications, New Delhi, 2004, pp. 15–16.
38. Rajni Kothari, *Rethinking Democracy*, Orient Longman Publications, New Delhi, 2005, pp. 6–7.
39. Ibid., p. 8.
40. Ibid.
41. Sudipta Kaviraj, 'Crisis of Nation State in India', *Political Studies*, Vol. XLII, 1994, pp. 115–29.
42. Francine R. Frankel, op. cit., pp. xvii–xviii.
43. Jayant Lele, op. cit., p. 173.
44. Ibid., pp. 19–21.
45. Ibid., p. 175.
46. Ibid., p. 173.
47. Francine R. Frankel, op. cit., p. 620.
48. Ibid., p. 621.
49. Ibid., p. 624.
50. Ibid., p. 625.
51. Rajni Kothari, 'The Congress Revisited: A Decennial View', *Asian Survey*, December, 1974, pp. 1035–54.
52. Ibid.
53. Ibid.
54. Niraja Gopal Jayal, op. cit., 2001, p. 571.
55. Deepak Nayyar, *Governing Globalization: Issues and Institutions*, Oxford University Press, Oxford, 2002.
56. Justice Jeevan Reddy Lecture delivered by a former Supreme Court Judge, in the seminar on 'Right to Strike and Judiciary Role' held in Hyderabad on 26 July 2005.

57. Jayant Lele, op. cit., p. 207.
58. Atul Kohli, *Democracy and Discontent: India's Growing Crisis of Governability*, Cambridge University Press, London, 1990, pp. 4–9.
59. Ibid.
60. Rajni Kothari, op. cit., 2005, p. 159.
61. Jayant Lele, op. cit., p. 155.
62. Ibid., p. 158.
63. Ajay Gudavarthy, 'Democratic Governance or Governing Democracy?', source: *http://bibliotecavirtual.clacso.org.ar/ar/libros/sursur/democratic/08guda.pdf*
64. Neera Chandoke, 'Revisiting the Crisis of Representative Thesis: The Indian Context', *Democratization*, 2000, source: *www2.ids.ac.uk/gdr/cfs/.../Chandhoke_Crisis%20of%20Representation.pdf*
65. Patrick Heller, 'Degrees of Democracy: Some Comparative Lessons from India', *World Politics*, Vol. 52, No. 4, July, 2000, pp. 484–519.
66. Akhil Gupta, 'The Political Economy of Post-Independence India: A Review Article', *The Journal of Asian Studies*, Vol. 48, No. 4, 1989, pp. 787–97.
67. Ibid.
68. Patrick Heller, op. cit., pp. 487–88.
69. Rajni Kothari, op. cit., pp. 12–13.

5 The Protests

The Nature, Issues and State Response to Forms of Protests in Hyderabad City[1]

The main focus of the paper is to understand the protest movements in Hyderabad city, in order to explore the relevance of protests in a democratic country like India. The paper focuses on several forms and attitude of protests and their consequences and looks at the government's response towards protests and protesters. The study is based on information collected from several eminent personalities and activists involved or concerned with such protest movements. The papers focus on four cases (protest movements) and their forms of protests and response of the state: executive, legislature and judiciary. In the light of these, it tries to analyse the relevance of people's movements.

The past three decades have witnessed the emergence of grass-roots movements for protection and promotion of human rights all over the world. India is no exception to this worldwide phenomenon. These movements did influence the democracy of India, especially in the last decade of the 20th century. These protest movements sprang up widely to assert democratic rights and challenged the path of development and the state policies in India The politics of confrontation became an alternative way for many people to exert influence over government and seek redressal of their grievances. Protests are so common that they not only supplement formal procedure, but also displace them and can ever render them irrelevant. Protests are also used in the development of civil societal activism, at one level, and politicization of the people, at another level. Even in a democratic country like India, protest movements witnessed civil societal mobilization of the masses into political activism and influenced the governmental policies.[2] To explore further, the study focuses on protest movements in Hyderabad city.

Hyderabad is the capital city of Andhra Pradesh, well known for its culture of protests as during the last six decades, Hyderabad, in particular and the Telangana region, in general, have been witnessing several movements like the peasant struggle, Naxalite, women, anti-liquor agitation, Dalit and tribal movements. This is largely because the city has a number of public institutions where people's demands can be placed from time to time. In these important public institutions, bureaucrats and eminent political leaders play valuable roles in policy making. People from different sections, castes, trade unions, women, and student unions from all over the state take part in protests. The advantage of having such protests in the city is that it can attract the attention of mass media regarding their demands. Many of these protest movements have taken place in areas specifically allotted for processions, meetings and rallies.

Mostly protests in the state take place when the Assembly is in session, because that is the time when protesters can influence the government more. They can attract the attention of the Assembly where the Opposition legislature party plays a vital role in pressurizing the government to solve the problems. The political parties and various organizations always try to find out innovative methods to pressurize the ruling government and register their protests against the government. The forms of protests include half-naked demonstrators, empty-pot rallies, effigy burnings and even posing as beggars small meetings distributing leaflets and posters and submitting memorandum, press conferences, press statements, long marches on foot, holding meetings at public places, mass rallies, processions, observing protest days, political drama, mass deputation, torchlight processions, demonstrations, hartals, strikes, picketing, satyagraha, dharna, fasting unto death, self-immolation, destruction of public property, holding up of transport, uprooting of railway tracks, wires, localized attempts to throw off state authority and run a parallel administration, and even declared or undeclared warfare in a region,

An analysis of the participation of the common people and their socio-economic background shows that most of them are from the middle or lower middle classes. Mostly mobilization is done by the activists or political groups. The activists try to mobilize the masses before they stage the protests. Before the activists start their protests, they try to mobilize the masses by focusing on the problems arising from the policies of government which impair their democratic rights. The mobilization process takes place at different levels. At the village level, they use traditional instruments like drums, mrudangams, songs, *burrakatalu*, distributing pamphlets, and street plays to mobilize the common masses. They hold meetings in the villages, addresses by opposition political parties, interest groups, non-governmental organizations and several activist groups like CITU, MRPS, *Telangana Prajasamithi*, Human Rights Groups, *Mala Mahanadu*, and Mahila organizations, trade unions and Dalit organizations. Most of the activists come from poor, middle class and village backgrounds. As a part of the effort to understand the dynamics of protests, some concerned persons were interviewed.

As M. Kodandaram[3] (dated 4 April 2004) said in an interview, 'We observe economically rich and socially prosperous people participating in protest movements. If any anti-people policy is made by the government, first of all a few individuals having the capability to comprehend the problem, articulate the problem and those endowed with good organizing capacity come forward and start mobilizing the people and creating awareness among them through their speeches in public meetings. The conscious people come together and form organizations in order to put the problems in front of the government. On the other hand, some activists who are already working in some political organizations and political parties come forward to work actively against the government's anti-people policies.'

As any protest movement itself is a long process, the activists first start negotiations with the officials who represent the government. The suffering people, individually or collectively, give the memorandum to the ministers concerned in order to solve the problem. If it is not fulfilled, the people go for 'dharna' in which they raise the problems that they face. Also, organizations try to gain support from other organizations and from several opposition political parties to realize their demand. If the problems get solved at the level of negotiations, there itself they stop the protest. If it is not realized, the activists catch hold of local leaders and boycott the government decision and put pressure on minister concerned of their area through whom the protesters hope to get a solution. Protesters also take help of sister organizations having direct or indirect relations with influential political parties or leaders to get their problem solved.

First, protest movement starts at the village level by a few people with scant resources. They try to give memorandum to the village assistant and village sarpanch through whom they are able to pressurize the Mandal president and Mandal Revenue Officer and later the activists stage dharnas, in front of the Mandal office and boycott the officials and representatives of the particular Mandal. If it helps in solving the problem, they stop the protest movement at the Mandal level itself. If it is not solved, they take the protest to the district level. At this level, they need more support from people and political parties and sister organizations to consolidate their protest movement, after giving the memorandum to the collector or district magistrate. They also hold rallies, processions and strikes in front of collectorate through which they create consciousness among the people.

They also take up the issue with the minister of their district. It is at this level that they mobilize the people from neighbouring districts with the help of several opposition political parties and other sister organizations and social activists. After this stage, the protest moves to the state level, because they hope that they could pressurize and influence more at that level.

S.R. Sankaran,[4] when asked about the protest movements, says that these initially start at the village level by an appeal to the officer concerned and protesters wait for a few days for a positive response. If the problem is solved, they stop protesting. If it is not solved, they go for a strike in front of the district collectorate or other district offices to express their grievances to the officers concerned. He says that success or failure depends upon the commitment of the activists, people's involvement, willingness of people to participate, capability of the activists and mobilization of masses and seriousness of the issues that they have taken up.

He divides the protest movements into two types: (i) the organized form of protest, and (ii) revolutionary or militant form of protest. The former type of protest lasts long from the beginning of protest till the problem gets solved. Such kind of protests follow certain rules, norms, principles and go through proper channels. The activists work within the constitutional provisions. The latter type of protest see activists following illegal means of protests like burning of buses, disturbing government offices, indulging in traffic jams, killings, blasting the public institutions, and so on. He says that the administrators are of two kinds: some of them sympathize with the problems taken up by activists working in particular organization or political party, and some are against such protests.

The first kind of officers tries to acquaint the activists with different aspects of the problem and ask them to observe patience. They (officers) listen to their problems and ask them to wait for some time till the discussions and negotiations take place to solve the problems and also try to place the issue before the higher authorities and minister concerned. They try to convince both the government and the organization to have negotiations to get the problem solved. The other type of administrators are arrogant and hostile towards protests and protesters. They respond in a rude manner and challenge the activists by forcing them to indulge in illegal forms of protest and inform the police to arrest the activists. This kind of attitude of the officers leads to illegal kind of protest.

Funding of the Protest Movements

B.V. Raghvulu[5] thinks that protest movements need resources to sustain. The organizations collect funds in three ways: (a) based on a genuine problem, they (organization) collect the funds from those who are facing the problems through donations; (b) political parties collect the funds in the name of people's protests, in which the parties would expect some kind of involvement in protests; and (c) non-governmental organizations (NGOs) get financial support from foreign governments, international organizations and other political organizations for supporting the protest movements. He further argues that when the protest movements of common, middle class people are funded by themselves, then they exert more influence than in any other kind of protest movement.

According to Kancha Illaiah,[6] caste plays a major role in protest movements. Due to untouchability, suppression and oppression, unequal treatment, starvation, drought, discrimination in the name of caste, Dalits form organizations and protest against social evils as well as for protection of their rights. He opines that in a democracy, people usually express their anger through protests to get their grievances redressed because they have the right to association and strike through the court of law. A woman activist, Padma,[7] draws the attention to the attitude of police towards protests and protesters. Treatment of the police towards protesters differs from person to person depending upon the leader, cadre and organization. If a particular activist belongs to an affiliated party or organization, the police treat him or her (them) 'generously'. If they do not belong to any politically-affiliated organization, the same police treat them in a coercive or brutal manner, harass the activists and file cases against them without any evidence.

The nature of the protest movements depends upon the cause, class and the context. For instance, protests in different industries in Hyderabad sees impressive participation. As one of the workers of Bharat Heavy Electrical Limited (BHEL), Vaijyanath,[8] says, 'the first step is gathering of workers in their workshop through mobilization and thereafter, the next step of the protest is giving a memorandum to the additional general manager of the block. The next step is to arrange a meeting in front of the main gate, which is called "gate meeting", in order to put forward their grievances in front of the managing committee. From this stage, the real (concrete) form of protest starts. All these processes take place under the guidance of the elected workers of the trade union. The trade union gets support from other sister trade union organizations and political parties. Workers give 14 days' deadline to the management committee or administrative body. Next step of protest is that workers attend duty with black colour badges and if it does not solve the problem, they start boycotting duty for one or two hours in every shift. If it is still not solved, they boycott work for one shift (duty). At the last stage, with the help of other political parties and sister organizations, they start holding public meetings in towns and rallies in order to pressurize the management'. He adds that the last stage of protest is to take it to Dharna Chowk, with the help of other trade unions in the state.

Social activist, Khasim,[9] says that protests are of two types: (i) ideology-based, and (ii) need-based. In the former kind of protest, they propagate their ideology with the issues that they take up through which they fight against the anti-people policies of the government. This approach is adopted by different organizations affiliated to different political parties like Leftist parties, rightist parties and people from different religions, caste-based organizations, etc. The need-based form of protest is spontaneous. In this, they fight with the government with the help of other sister organizations. In this kind of protest movement, activists usually emerge from the affected (groups) people such as students, workers, women and slum-dwellers. They take up the issues like bus fares or increase of student fees. There may be protests against some officials or ministers who indulge in lumpen and corrupt activities. They all come under temporary or transient kind of problems. Ideology-based protest movements succeed in drawing the support of other political parties, as well as academicians. But the need-based organizations or sporadic groups face shortage of resources because their demand is temporary and if the problem gets solved, organizations stop resisting. The police also treat the activists in a different manner based on the strength of the organization and the activist's personal image.

Woman activist, G. Shyamala, says that after putting pressure on the government through several forms of protests, they resort to blocking of roads as a critical step. She adds that it is necessary to think about the problems of society as a whole than considering the problems of only a small section of the people.[10] Another respondent, Laxman Swamy,[11] says that blocking the roads and breaking the law are impermissible and ineffective means of protest. Yet another respondent, Veeresham, says that blocking of roads is quite common in protest movements and that most of the effective forms of getting the problem solved lie in entering into negotiations with the government authority.[12]

A few respondents argue differently. They say that after all other forms of protests have been exhausted, at the last stage, they resort to blocking the roads. Although this may cause inconvenience to some people, but in the long run, it may be justified in solving the problem of a certain section of people. Activists take several forms of protests to attract the people from all parts of the society and make use of the media to highlight their problems so as to pressurize the government in a democratic manner. If it is not possible, use of force or taking to illegal forms of protests is the logical step. Another respondent says that earlier when the activists gave notice to government, or management, they used to respond immediately. But in the recent past, the ruling authority is not responding because governments have been following conditions laid down by the World Bank and dictates of developed countries like United States and United Kingdom.

Observance of Protests and its Consequences in Hyderabad City

In the city of Hyderabad, there is not only a particular place allotted but there is also a route prescribed for processions and rallies. Protests cause traffic jams quite often, because the state government has been trying to reduce the length (distance) of the road (Sundarayya Vignana Bhavan and Indira Park) on which to take out processions and rallies. During the time of rallies, protesters raise slogans against the government and its policies. Slogans like ‘government, down-down, we want justice, stop anti-people policies, CM, down-down, long live unity’ are normally raised. The protesters form circles (human chain) and through slogans intensify the voice and proceed to Indira Park to hold meetings. Mostly they bring people from villages who usually belong to the poor and middle classes, Scheduled Castes and also from the slum areas in Hyderabad city. During the time of the rally, the police come to regulate the protest. The number of police personnel deployed depends on the seriousness of the demand or problem, organization and strength of the people involved in the procession. Among the protesters, a few members lead the mass of people participating in it. While taking out the procession, the activists try to go in a systematic manner and encourage the protesters to raise slogans against the government. During the protest, they distribute water packets and if needed also distribute food to the fellow activists

Those who are working in CITU, SFI, DFI, and KNPS, etc., usually get some payment but other organizations such as MRPS, *Mala Mahanadu*, trade union organizations and Telangana movement, women's movement attract voluntary participation without offering any kind of financial assistance. They are participating voluntarily because of the sentiment of caste, class, and regional feelings. Most of the youth in Communist party-led organizations receive training classes on the ideology and philosophy by intellectuals, human rights activists and party leaders. This adds to their participation and organizational capabilities during protest movements. Organizations usually get financial support from several political parties and businessmen, political leaders and also at times from bureaucrats, private organizations and moral support from human rights activists, other sister organizations, eminent academicians, political parties, sympathizers and sometimes from the international organizations.

During the time of the Telugu Desam government, there were many protest movements, but at present under the Congress government, protest movements are less. The Telugu Desam government followed the advice of World Bank and other multinational corporations, neglected agricultural development, farmers, unemployed youth and women. The government, instead of creating employment opportunities for the youth, took to privatization of educational institutions, increasing power tariff charges, reducing the subsidies to farmers and poor people and neglected the Telangana region. On account of all these factors, different sections of the people started asserting themselves through different forms of protests. The members of organizations involved in protest movements included CPI, CPI (M), PDSU, SFI, ABVP, Dalit and student organizations. Even Naxalite groups resorted to protests but took to violent protest, such as burning RTC buses, police stations, killing political leaders, officials and ministers. These forms reached their peak when they attacked the convoy of Nara Chandra Babu Naidu, the then Chief Minister of Andhra Pradesh. (This is popularly known as Alipiri Incident).

The Communist Party and other political parties took to agitations with the help of other organizations against the increase of power tariff charges by the Telugu Desam Party. Activists used several forms that included *Bijli Bandh*, signature campaign, distributing pamphlets, organizing public meetings in rural and urban areas, rallies, mock assembly, and so on. The Telugu Desam Party tried to stop the agitations with police force. Many activists were arrested and beaten up during the power tariff agitation. There was also police firing in which three activists were killed. This showed how the government used force to silence the protest movement. Under the leadership of K. Chandrasekhar Rao, founder leader of Telangana Rastra Samiti, the demand for a separate Telangana state sprang up. He started his movement by conducting meetings at different levels. He started mobilization and started pressurizing the government to implement government order 610, and demanded policies in favour of Telangana region. One student union activist said that the TRS grew in strength partly because of Chandrasekhar Rao, who drew the people through his attractive speeches, dharnas, boycott, demonstration and public meetings, etc.

The present situation is different as TRS and Communist parties joined the UPA government at the centre as well as the state. The Telugu Desam Party and Bharatiya Janata Party have not been able to muster strong opposition to the Congress government. Even the Dalit protest movements are unable to question the government due to internal conflicts among themselves regarding categorization of SC reservations. Notwithstanding these developments, there has been a protest movement of a wide-ranging stratum of the society. The main protest movements are now confined to arranging of press meetings, distributing of pamphlets, giving public speeches, etc. The recent past has seen, small protests like those by Anganwadi workers, village workers and daily wage labourers, students, Hindi pundits, toddy workers, medical employees, MRPS, *Mala Mahanadu*, slum area dwellers, women, backward classes, hotel workers, rickshaw workers, blind and deaf people, industrial workers, against proposed execution of Nepal Buddhist monks by the Chinese government, by *Kula Nirmoolana Porata Samiti* for fulfilment of election promises given by the Congress party and government employees. Congress party activists also protested against Telangana Rastra Samiti, because of K. Chandrasekar Rao's statement against Sonia Gandhi, especially by the Congress MLA and former legislature party leader P. Janardhan

Reddy, which led to a traffic jam and two persons died in Hyderabad. Then the rally and demonstration and another public meeting under the leadership of Manda Krishna. In the public meeting conducted by Manda Krishna, three children died due to heat stroke. Again, under the leadership of P.V. Rao, activists resorted to "rail roko" (stop the trains) in Secunderabad railway station, seeking implementation of Supreme Court's judgment regarding the categorization of reservations for Scheduled Castes. However, the protests that took place in this short period were mixed in character and less organized. Most of the agitations were aimed at pressuring the government to carry out its electoral promises.

Protest Movements: The Trends

While analysing the causes of the protest movements, the dynamics and overall pattern also need to be looked into. The following are certain select movements that took place during the study period. They provide insights for a deeper understanding of the micro-movements.

Case 1

While discussing different examples of protests, one incident that occurred on 24–25 November 2004, involved a group of youth from Tibet pursuing their higher education and north-eastern students and sweater sellers together resorting to an agitation. They were protesting against the Chinese government's decision to execute 'Tulku Tenzindelek', who was an influential Buddhist teacher campaigning for social and religious development in China. The Chinese government arrested him in 1988 for building a monastery without 'approval of the state'. On 2 December 2002. Kardze International People's Court sentenced him to death. The Chinese government proposed to execute him on 2 December 2004. Against the decision of execution, members of the regional Tibetan Youth Congress and Friends of Tibet undertook a relay hunger strike on 25–25 November 2004 near Dharna Chowk. They were found raising slogans like 'join our campaign, save an innocent person, save Tulku Tenzindelek from execution'. They requested for signatures in favour of Tuluku through an online petition. Anjaneya Reddy, Managing Director of National Hydroelectronic Power Corporation (NHPCO), lent his moral support to them. This protest is an example of protest of people of one country, staying abroad for an issue in their country.

Case 2

On 11 March 2005, under the banner of Madiga Reservation Porata Samiti (MRPS) led by Kanakaraju Madiga, a relay strike was undertaken for one week. As part of the protest, they undertook a half-naked dharna and on another day polished shoes. Their main demands included stopping all the admissions and recruitment of Scheduled Castes (SC), category reservation until the problem was settled. They wanted the government to send delegates to New Delhi to meet United Progressive Alliance chairperson Sonia Gandhi and stay in New Delhi till Parliament amends the constitutional provisions in favour of classification of the Scheduled Castes into ABCD. They started the protest from the village level. They organized village committees, mandal committees, district committees and state committees. They mobilized the people through traditional instruments like *dappu*, folk songs, dances, *kolatam* and speeches. On 14 December 2004, under the leadership of Manda Krishna, thousands of people participated in the rally. From there, they decided to go to the state Assembly but were prevented by the police. They could not reach the Assembly as the police closed the way and the activists stayed on the road and did not move for quite some time. Not only students, youth and farmers, but women groups from the Madiga community too participated emotionally in the protest. The protest also included dance in favour of categorization in a rally as a form of agitation. They gave slogans in favour of ABCD classification among the Scheduled Castes. They reiterated 'we give our life but we shall achieve categorization.' They also raised slogans like 'beat the drum, make the category lawful', 'stop filling the SC backlog posts', 'we want justice', 'YSR, down-down'. To maintain law and order, police arranged Intelligence to ensure that people do not get involved in unlawful activities, and arranged water cannons, tear gas, horses, and fire engines. The Telugu Desam Party and Bharatiya Janata Party supported the dharna, and their state presidents participated in it. The demand for ABCD classification had been so effective that the protest was able to muster enormous numbers. The government of Andhra Pradesh finally not only agreed to it, but made a policy to that effect. The High Court of Andhra Pradesh also ratified it but that was challenged in the Supreme Court. The Supreme Court did not uphold the judgment of the High Court. This calls for an amendment to the Constitution. The MRPS is continuing its mobilization for a constitutional amendment. Notwithstanding the demand for the amendment and the outcome, the MRPS protest is one of the exemplary protests which could build up so much pressure that the political executive had to respond to the protest. The controversial issue of categorization among Scheduled Castes once again aroused and pressurized the government and tried to make the people and government rethink on the issue of categorization.

Case 3

The Road Transport Corporation (RTC) employees undertook a protest to save the RTC from privatization. All the unions of the Andhra Pradesh State RTC formed a joint committee to fight against anti-APSRTC workers. They demanded an increase in their salaries, to make the temporary employees permanent, negotiations, constituting a cabinet sub-committee to discuss the issue relating to problems of RTC employees and other demands. Here, different organizations came together and formed a joint committee to fight against anti-government policies, demanded reducing the tax on city services from 7 per cent to 5 per cent and on distinct services from 5 to 2 per cent, reduction of sales tax on diesel and particularly to oppose privatization. They held meetings in front of bus stands. These processions were led by local leaders of RTC employees' associations. The government did not budge. So they went on dharna in Hyderabad, followed by a rally from Indira Park to RTC crossroads. Protesters burnt the effigy of then Chief Minister Y.S. Rajasekara Reddy. Later, the government constituted a three-member cabinet sub-committee to look into the problem. Negotiations had been held between the government and RTC employees' joint committee. But no positive outcome came out; at last, the RTC employees gave a call for bandh. In the meantime, a public interest litigation (PIL) was filed in the High Court which called upon the government to take up all the necessary measures to see to it that there was no inconvenience to the common people, employees, businessmen, women, school children and others. As workers insisted on the strike, the Andhra Pradesh High Court intervened and insisted that the workers call off the strike, as the common people were suffering. It also advised the government to solve the problem within 25 days. This entire process took seven months to be settled. While the government slowed down the process of privatization, it is again talking of privatization.

Case 4

The junior doctors' protest movement has been one of the most controversial, but effective, protest movements in the recent past. More than 11,000 junior doctors studying in different government medical colleges in the state undertook an indefinite strike by boycotting even the emergency services. They started the protest against proliferation of private medical colleges. They held that the private colleges have poor infrastructure and unqualified faculty and the government failed to protect the quality and standards of medical education. They organized it under a committee of representatives of the Andhra Pradesh Junior Doctors Associations (APJUDA), drawn from different medical colleges. All of them met at Osmania Medical College and decided to form a joint action committee to fight for the standards. A decision was taken to intensify the agitation and to put pressure on the government to attend to these problems. Continuing their agitation, the doctors let black balloons into the sky at Osmania Medical College, symbolic of their anger against Chief Minister Y.S. Rajasekar Reddy for forgetting the promises that he made to the doctors before the elections. It may be recalled that Rajasekar Reddy not only addressed the striking doctors during the Telugu Desam Party regime, but promised to fulfill their demands. The Congress government was elected in the ensuing elections but he went back on the promise, inviting another protest movement. The junior doctors followed several forms of protests such as silent rally, enacting a skit, carrying an effigy of the Chief Minister of Andhra Pradesh for forgetting his promises. The Andhra Pradesh government held that if the doctors on strike did not end it, the government would recommend to Medical Council of India for cancellation of their registration. The government declared the strike illegal and decided to invoke provisions of the Essential Services Maintenance Act (ESMA). Many senior citizens from across the country were not happy with the government's decision. The government started calling new MBBS graduates for walk-in interviews to replace the junior doctors in hospitals across the state. This whole protest was quite different from other protest movements in Hyderabad. This was mainly initiated by junior doctors who were students. The government of Andhra Pradesh did not respond in favour of junior doctors and ignored their protest movement. In the course of protest, one of the leading private medical practitioners went to court and filed a PIL, drawing the judiciary into the controversy. The court took a serious note of the strike and asked the junior doctors to call off the strike, which they did. The protest continued in other forms like giving memorandum to temple pujaris, over-time duty, serving in slum areas and explaining the causes for the strike, boycotting the emergency wards in the hospital, etc.

A Division Bench of the Andhra Pradesh High Court, comprising acting Chief Justice, Bilal Nazki and G. Chandraiah, pulled up the junior doctors for continuing the protest when the matter was under consideration and expressed concern over the plight of the patients in government-run hospitals across the state. The High Court asked the Medical Council of India for the justification of the registration of those striking doctors and asked why the Council should not cancel their registration for disrupting health care services. The court said that it would look into their complaints if only the junior doctors stopped their protest. The junior doctors resorted to novel protests by visiting the patient wings in hospitals and treating the patients after the duty hours and conducting medical camps in the slum areas, partly to mobilize public opinion. The medicos explained to the people the circumstances under which they had resorted to an agitation. Junior doctors decided to work overtime to draw the attention of the government and also the High Court. As a part of continuation of protest, they organized campaigns and seminars.

A seminar was conducted in Hyderabad by the Bar Association of High Court on 'the Right to strike and role of the judiciary'. This seminar raised several questions about the forms of protest, particularly the right to strike. It reflected the changing nature of the discourse and also the character of Indian democracy. In the inaugural speech, Justice B.P. Jeevan Reddy[13] observed that the right to strike against low wages, for bonus, against slavery and improving conditions has been accepted in the United States and the United Kingdom. The working class achieved this right all over the world. The scheme of Industrial Disputes Act, 1947 had given the right to strike to Indian citizens and the Constitution recognized the right. He added that the court intervention in the case of RTC employees' strike and medical doctors' strike, under Public Interest Litigation, amounted to interference in the conflict between the working class and employer. He maintained that a balance between public and private interest needed to be stuck. The judge suggested getting the problems sorted out through negotiations. He resented the judgment of the Andhra Pradesh High Court and held that if that court goes on giving judgments against the workers, employees and their protest movements, it would diminish the overall faith in the judiciary. G. Haragopal,[14] in his talk, noted that 'no worker is interested in protests except when he feels compelled. Employees go for strike under unjust conditions. We should recognize the imbalance of power between the labour and capitalist, employer and employee'.

He added that strike is admissible in contemporary jurisprudence. 'Such rights are denied only when governance becomes difficult. The court should maintain an equilibrium between both the workers and employees, citizens, on the one hand, and the state, on the other'. He added that law is a balancing force, in favour of collective good. He also stated that the court should carry public opinion with it. If such an approach is not adopted, it would lead to a crisis of governance. In spite of mobilization of public opinion through varied methods of agitations, the court stuck to its position on the ground that the strike violates the rights of the patients, and the junior doctors were left with no option but to withdraw the strike. The office-bearers and the leaders who led the strike were pushed into wilderness. The civil liberties and human rights activists did not know the way out. It landed the junior doctors in a stalemate. The frustration and suffocation that they suffered seems to be something which a democratic system needs to be concerned with.

The findings of the analysis of the nature of protest movements suggest that they not are not only against the government, but also against certain powerful sections of the society. For instance, the protest movements of one sub-caste against another sub-caste, group of individuals against another group, one region against another region. These movements or counter-movements do pressurize the government or administration to use its power to reformulate the policies. The state, caught between the pressure and counter-pressure, is finding it increasingly difficult to decide and govern the society. This crisis does affect the democratic system and its modes of governance. As the systems fail to respond, the movements take to different forms of protests, which include Bijli Bandh, signature campaign, pamphlet distribution, public meetings, 'rail roko' (stop the trains), cycle rallies, marches, humorous skits and pranks, performances of plays, parades, mock funerals, demonstrative funerals, homage at burial places, walkouts, social boycott, singing, religious processions, deputations, mock awards, group or mass petitions, public speeches, letters of opposition or support, declarations by organizations and institutions, picketing, mock elections, display of portraits, prayer and worship, symbolic lights, display of flags and symbolic colours, suspension of social and sports activities, boycott of social affairs, student strikes, withdrawal from social institutions, refusal to pay debts and dues, sit-in, stand-in, pray-in, parallel government, seeking imprisonment, boycott of elections, hartals, sympathetic strike, silence rallies, dharnas, mock assembly, courting arrest, etc. These forms of protests indicate both creativity and desperation.

In the process of protests, negotiations, discussions, debates, criticism and, seminars are held by several organizations and to counter these responses, government would give clarifications, set up inquiry committees to study and give advice. The protest movements suggest that Indian democracy is in a crisis. This crisis is also rooted in multi-lingualism, caste and religion. The protest movements have gone up and are bound to become far more serious as globalization spreads. Bikhu Parekh held that 'due to the globalization process, welfare policies have been undermined, educational institutions are becoming privatized, agriculture sector is marginalized'. He added that as a result of these, 'all sections of people are becoming frustrated'. The protests are spreading to common men, employees, workers, Dalits, women and also mass resistance.

Strikes by MRPS, APSRTC and junior doctors indicate that as governance is becoming complex, and political executive is not able to respond, the judiciary is stepping in. The judiciary is respected as it symbolizes justice. In all the three cases, the *Madigas*, the APSTRC workers and young junior doctors were extremely unhappy with the judicial pronouncements. In a democracy, the faith in the impartiality of the institutions is important. The legislature and executive have a credibility crisis but if the faith in the judiciary gets a setback, the crisis of democracy will be far deeper and, in the long run, counter-productive. It is time that Indian democracy learns to respond to the macro and micro-movements in time and in favour of the people. The democratic movement is generally considered as a backbone of the human rights movement. Democratic movements consisting of workers, peasants, middle classes, employees, youth and student organizations are involved in mobilization of various sections of the population in their struggles that are intended to improve their lot. There are several types of struggles that have been taking place in the society. There are class struggles and sectional struggles within the same broad class category and also struggles involving issues of gender, caste, religion, language, culture, region, etc. In these struggles, one set of persons clashes with another set. Organizations of toiling people not only struggle on specific class or sectional demands, but these movements are also considered as the training school for raising the consciousness of its members. Most of the struggles are won or lost depending on the strength of mobilization within the organization, supplemented by outside support that becomes critical at some point of time.[15] This part of the study studied democracy by understanding forms of protests and its impact on the people and their assertiveness.

Notes

1. Case Study of Protest Movements, Dharna Chowk, Indira Park, Hyderabad, September, 2004 to August, 2005.
2. Rajni Kothari, *Repression and Resistance in India*, Vol. 1, Popular Prakashan, Mumbai, 1990, pp. 3–5.
3. Professor in Political Science, Osmania University, Hyderabad, Human Rights and Separate Telangana State activist, interviewed on 15 March 2005.
4. Retired IAS Officer, Convener of Committee of Concerned Citizens, Andhra Pradesh, interviewed on 24 August 2005.
5. General Secretary of CPI (M), Andhra Pradesh, interviewed on 12 June 2005.
6. Professor in Political Science, Osmania University, Hyderabad, interviewed on 14 April 2005.
7. President, Democratic Women's Organization, Andhra Pradesh, interviewed on 5 June 2005.
8. General Secretary, Samata Sainik Dal, Andhra Pradesh, interviewed on 7 June 2005.
9. President, Telangana Student Union, Andhra Pradesh, interviewed on 22 May 2005.
10. Women activist, interviewed on 23 March 2005.
11. Student from Osmania University, interviewed on 15 March 2005.
12. Retired Lecturer, interviewed on 6 May 2005 at Hyderabad.
13. Former Judge, Supreme Court of India, Seminar on 'Right to Strike and Judiciary Role' held in Hyderabad on 26 July 2005.
14. Dean, School of Social Sciences, University of Hyderabad, Andhra Pradesh, India, Seminar on 'Right to Strike and Judiciary Role' held in Hyderabad on 26 July 2005.
15. D.L. Sheth, 'Globalization and New Politics of Micro Movements', *Economic and Political Weekly*, Vol. 39, No. 39, January, 2004, pp. 45–56.

6 Human Rights Implications of Dalit Self-Assertion in Telangana

In the 1980s, the Dalit movement in Telangana picked up pace. Opinion makers like teachers, advocates, lecturers, writers and singers from among the Dalits were active in mobilizing and organizing masses from the community. Organizations, like Ambedkar Youth Associations, DAFODAM, teachers and lecturers' organizations, were active in this whole process. In the 1980s and 1990s, a lot of Dalit literature come up, singers and writers emerged and several agitations were taken up against caste oppression, atrocities on Dalits, discrimination, untouchability, *vetti* (forced labour), and problems of Dalit women, but these assertions and voices from the margins, have been replaced or weakened by other identities. This paradigm shift has taken place particularly in the region of Telangana due to four reasons: caste and class differences; globalization and its impact on development and opportunities; the *Madiga Reservation Porata Sammithi* (MRPS) and its mobilization of one particular sub-caste – *Madiga*; and the separate Telangana statehood movement. The emergence of these movements created consciousness among the Dalits, but has been a setback to the Dalit movement in the region.

In the 1980s, most of the Dalit activists, singers, writers and teachers were part of the Left movement, either radical Left or Left movement. When there was a debate on the relevance of Marxist ideology or the relevance of class, most Dalit activists differed with the ideology of class and argued that, in the name of class, the problems of Dalits based on caste and leadership have been ignored and not articulated. This development reflected in the shift of Dalit leadership from the Marxist movement to Dalit movement. For some time, the Dalit movement was active and mobilized Dalits against the atrocities on them, but after globalization, the leadership from Dalits was in a crisis as there was state repression on them. There was no mobility of Dalits, no support base for them and there was the emergence of culture NGOs (non-governmental organizations) in Andhra Pradesh due to globalization. This culture of NGOs made Dalit leaders and writers join NGOs, either for their personal benefits or intending to make use of the fruits of globalization for the well-being of Dalits in the region. The other reason could be the MRPS movement to achieve categorization among Scheduled Castes (Dalits) in Andhra Pradesh. It further divided the Dalits in the state, though it created enormous consciousness among the Madiga community. Because of these reasons, Dalits were in search of an organization to work for the democratic cause as naturally Dalits are being exploited and dominated by the upper castes. They are conscious about their rights and waiting for the leadership or organization which upholds the democratic cause. These political, social-economic disparities among the Dalits, globalization, negative impact of development and the conflict between caste and class pushed Dalits to wait for the organization. When they were in search of such an organization, they found a democratic movement, i.e., the Telangana statehood movement. All these developments forced them to join the Telangana movement in the decade of 1990s. When K. Chandrasekhar Rao launched TRS, the Dalit teachers, advocates, lecturers, writers and singers had little option but to support TRS and Telangana movement. That's how the Telangana movement today witnesses folk culture: songs, writings, (*Dhoom-Dhaam*) and poetry. People like Gaddar, Andesri, Guda Anjaiah, Goreti Venkanna, Vimaakka and hundreds of writers and singers from Dalits have emerged.

So, the Telangana movement replaced the Dalit movement but scholars and writers argue that it lacks a democratic face as hundreds and thousands of students, writers, teachers and activists from Dalit background were active in the movement but confined it to the level of participation in the agitations and there is no space in decision-making. Of course, there are cases where Dalits are active and are respected, but that is not enough. Hence, there should be a parallel Dalit movement along with the Telangana movement. This would once again give an opportunity for Dalits to mobilize, organize and agitate for their rights. It is argued that the Dalit leadership in the region has not been able to take up the issues or problems of Dalits seriously after 1990s. If the same continues, there will be serious problems for Dalits in the future in Telangana. When I wrote a paper on the 'Human Rights Implications of Dalit-Self Assertion in India', I focused on certain problems and the agitations of Dalits in Telangana region, but those kinds of assertions are missing in Telangana region. It is the right time to take those issues and mobilize Dalits in the region. This unit thus deals with the assertions of Dalits in the region during 1990–2000.

The present study is an attempt to assess the rising consciousness among the Dalits in Medak district of Andhra Pradesh. The nature and evolution of the Dalit movement is reflected in the impact created by two major incidents in the Telangana region and one incident in the region of Andhra, both of which resulted in violence against the Dalits and their self-assertion (visible in the refusal of killing of animals in front of the goddess). One was in Psundur village in Prakasham district; second, in Jhadimalkapur village in 1996; the third was in Allapur village, Narayanakhed *mandal,*[1] in Medak district (movement against denial of temple entry) in 2004. Based on these undemocratic episodes, the way the Dalit movement shaped and reshaped its agenda, its political discourse and the strategy of transformation in the Telangana and Andhra regions is the focus of this study. The comparison of these movements is very important in understanding not only their structure, but also the nature of the ongoing social transformation in the region. It is also an attempt to understand the consciousness among the Dalits and to elucidate, based on these three case studies, how these groups struggled against Hinduism to Christianity as well as factors that account for their disavowal of their own culture and religion. The study also seeks to analyse these developments in the light of Ambedkar's[2] understanding of Indian democracy: values, reality and its formal and substantive dimensions and also its vitalities and vulnerabilities. Such an approach would provide an insight into the unfolding reality and also reconceptualize Indian democracy.

Introduction

Human rights are much discussed in contemporary India. They have been more intensely debated in the wake of growing atrocities against this historically deprived community. Dalit human rights have become an international issue and organizations like Human Rights Watch, Amnesty International, Minorities Rights Group and Anti-Slavery International are engaged in the discourse. The issue is being raised in international bodies such as the UN. Violations of Dalits' rights are one of the systemic problems in India. The socio-economic milieu of Indian society is inherently hostile towards the protection of the human rights of Dalits. It is social stratification through the caste system which promotes and perpetuates societal violations of Dalit human rights.[3] In this regard, my study seeks to understand Dalit human rights and their self-assertion, to comprehend the nature of the violation of Dalits' rights, their consequent growing political self-assertion and the overall trends in the Dalit struggle for dignity, self-respect and freedom.

The post-Emergency[4] period marked a new phase in the political history of India. It saw heightened social and political articulations and an intense ideological contestation through a wide assortment of issue-based mobilizations and struggles in different parts of the country. Farmers' movements, Dalit mobilization, the renewed struggles of the agrarian poor, women's discourse, and a new phase in student politics and civil rights articulation in a number of states were a part of this new development. There were demonstrative of a vibrant civil society in the post-Emergency period. The state of Andhra Pradesh was no exception to this rule. A massive mobilization of different sections of society, and students and rural youths in particular, marked a new phase in the grassroots politics in the state. The organization and political articulation of the rural poor took a more visible form and moved to the centre of political discourse. These articulations posed an ideological challenge to mainstream politics, in general, and to the Indian National Congress (INC), which has been a dominant power in state politics since the formation of the state in 1956.[5]

Brief Sketch of Telangana and Dalits

The Telangana region is located in the western part of Andhra Pradesh. It was formerly part of the state of Hyderabad, ruled by the Asaf Jahi dynasty (the ruler was known popularly as the Nizam) from the 18th century until independence. It came out of the ruins of the medieval Bahamani and Qutub Shahi kingdoms and formed a polygonal tract occupying the centre of the Deccan Plateau. The Nizam's state[6] comprised three linguistic regions: Telangana, Marathwada and Karnataka. For the purpose of administration, the entire state was divided into four *subas* (i.e., districts): Warangal and Medak (Telangana) Aurangabad (Marathwada) and Gulbarga (Karnataka). The Telangana region that formed a part of the Nizam's dominions represented the unique Deccan culture.[7] While India achieved independence in 1947, the Hyderabad state did not get freedom until 1948. After police action under the leadership of Sardar Vallabbhai

Patel, the state was merged with the Indian Union. In 1956, the region was merged with the Andhra regions (it was a part of Madras presidency) based on language, i.e., Telugu.[8]

There is a widespread feeling that the aspirations of the Telangana people were undermined in all spheres, i.e., social, economic and political, which resulted in the demand for a separate Telangana state.[9] This is an agitation that is still going on. Telangana is supposed to be a backward region; the regional backwardness is also reflected in the deprivation of Dalits there. This study focuses on Medak district as a whole and Narayanakhed and Zaheerabad mandals in Medak district, in particular. Despite six decades of democracy, the conditions of Dalits have not changed qualitatively. This raises a question about the function of democracy in the country.

Historical Context of Telangana Region

In Telangana, given the above historical specificities of the Nizam's domination, the trajectory of change took a different shape. The ruling class or the landed gentry of the region, consisting of Muslim jagirdars and Hindu deshpandes, bestowed citizens with hardly any civil or political rights. This historical legacy of an oppressive class of landed gentry created problems for the rural population through the illegal eviction of farmers. The extraction of free goods and services (known as *vetti*) was used by the ruling class and this led more to the denial of Dalits' rights than to dignity and self-respect.[10]

In terms of social movements, the articulation of the civil society on the issue of Telangana is enormous. There has been a mobilization of the rural poor and youth by the radical Left on the basis of class; the developed coastal region has witnessed an emotional mobilization on the socio-cultural identity of caste. The relationship of these subaltern mobilizations to the larger political processes – political parties, their social basis and public policies – has been quite complex. The agrarian and Dalit movements in Andhra Pradesh brought the following issues on to both civil society and the political agenda: one, land distribution; two, wage increases for agricultural labour; three, farm servants; and four, *beedi* workers, *tendu* leaf collectors, and caste/class-based socio-economic oppression (of which *vetti*, or forced labour, was an important dimension). This movement influenced even Medak district.

This study focuses on Dalit self-assertion in Medak district. Medak district was originally known as Methuku Durgam and was subsequently changed to Methuku on account of the fine rice produced in this area. Medak district earlier was part of the Kakatiya kingdom. Finally, with the fall of the Qutubshahi dynasty, the Asif Jahis annexed it with the Mughal Empire. During the formation of Hyderabad state, this district was detached and was included in the Nizam's dominion. It finally became a part of Andhra Pradesh with effect from 1 November 1956 after the re-organization of states following independence in India.[11] Though the district is very close to Hyderabad, the capital city of Andhra Pradesh, the social practices relating to religion and caste – like *Jogini system, Vetti, Banamati*, child marriages, untouchability (in schools, students sit in separate classrooms), etc. – remain widespread. They indicate, in the eyes of Dalit activists, that Dalits have been treated in an inhuman way in the districts of Telangana region as several writers or social scientists like Professor Haragopal (also a human rights activist) and Professor Gopal Guru argue.

Understanding Concepts of Dalit, Caste and Untouchability

The term 'Dalit' is derived from the Sanskrit root '*dal*', which means burst, split, broken or torn asunder, downtrodden, scattered, crushed, destroyed.[12] The word was first used by the British, and then by Dr B.R. Ambedkar in his Marathi speech 'The Untouchables', published in 1948. Later, the Dalit Panthers revived the term in their 1973 manifesto, extending its definition to include 'Scheduled Tribes, neo-Buddhists, the working people, the landless and poor peasants, women, and all those who are being exploited politically and economically in the name of religion'.[13] Literally, the meaning of Dalit is 'broken' people who lie at the bottom of India's caste system. Dalits are discriminated against, denied access to land, forced to work in degrading conditions, and routinely abused at the hands of the police and higher caste groups that enjoy state protection. In what has been called India's 'hidden apartheid', entire villages in many Indian states remain completely stratified, with the untouchables segregated.[14] It is important to explain the significance of the concept of 'Dalit' in this context. There has been an intense debate on this question, resulting in two important viewpoints. One is that the socially, politically and educationally oppressed sections of the society are Dalits. Another is that Dalits consist of only those sections of Indian society that have suffered or continue to suffer as untouchables. Dalits have been called by various names: untouchables, *harijans* (children of God – a name given by Gandhi), exterior castes, depressed classes, outcastes, pariahs, etc. In more ancient times, terms such as *Mlecha, Chandala,*

Panchama, Nishada, Avarna, Antyaja, Atishudra, Paulkasa, etc., were in use.[15] Dalit communities in India are extremely heterogeneous groups, divided into hundreds of castes and sub-sub-castes and spread over every nook and corner of India.[16] The term 'Dalit' refers here to the Scheduled Castes and Scheduled Tribes who constitute around 23 percentage of the total population in India. According to the 2001 Census, Scheduled Castes (Dalits) comprise 16.2 per cent of the total population of India; that is, they number over 17 crores. Scheduled Tribes comprise 8.2 per cent of the population; that is, they number over 8 crores. Both together constitute 24.4 per cent of the Indian population; that is, they together number over 25 crores.

Caste is specifically an Indian expression of institutionalized inequality and indignity. As Ramaiah argued, 'In the name of caste, society is divided into two categories: power and vulnerability; privilege and oppression; honour and denigration; plenty and want; reward and deprivation. Untouchability is a part and parcel of the caste structure; it is an economically and socially exploitative system worse than slavery.'[17] India's caste system is perhaps the world's longest surviving social hierarchy with permeating graded inequality. A defining feature of Hinduism is caste which encompasses a complex ordering of social groups on the basis of religion and rituals. Differences in status are traditionally justified by the religious doctrine of *karma,* a belief that one's place in life is determined by one's deeds in a previous lifetime. Ambedkar saw the caste system as a serious obstacle to the path to democracy. According to him, democracy lies not just in the form of government, but also in term of association between the people who form the society.

According to S.R. Sankaran,[18] Indian society is divided and degraded on the basis of the caste system and therefore cannot truly be called democratic. G. Haragopal and B. Chandrasekhar Rao (2000) observed that 'the problem of caste is very complex as the ideology of Hinduism is rooted in hierarchical and authoritarian worldview. Every caste occupies a place, either lower or higher, in the ladder. In the attempt for a change, each caste resists the domination from the castes below'.[19]

As Lata Murugkar argued, it is a unique phenomenon in the world. For long, according to the *Chaturvarna* system of the Hindu religion, the untouchables have been regarded variously as *avarnas, atisudras, antyajas or panchamas* – a fifth order of sorts, beyond the pale. The stigma of untouchability is attached to this community because of the so-called polluted state related to its members' 'lowly' occupations as sweepers or cobblers. Untouchability has been considered a congenital stigma which cannot be eliminated by any rite or deed. For centuries, the untouchables suffered from many kinds of religious, economic and social discrimination. They were not allowed to study the sacred scriptures or worship in the temples of higher-caste Hindus. Even their touch was considered defiling by the caste Hindus; hence, they were not allowed to bring water from tanks and wells of the latter. Their women were not permitted to cover their breasts. They were restricted in dress, speech, food and manner. Any violation of the customary norms of behaviour was visited with punishment – from severe ostracism to decapitation.[20] Sukhadeo Thorat observes that such a system leaves no scope for individual choice including in matters of occupations. The Hindu social order does not recognize equal need, equal work or equal ability as the basis of reward for labour in the distribution of goods and opportunities. It is believed that those who are considered as the highest must get the best and those who are classed as lowest must accept the least and worst. This entrenched inequality leads to the unending spiral of violence against Dalits.[21]

Regarding untouchability, the National Commission report, 1997, for Scheduled Castes and Scheduled Tribes (SCs and STs) underscored that untouchability – the imposition of social disabilities on persons by reason of their birth in certain castes – was still practised in many forms throughout the country. Untouchability is a dominant factor still continuing in the matter of social relationships. Untouchability takes the form of barriers in bathing, eating, drinking, worshipping and having access to common property. It puts a ban on all common forms of participation. In the use of public facilities, the spirit of discrimination manifests itself in the exclusion of conveyance and access to land, water and other livelihood resources. Dalit women face double discrimination on the basis of caste and gender in all spheres of life and are subjected to gross violations of their physical integrity, including sexual abuse by dominant castes, with impunity. They are socially excluded, abused and economically exploited. The practice of 'divine prostitution' (Jogini/Devadasi system in temples in India) continues even today, despite laws prohibiting this menace affecting Dalit women.[22] Dr Ambedkar observed that untouchability was more than a religious system. It was also an economic system worse than slavery. Prof. Nancharaiah observed that those considered as untouchables were denied the right to education, the right to owning land and the right of wearing jewellery. They were also denied the right to bargain for a decent wage and they were obliged to accept whatever was paid by the upper castes, who were the dominant feudal landlords in the caste hierarchy. They had to perform a number of duties in the villages without any remuneration.[23] These three models are interrelated and were causes for the deprivation of Dalits.

Emergence of the Dalit Movement in Telangana Region

The 1920s saw the emergence of the Dalit movement as a conscious, organized force in the social and political life of Dalits. In the 1920s, after the Dalit Panthers movement saw a qualitative leap forward, Jyotirao Phule, Peryar Ramaswamy and Ambedkar fought for self-respect, and a decent and dignified life. The earlier Dalit movement emerged in Maharastra. Later, it spread to the entire country. At the global level, the turbulent post-war era was marked by the challenge of the Russian Revolution and by the Montague-Chelmsford reforms. It was a period of advancing mass struggles and ideological upheavals in India.[24] The Dalit movement also started during the same period.

During those days, Dalits in the Telangana region faced pressure to identify themselves either with Hindus or with Muslims. In some ways, Dalit-Muslim relations in the Hyderabad area itself were close, yet it was a closeness characterized by ambiguity. The relationship was expressed in a saying quoted by one Dalit activist: the Dalit colony is where the Muslims' 'in-laws live'. That is, the Muslims took wives/girls from the Dalits. The Devadasis from these communities – Malas, Madigas, Basavas and Matangis – often had relations with affluent or noble Muslims in Hyderabad city. When the Dalit reformers tried to stop these customs in the 1920s, one consequence was increasing Muslim antagonism. 'Muslims were always after our girls' was a frequent complaint among Dalits. The 'closeness' thus had a clear element of sexual exploitation in it, as Muslims did not need to respect the dictates of untouchability. This could be seen in the naming of Hyderabad itself after a Dalit girl (Bhagyamma), who is said to have been brought into the harem of the founding prince. In this narrow and communalized framework, a small but vigorous Dalit movement developed after 1910, primarily led by Hyderabad Dalits, particularly the Malas.[25] Two leaders stood at the forefront of the movement: Bhagya Reddy Varma, with an organization called Manya Sangam, and Ariga Ramaswamy.[26] They worked with the help of Manyasangam and concentrated on internal social reform: attempting to ban liquor consumption, meat eating at social functions, and the abolition of the Devadasi system. This group also found itself in conflict with the traditional caste called 'Chanduris' or the overseers of the Malas, and throughout the 1920s there were attempts to reform the oppressive system. This development was partly due to the formation of a Dalit middle class which began to enter social life. The radicalization among Dalits throughout South India brought with it an Adi-Hindu ideology. In 1924, Ariga Ramaswamy formed the Adi-Hindu Jatiyyonati Sabha and Bhagyareddy Varma transformed his Manya Sangam into the Adi-Hindu Social Service League. This became the main organization of the Dalits of Hyderabad.[27] As T.V. Narayana, a Dalit leader, said, 'In the 1920s, generally in Telangana, Dalits used to work in the reformist organization of Arya Samaj that had worked against the conversion of poor people into Christianity and for conducting inter-caste marriages, mixed dining facilities, free education to the poor people, widow remarriage, etc. As a result, there were no conversions into Christianity in the region of Telangana, as there were in the Andhra region.'[28]

Socio-economic Status of Scheduled Castes in Telangana Sub-region

In the Andhra sub-region, the status of Dalits is comparatively better than that in Telangana. The atrocities against Dalits in Chundur, Vempenta and Karamchedu stand as examples of increasing Dalit repression in Andhra. These violent acts against the Dalit communities were intended to suppress the growing awareness among them. The increasing consciousness among these sections posed certain questions to the well-established hierarchical order of the upper castes, and to class collaborations. In the case of Telangana, the Dalit sections continue their struggle for a dignified existence (owing to prevailing economic conditions). As mentioned earlier, the Dalit sections under the Nizam's rule were subjected to *vetti* practices. It was compulsory for every family to send a man from their home to work in a feudal lord's house. Though the Nizam's days are over and India has entered the 21st century, this feudal legacy persists in the Telangana villages. Because of unfavourable agricultural conditions and poor irrigation facilities, agricultural workers get employment for only four months a year. *Vetti* thus became one of the options to cope with the financial crisis. Sending smaller children to *vetti* in return for the money borrowed from the village moneylenders for medical or some other emergency needs are also in vogue. A survey done by an NGO, Deccan

Development Society (1996), among 55 villages revealed that 481 children and 483 adults were still working as *vetti* labourers in Medak district itself. In total, 9,000 male children and 12,000 adults were working under *vetti* in Medak district.[29] Atrocities carried out on the Dalit sections are reported in the newspapers regularly. There are also humiliations like the 'two glass system'[30] in hotels, and Dalits being burnt alive under the pretext of practising witchcraft. These are still commonly seen in the rural parts of Telangana.[31] In short, Dalits are denied their rights as human beings. The following cases indicate the state of Dalit rights and the growing self-assertion of Dalit youth.

Case 1: Assertion of Dalits in Psundur

In Psundur village, an upper caste mob attacked the Dalits and brutally killed eight Dalits. Some bodies were cut into pieces and some bodies were thrown into the river. The level of brutality was unprecedented. This was followed by a sustained struggle for justice. It went up to the judiciary and the Dalits succeeded in setting up of a separate court in the village where the massacre took place. From the month of August, 1991, the hearing went on till 31 July 2007, when the judgment was given. The Public Prosecutor who argued for the Dalits held that one major issue was the 'propaganda' by the 'fascist *hindutva* forces' in favour of upper castes who were responsible for the Psundur massacre. It is to be noted that as of today, the seven accused have still not been arrested and 33 witnesses and 33 of the accused have passed away as there was delay in the judgment. As many as 123 members were released on the grounds of innocence, 21 of the accused were given the life sentence (imprisonment) and 30 members were given one-year imprisonment. It took 16 years to deliver the judgment. The special court did not consider the Psundur case as a trailblazer and held that those who killed by the upper castes were not from the Scheduled Castes or Harijans. The Division Bench felt so on the grounds that their names were not typical Dalit names as they were drawn from the Bible. The partial success in getting justice is an outcome of Dalit, civil liberties and human rights movements. The issue of solidarity of the movements becomes extremely crucial in shaping and reshaping the agenda and political discourse of the Dalit movement and in evolving the strategy of transformation. It also determines the nature of social transformation in times to come.

The response of the state and the dominant section of the civil society fell short of the expectations of Dalits. From the beginning of the incident till the delivering of the judgment, the state was not firmly in favour of the Dalits. This negative disposition of the state strengthens the argument that the only alternative is to continue the struggle. Gopal Guru argues that the role of the state in protecting the human dignity of the Dalits is unsatisfactory. It has not been able to stop the practice of untouchability. Jean Dreze feels that just as the consciousness of Dalits is growing, the atrocities are also growing. The state and its administrative apparatus can play a positive role but the experience is totally contrary to expectations. The entire law-enforcing agency has no respect whatsoever for the law, not to speak of safeguarding the civil rights of the Dalits. The Psundur massacre took place as Dalits of these districts are better educated, assertive, and identity-conscious than the Dalit communities of other regions or other districts. Hence, Balagopal argues that the younger generation from this region started rejecting social and political subordination to the forward castes. It is this socially and politically effective advancement and assertiveness of the Dalits that the forward castes find intolerable, and this resulted in the massacre of the Dalits in Psundur. Sukhadeo Thorat argues that there are established techniques adopted by a section of the dominant castes to reinforce their superior power over the Dalits when they question the existing system in which they are suffering for centuries, or assert their rights. It generally occurs with more force when upper castes feel threatened or the *status quo* is challenged by the Dalits seeking basic human rights. Haragopal holds that education could enhance the status of the Dalits socially, economically and politically and lead to equalizing opportunities, thereby deepening democratic foundations, and strengthening social harmony.[32]

Case 2: Dalit Self-assertion in the Village of Jhadimalkapur

The Durgamma Jatra festival, held in Jhadimalkapur village in Medak district every three years, involves the slaughter of 35 to 40 buffaloes. The same Dalit family in that village has been forced to perform the animal sacrifice for generations. Recently, one of the family's youth refused to perform the sacrifice. Rathnam, one of the very few young educated Dalit youth in this village, said, 'We Dalits have traditionally been forced to perform the animal sacrifice for generations.' He added, 'It would have meant slaughtering 35–40 buffaloes in two-and-a-half hours.' He did not believe in the ritual. He also regarded it as something imposed on his family merely because they were Dalits. He urged his fellow Dalits not to participate in it. Rathnam said his father was already in his sixties and his father himself had never enjoyed performing the ceremony. On the festival day, he was supposed to use a huge knife weighing nearly 5 kilograms. He had to kill each buffalo in less than four minutes. The person doing this job is not supposed to make any noise while performing it. If he does, he is beaten with sticks. After killing the animals, he has to carve the animals into pieces and finally bury the remains. These go into pits dug, filled and covered up by members of the Dalit community. This job has to be completed in 10 hours. There is no payment for this work. The person who performs it is also thrashed severely if he fails to finish the task on time. In 1993, Rathnam stayed away from the village and avoided assisting in the ceremony. According to his account, he didn't dare enter the village for six months after. When he did, no one spoke to him, not even co-Dalits. They were afraid. (Some of them also believe in the ritual.) After some time, he had no option except to resume this slaughter.

In 1996, at the time for the Durgamma Jatra festival, the leaders of the upper castes approached him again. Rathnam had not changed his views. His family supported him. Rathnam's father had done the slaughtering job for 18 years. He could not take the strain any more. In 1996, Rathnam was working as a compounder (assistant to doctor) in a nursing home in Zaheerabad town – the *mandal* headquarters of his village. The upper caste leaders sent for him and insisted that he had to perform the ceremony. Rathnam informed the collector and the superintendent of police of the problem. This angered the village elite. On 12 May, they summoned his family in Jhadimalkapur and warned them, 'Tell us by this evening whether he will kill the buffaloes or not. If he does not do so, your son will not live much longer.' At that time, Rathnam used to commute from Zaheerabad to his village by bus. That day his mother sent his younger brother to inform him not to come home, so he did not. The same night, approximately 100 people from the upper castes went to his home drunk and abused his family late at night. Rathnam's family was isolated. Even a few Scheduled Caste community people expressed their view that 'we depend on the upper castes so much, how can we confront them?' Then the upper caste visitors went away, and a caste *panchayat* (council) was held. The verdict was swift. The whole family was boycotted. Anyone speaking to them would face 25 beatings with *chappals* (footwear/slippers) and pay a fine of ₹ 5,000.

This was the only family in the village which disobeyed the tradition. One of the respondents said, 'This profession has been going on for ages. The Scheduled Caste people of this village have been given

10 acres of land as *eenam land* in return for their doing this work.' He added, 'They should do this job as a part of village rituals.' The upper caste leaders of the village asked one of Rathnam's relatives, Nagappa, to perform the ritual. Rathnam informed the collector and the superintendent of police. The latter warned the villagers against such a practice. Soon after, there was an attempt to murder members of Rathnam's family. Therefore, they moved out of Jhadimalkapur village to Zaheerabad.[33]

As 31 May, the day of the sacrifice, approached things heated up. The whole village was tense and anxiously waited to see what would happen. Even a television crew from Hyderabad visited the village, hoping to catch the event on camera. The members of the crew were severely beaten up, which caused an uproar in the state legislature. A police picket at the village was also attacked. Cases were filed against 19 upper caste people and some backward class persons. But powerful networks were soon in action. Narsimha Reddy (Former MLA of Zaheerabad) and others held a *dharna* in front of the police station. He was the supporter of the then Member of Parliament who remained in the background, but supported the upper castes. The protest was directed against police repression. The police arrested the protesters but released them shortly afterward. The upper caste people of Rathnam's village waited to kill him, but he escaped. Thereafter, there was tension in the village and Rathnam's father died after four months. This entire movement was under the banner of DAFODAM, Ambedkar Youvajana Sangam and the A.P. Study Circle of Zaheerabad under the leadership of Ananthaiah (activist and lecturer-principal at Jogipet), Ramchander Bheemvamshi (artist and teacher at Zaheerabad), Narsimulu (activist and teacher at Zaheerabad) and other local and state Dalit leaders. Due to the powerful movement to counter this practice and to promote the protection of Dalit rights, the government promised 3 acres of land, a house, and a job to Rathnam, who opposed this particular *vetti* or forced labour. Therefore, this protest was also against *vetti*. But as of now, the government has not fulfilled its promises.

Rathnam is staying in Zaheerabad in a rented house, and has converted to Christianity. However, the movement also started addressing environmental degradation as well as Dalit dignity. Many associations, NGOs and political parties congratulated Rathnam for his refusal to take part in the superstition of animal sacrifice. The Arya Samaj, Menaka Gandhi and other public bodies and persons expressed their appreciation. However, no organization or individual has helped him materially. Also, many people seem not to have understood that his movement was for self-respect, dignity, and freedom from forced labour.[34]

Case 3: Assertion of a Dalit Student in Allapur Village

The village of Allapur is located 9 kilometres from the *mandal* headquarters of Narayanakhed in Medak district. There is no paved road to this village. Here, it is primarily the Reddy and the Balija castes (about 135 families) who wield political, economic and social power. There are 30 Dalit families. All the upper caste people own 30–40 acres of land but most Dalits do not have land, and those who do usually have about an acre. Because they lack land, the Dalits work on the estates of the upper castes. As wages, Dalit women get ₹ 15 and Dalit men get ₹ 30 per day. They have nowhere to go. Among the Scheduled Castes, there are only six members who are highly educated, meaning that they have studied up to 10th class, intermediate and graduation. The other Dalits work as labourers (without taking any money) and forced labour in the houses and lands of the upper caste and Backward Classes. In this village, many discriminatory practices are common, including the two-glass system, the denial of entry into temples, and the denial of the right to wear *chappals*. The Dalits are expected to follow blindly whatever the upper caste people order. With growing access to education, some Dalit youth started questioning the entrenched practices of the oppressive Hindu social hierarchy.[35]

In 1995, one Dalit student, B. Tukaram, entered the Hanuman Temple, which triggered a social boycott of Dalit families by the upper castes in the village. Tukaram was educated; he had passed the intermediate examinations (prior to college) at the Andhra Pradesh Social Welfare School (APSWR) at Hathnoora, Medak district. He went to the temple to perform *puja* by breaking a coconut to invoke the blessings of God for passing his intermediate exam. The strong belief of the upper caste residents of this village, however, was that the Dalits are untouchables and they therefore should not enter the temple and offer prayers. Tukaram's act was construed as an offence to upper caste beliefs. Enraged by this, the village elders called for a *panchayat* and decided to boycott 26 Dalit families in the village. In the *panchayat* held by the upper castes, Tukaram's parents apologized to the upper caste representatives, but Tukaram was not willing to apologize, nor did he agree to their demand that he touch their feet. From the next day on, Dalits were not allowed to visit restaurants or shops, or use the borewells to get water. Even the domestic animals of the Dalits were not allowed to pass through their streets in the village. If Dalits violated these sanctions, they would have to pay ₹ 500 as fine and be beaten up with slippers. The Dalits notified the Ambedkar Yuvajana Sangam in Narayanakhed. Leaders of the association visited the village to find out the particulars about the social boycott. They met both the upper caste people and the Dalits. Both agreed to a compromise. But on the very same day, the upper caste people met under the guidance of the school teacher, who was from the Reddy community, and unanimously decided to continue the social boycott. The next day, the media visited to cover the news. The upper caste people openly told the media that they had socially boycotted the Dalits, as entry into a Hindu temple by a Dalit was against the Hindu tradition.[36] The incident had taken place on 24 May 2005, but the local police or district administration did not know about the incident in Allapur village till the media (electronic and print) covered the news. After the media's coverage, the population of the district and state were informed about the Allapur social boycott. Thereafter, Dalit organizations demanded the initiation of legal proceedings against the upper caste men, and extension of welfare schemes to the socially boycotted. Later, several political leaders and district administrators visited Allapur village. They included Justice Punnaiah, district collector, superintendent of police, Raghavulu, CPI (M) general secretary, Nalla Surya Prakash (BSP), and others. At last, the police filed cases against the upper caste people. After 20 days of social boycott, some unidentified persons hacked Govind Reddy (40), a farmer, to death in Allapur village. The victim was one of the 20 persons who had been arrested in connection with the boycotting of Scheduled Caste persons. Due to pressure by local political leaders, police filed charges against the Dalits of the village for the murder of Govind Reddy. Twenty Dalits were arrested. In reality, Govind Reddy was murdered by his own brother due to a land dispute. This came out in the interrogation conducted by the district superintendent of police. The state-level Dalit organizations staged protests against the filing of the cases against Dalits. Several political parties, activists of KNPS, NGOs, civil society groups, democrats and human rights activists raised their voices. CPI (M) and TRS sent fact-finding committees to Allapur village. In the Legislative Assembly, members pressured the government to distribute land, announce financial assistance to construct houses for Dalits and also offer financial assistance to those Dalits who were socially boycotted. Although the government agreed to provide financial assistance for small houses, they have yet to extend any sort of assistance to Dalits.[37]

These three cases indicate how Dalits are becoming conscious of their rights. As Dalits are exposed to the larger world through higher education, which has become possible through reservation, Dalits have been able to move forward. Increasingly, they want to live with dignity and self-respect, and do not want to submit to anybody. Psundur (also sometimes called Chundur) and incidents of oppression such as in Karachedu and Vempeta are not only a result of upper caste power but also changing Dalit consciousness and movements in Andhra Pradesh. The growing self-assurance indicates that Dalits from coastal regions are increasingly educated, assertive and conscious of their rights. As they had an early exposure to education, they are able to challenge the evils of the social system. Balagopal observed that 'the younger generation has started rejecting the social and political subordination to the forward castes. This kind of attitude on the part of Dalits was intolerable to the forward castes. It led to assaults on 17 members from Dalit community in Psundur'. As a result, the Dalits of Psundur in Andhra Pradesh have started a massive movement.[38]

Both of the above given cases were the result of forced labour in the name of caste. The suppression and inhuman treatment of Dalits are not seen in their totality. On closer inspection, one sees in both the cases, two young men who had received some education and were influenced by Dalit movements in the states. They dared to defy what they perceived as oppressive practices as a result of their growing democratic consciousness. Another reason for their decision might have been that while they were attending government colleges, in course of interaction with their friends, they might have realized that they were being treated in an inhuman way by the upper castes.

The government enacted the SC and ST (Prevention of Atrocities) Act, 1989; under which special courts have been set up at the district level. The nation should enlarge the space for each culture for its diverse development and in the areas of social, economic, educational, and other activities. These are all necessary, as the Dalit community has been kept away from sources of both social and economic status for a significant time, a fact which is used to justify Dalits' economic and social backwardness.[39]

Conclusion

Atrocities against Dalits are not new. Eminent Dalit scholar Gopal Guru observed that the violation of Dalit human rights through violence against the Dalit community flows from the conservative ideology and political apparatus of the Hindutva forces. He also argued that when this ideology is coupled with the demand for Dalit status, the result is a violation of the human dignity of Dalits. The ideology of untouchability is based on a concept of the 'purity/pollution line' and justifies practices discriminating against Dalits.[40] These are established techniques adopted by a section of the dominant castes to reinforce their superiority over Dalits. The ideology gains particular prominence when upper castes feel threatened or the status quo is being challenged by the Dalits seeking basic human rights.[41] A number of instances from different parts of the country show that it is Dalit men and women who become the target for upper caste violence when the former dare to protest against the infringement of their rights. The Karamchedu Massacre, the Psundur carnage, and the Kirlanji rapes are a few instances of this trend. As Thorat argues, Dalits who question upper caste norms are also subjected to subtle, but no less oppressive, tactics including social ostracism. Dalits find that their access to work, land, credit, merchandise and public facilities may suddenly be cut off. Since the upper castes control the rural economy, it is difficult for Dalits to assert their rights without jeopardizing their livelihood.[42] The state response to violence against Dalits has not been as supportive toward Dalits as the law seems to envisage. Gopal Guru argues that the role of the state in protecting the human dignity of the Dalits is unsatisfactory in the sense that it has not been able to stop the practice of untouchability.[43]

The Indian Constitution guarantees certain rights to all citizens and places upon the state an additional charge to protect and serve the interests of the poorest and most socially disadvantaged groups so that they may gradually attain positive liberty. But in reality, crimes against Dalits rarely result in conviction, owing to the state's failure to investigate and prosecute such offences. State authorities generally ignore the provisions of the Acts in carrying out investigations. The cases mentioned here show how this dereliction of duty happens and how, by siding with the upper castes at key points in caste conflicts, police and other state officials sabotage Dalit mobilization and subvert the course of justice. Although the state has carefully legislated to protect the rights of Dalits, these legal provisions are not carried into force because the administration is caste-biased, as Thorat points out.[44]

The furore raised by these cases is further evidence of the overall trend towards democratization. The aspirations of Dalits, as articulated by Phule and Ambedkar, can only be fulfilled when subjects assert their rights by raising their voices against centuries-old oppression in the name of tradition and custom. The cases pointedly make clear that unless civil society comes to the rescue of the oppressed, social transformation and Dalit upliftment will remain a dream. Tentative promises by the government and other organizations, which are never realized in real terms, can only aggravate social oppression and human degradation. Only a sincere effort from educated Dalits, the government and civil societies can realize Ambedkar's dream of achieving liberty, equality and fraternity. Despite the Indian Constitution's solemn commitment to freedom to redeem oppressed groups such as Dalits from all bondage, forced labour, atrocities and all other forms of exploitation, practical enforcement of this policy remains a distant dream. The Dalits remain the most exploited section in Indian society.

To overcome this kind of oppression, S.R. Sankaran[45] has suggested measures for enhancing the quality of Dalit rights, that include land restructuring, better wages, equitable shares in emerging opportunities and well-targeted socio-economic programmes backed by effective implementation of special laws in their favour; not just 'safety nets' or measures with a 'human face'. Many parties have started preparing an action plan encompassing various aspects like compulsory education, common education schools, provision of irrigation sources to Dalit families for cultivation of land, and involving Dalits in decision-making. As a result, today many political parties have initiated efforts to bring out a Dalit empowerment policy and have promised to give 3 acres of land per family to the nearly 10 lakh Dalit families in the Telangana region. Several political parties have also promised to fight for reservation in the private sector to ensure that Dalits are not discriminated in the employment market.

It can be concluded that although democratic and independent India has generated enabling conditions permitting Dalits to occupy the offices of power, there has not yet been any significant change in their socio-political status at the grassroots level. On the contrary, the patronizing tendencies of co-option and the marginalization of assertive or potentially assertive Dalits by dominant castes, classes and parties have subjugated Dalit self-assertion, resulting in the perpetuation of upper caste hegemony. Dalit political self-activism has to be able to dismantle these social cobwebs so that Dalits can enjoy the fruits of democracy in their own right, without any patronage. I argue here that it is the responsibility of Dalits, Dalit intellectuals and, administrators of the Dalit community to create awareness among Dalits about their rights, self-respect, dignity and a decent life. Not merely

Dalits, but also the civil society associations, should play an important role in transforming the society. The cases discussed in this paper highlight the aspirations of young, educated Dalits. Actions like theirs may accentuate the process of social transformation, despite the hazards and hardships that are inherent in this transition from subjugation to dignity and freedom, which Ambedkar postulated as necessary conditions for substantive democracy. Thus, the study argues that the spirit of social transformation, equality and dignity should be reflected in Telangana region after formation of the state. In this regard, the next unit would focus on the Telangana movement and its relevance in contemporary politics to comprehend or assess democracy critically.

Notes

1. Group of villages.
2. Political activist, legal scholar and drafter of the Indian Constitution.
3. R.D.M. Maurya, 'Human Rights Violations and Atrocities on Dalits', in *Restoration of Human Rights and Dignity to Dalits: With Special Reference to Scavengers in India*, edited by Gopal Singh and Ravindra Gadkar, Manak Publications, New Delhi, 2004.
4. Imposed by Prime Minister Indira Gandhi in 1975.
5. K. Srinivas, *Caste, Class and Social Articulation in AP: Mapping Different Regional Trajectories*, Overseas Development Institute, London, 2002, pp. 1–6.
6. They ruled the state which comprises Telangana, Bidar and Mysore.
7. M.D. Tajuddin, 'Role of State and NGOs in Issues of Food Security: A Case Study of DDS', Medak district, Unpublished dissertation, Centre for Regional Studies, University of Hyderabad, 2004, pp. 5–6.
8. Ibid.
9. Demand for Telangana state came up when Andhra Pradesh was formed as a separate state in the 1950s.
10. Ibid.
11. Ibid.
12. James Massey, *Downtrodden: The Struggle of India's Dalits for Identity, Solidarity and Liberation*, WCC Publications, Switzerland, 1997, p. 1.
13. John C.B. Webster, 'Who is a Dalit?', in *Dalits in Modern India: Vision and Values*, edited by S.M. Michael, Vistaar Publications, New Delhi, 1999, p. 68.

14. R.D.M. Maurya, op. cit., pp. 77–78.
15. G. Haragopal, 'Rights of Dalits: Law and Reality', *Indian Journal of National Human Rights Commission*, Vol. I, New Delhi, 2002, pp. 133–34.
16. Raj Kumar, 'Dalit Culture: A Perspective from Below', *Social Action*, Vol. 50, No. 1, January–March 2000, p. 17.
17. Avatthi Ramaiah, op. cit., pp. 1–4.
18. Committed retired IAS (Indian Administrative Service) officer.
19. G. Haragopal and B. Chandrasekhar Rao, 'Dalit Consciousness in Andhra: A Hypothesis', *Indian Journal of Human Rights*, Vol. 4, Nos 1–2, 2000, pp. 137–45.
20. Lata Murugkar, *Dalit Panther Movement in Maharashtra: A Sociological Appraisal*, Popular Prakashan, Bombay, 1991, p. 1.
21. Sukhadeo Thorat, 'Human Rights of Ex-Untouchables in India: Violations and Enforcement', *Indian Journal of Human Rights*, Vol. 4, Nos 1–2, 2000.
22. Report, National Campaign on Dalit Human Rights, New Delhi, 2006, p. 5.
23. G. Nancharaiah, 'Development Policy and Social Change with Reference to Scheduled Castes', in *Human Rights of Dalits: Societal Violation*, edited by R.M. Pal Bhargava, Gyan Publishers, New Delhi, 2001, p. 53.
24. Lata Murugkar, op. cit., p. 105.
25. Interview with P.R. Venakataswamy, activist, on 11 September 2006.
26. Gail Omvedt, *Dalits and Democratic Revolution: Dr Ambedkar and the Dalit Movement in India*, Sage Publications, New Delhi, 1994, pp. 121–22.
27. Ibid.
28. Interview with T.V. Narayana, Dalit activist, on 15 September 2006.
29. Source: *http://www.carped.org/project.php*, Centre for Action Research and People's Development.
30. Separate glasses for Dalits. After having tea, they have to clean the glasses themselves even though they pay the same amount as other upper castes pay. Interestingly, they sit outside the restaurant.
31. Suneeta Eluri, 'Political Responses to Right to Development: A Case Study of Telangana', Unpublished M.Phil dissertation, University of Hyderabad, Hyderabad, 2003, pp. 34–35.
32. K. Balagopal, 'Post-Psundur and Other Psundurs', *Economic and Political Weekly*, Vol. 26, No. 42, 1991, pp. 2397–99.
33. Interview with Ratnam, victim, on 1 September 2006.
34. Interview with B. Ananthaiah, Lecturer and Principal, Government Degree College, Jogipet and Dalit activist, Medak district, on 13 September 2006.

35. Tudum Rajender, Tudum, Velivesina Allapur Dalitulapi Akrama Hatya Kesula?, *Pratigatana* (counter reaction) KVPS, p. 12.
36. Interview with Tukaram, victim, on 17 September 2006, in Allapur village, Narayanakhed Mandal, Andhra Pradesh.
37. Interview with Sailu B., school teacher from Narayanakhed, on 25 September 2006.
38. K. Balagopal, op. cit., 1991, p. 2399.
39. Avatti Ramaiah, op. cit., p. 6.
40. Gopal Guru, 'Human Rights and the Dalits', in *Human Rights of Dalits: Societal Violation*, edited by R.M. Pal Bhargava, Gyan Publishers, New Delhi, 2001, p. 40.
41. Sukhadeo Thorat, Ghanshyam Shah, Satish Deshpande and Amita Baviskar, *Untouchability in Rural India*, Sage Publications, New Delhi, 2006, p. 133.
42. Ibid., pp. 137–38.
43. Gopal Guru, op. cit., p. 41.
44. Sukhadeo Thorat, op. cit., 2006, p. 147.
45. Retired IAS (Indian Administrative Service) officer.

7 The Telangana People's Movement

Demand for a Separate State and Democratic Rights

This chapter focuses on the ongoing Telangana statehood movement. This is divided into two parts. The first part focuses on territorial statehood and the second part on democratic statehood. The people and political parties who are supporting the idea of a mere geographical Telangana state feel that the problems of poor, marginalized and deprived people can be better addressed after the formation of a separate state, whereas people's organizations and individuals who are supportive of a democratic Telangana are keen on substantial development of marginalized communities. The egalitarian values like equality, liberty, fraternity, respect and dignity have to be ensured, protected and respected in the separate Telangana state critically. This study intends to depend on secondary and primary sources. It also depends on the writings and debates in the vernacular language, i.e., Telugu.

The Telangana region is located in the western part of Andhra Pradesh. It was formerly part of the state of Hyderabad, ruled by the *Asaf Jahi* dynasty (the ruler was popularly known as the Nizam) from the 18th century until independence. It came out of the ruins of the medieval Bahamani and Qutub Shahi kingdoms and formed a polygonal tract occupying the centre of the Deccan Plateau. The Nizam's state[1] comprised three linguistic regions: Telangana, Marathwada and Karnataka. For the purpose of administration, the entire state was divided into four *subas* (i.e., districts): Warangal and Medak (Telangana), Aurangabad (Marathwada) and Gulbarga (Karnataka). The Telangana region that was formed as a part of the Nizam's dominion represented the unique Deccan culture.[2] While

India achieved independence in 1947, the Hyderabad state did not get freedom until 1948. After police action under the leadership of Sardar Vallabhbhai Patel, the Nizam state was merged with the Indian union. In 1956, the region was merged with the Andhra region (which was a part of Madras presidency) based on language, i.e., Telugu.[3]

Introduction

Ever since the formation of Andhra Pradesh, there has been discrimination against Telangana in resource allocation, development schemes, education of locals, and employment generation. Injustice and discrimination are also evident in denying spaces for Telangana and Telanganites in decision-making economic, political, social and cultural spheres. In fact, this is only a continuation of the state policy, as Telanganites could not get their due share.

The state of Andhra Pradesh has a distinct place in the history of social movements in India, having witnessed movements by peasants, Dalit, tribals, women and Naxalites. The Telangana movement is not merely the demand for statehood, but also the demand for economic and cultural autonomy from the Andhra region. The rebirth of the Telangana movement in the 1990s raised the question of distribution of land, self-respect, self-rule and for an equal share in the political and economic domains, along with bifurcation of the state.[4] This movement is rooted in a historical context and development model. The regional disparities, in the economic, social and cultural spheres, are a part of reality. After formation of linguistic states, every economic or developmental model, be it the green revolution or globalization, further widened the differences and disparities and the reckless cultural urbanization led to imbalanced and unplanned development. This direction of the development model further sharpened the contradictions and created new tensions in Andhra Pradesh politics. The ongoing movement is a search for resolution of the contradictions.[5]

It is broadly believed that every movement has three facets in its activities to mobilize, articulate and represent people's demands. These are: sensitization, agitation and political process. The Telangana movement witnessed these three facets from the beginning of 1950s when Andhra Pradesh was formed. Without sensitization, there would be no strong agitation and vibrant political process. The process of sensitization starts with opinion-makers as they are apolitical.[6] This section articulates and communicates the demand to the people and mobilizes and motivates them towards agitation in order to solve the problems. The process of sensitization is never ending but there may be interruptions to the movement. People who are concerned with the demand participate in the agitations in support of the issue. Either it is legal/democratic or illegal/undemocratic – depending on the seriousness of the problem, nature of leadership and response of the state. Another facet is the political process in which political parties are launched and participate in the election battle, represent the people in the Assembly or Parliament and air the demands in the House on behalf of the people.[7] Prior to the formation of Andhra Pradesh, opinion-makers sensitized the people and participated in the agitation against exploitation and discrimination by Andhra rulers and are still sensitizing the people. It is a continuous process. To comprehend this whole phenomenon, this study is divided into two parts.

I

In the decade of 1940s and at the last stage of the Nizam's rule, the military administration brought outsiders (Andhra) to Hyderabad state as Telangana people were not qualified and lacked English language and administrative skills, despite the opposition from employees and students from the Telangana region. Those who came to Hyderabad state from Andhra felt victorious and misbehaved with the locals (Mulkis). Against the negative behaviour of Andhra employees, there was an agitation against them. In the agitation, seven students died in the police firing. Assuming that if Andhra Pradesh is formed, there would be the dominance of Andhra leaders in Telangana, the opinion-makers played a major role in mobilizing employees against the state and Andhra employees as well. There were agitations against the non-*Mulkis* in 1952. To enquire into this episode, the government of Andhra constituted a committee under the chairmanship of Justice Jaganmohan Reddy. Prior to the formation of Andhra Pradesh, the then Prime Minister Jawaharlal Nehru visited the Andhra region. During his visit, a few Communist Party activists demanded *Vishalandra* state but Nehru opposed the demand but later the government was compelled to constitute the SRC with Fazal Ali.[8]

It was possible as the Andhra elite were strong in terms of power and resources and influenced the SRC, but notwithstanding the opposition from Andhra, the report of the SRC opposed the merger of Telangana with Andhra region. However, the Government of India announced the formation of Andhra Pradesh – with certain conditions and contradictions. A Gentlemen's Agreement was a part of it. After formation of Andhra Pradesh, rulers who were party to the Gentlemen Agreement violated it. This proves the point that from the very beginning, the leaders from Andhra region did not allow the leaders from Telangana to grow politically, and those who had grown politically already did not get the support from the Andhra leaders. This anti-Telangana attitude led the people of Telangana to start an agitation in the late 1960s. The hostile attitude of the rulers from Andhra region explains the negligence of the region that led to the demand for a separate state. Many of them from Telangana region like Ravindranath started the fast-unto-death at Khammam and Mallikarjun, a student leader, and some others have started sensitizing the people of Telangana over the injustice done to them by Andhra leaders in the integrated Andhra Pradesh state. Madan Mohan started Telangana Praja Samithi. It witnessed around 400 students dying in police firing in the first phase of the movement. This approach made many opinion-makers engage in writing papers.[9] In the 1960s, activists who were working for the cause of a separate Telangana state got the support from educationists.[10] The third facet is the political process, which was reflected in the decade of 1960s. Marri Chenna Reddy launched TSS with the support of trade union and student leaders of Telangana. The TSS later contested elections and won a majority of seats in the Parliament elections, but within a short period, Marri Chenna Reddy merged TSS with the Congress party. This attitude of Marri Chenna Reddy betrayed the people's aspirations for a separate state. The movement became political. Counter to the Telangana movement, Jai Andhra movement was launched by Andhra leaders. The result was a five-point, and six-point formula. P.V. Narasimha Rao became the first Chief Minister in 1973 from the Telangana region to satisfy the political leaders from Telangana. For the time being, there was no movement because of the co-option and coercive politics of Indira Gandhi and NTR between 1980s and 1990s.[11] The decade of 1990s once again gave the scope for the second phase of the Telangana movement.

Due to pressure from the Telangana employees, NTR issued the GO 610 to ensure employment for Telangana youth.[12] In 1998, TJS was launched and argued that a separate Telangana was a democratic demand and upheld the implementation of GO 610, while opposing the establishment of corporate colleges in the region. It started the programme called village-to-village campaign (*Rachha Banda*). At this stage, opinion-makers created consciousness among the people and prepared the base for the movement. In the wake of these developments, the movement was taken up by KCR, who came out from the

TDP and as a protest launched the political party – TRS – in 2001. The issues relating to injustice being done to the Telangana region have been widely debated and discussed. Therefore, it was generally felt that it should be tested in the electoral process. Forty-five Telangana MLAs from the Congress party backed by YSR wrote a letter to the Congress chief demanding a separate Telangana state and a separate PCC for Telangana region. The Congress (2004) and TDP (2009) had a political alliance at different points with TRS and supported the demand for a separate statehood.

During the 2004 general elections, the Congress party convinced the TRS to have an alliance to contest elections. At that particular juncture, the Congress had an alliance with the TRS and an agreement was arrived at between these two political parties.[13] During the course of the campaign, AICC president Sonia Gandhi made a statement while addressing an election campaign.[14] The TDP alliance with the BJP said 'no to the formation of Telangana state' and CPI was 'in favour of the demand for Telangana state', yet there was no clarity on the issue of the formulation of a separate state at that stage. It was a straight fight between two alliances. One in favour of formation of state and other opposed to it. In the polls, the Congress party-TRS alliance registered an impressive victory. On the contrary, the TDP alliance lost the elections. The Congress party invited TRS to join the coalition government at the Centre. But the TRS insisted upon a categorical assurance and inclusion of the demand in the Common Minimum Programme of the UPA. The assurance was made a part of the Presidential Address to the first joint session for both the Houses of Parliament and was further reiterated by the Prime Minister after the formation of the UPA government.[15]

Later, the Congress delayed the process and constituted committee after committee.[16] Though the committee of Pranab Mukherjee favoured the state, no report was submitted to the government. Subsequently, the CPI changed its earlier stand and gave its consent in favour of the demand to the Pranab Mukherjee Committee and the TDP also gave its consent to UPA Sub-Committee. However, YSR changed his strategy and said 'the Congress Party and UPA were committed to the formation of second SRC and he would abide by any decision taken by Sonia Gandhi'. Privately, he pressurized the Congress High Command not to agree to the formation of Telangana State.[17] During 2004–2009, YSR used all the possible methods to suppress the movement, demoralized the leadership active in the movement and threatened the MLAs from Telangana region to maintain silence on the issue and fortified the leadership to quit TRS and join the Congress party. He partially succeeded in implementing his strategy to restrain the movement for the time being.

After the 2009 general election, the Telangana movement received a setback as intellectuals, writers, singers and activists felt that the TRS, which was formed for the cause of statehood and was supposed to reflect the voices of the people, was not doing enough. It lost a majority of seats it contested due to lack of effective strategy, no coordination among the parties in the alliance and dual nature of YSR. During the election campaign, the major political parties, except CPI-M, supported the Telangana cause, but there was no seriousness in TDP's commitment. All these contradictions within the alliance made people not to believe these parties and their political commitment. The Congress party under the leadership of YSR went to the elections promising that 'in principle they are not opposed to separate statehood'. The Congress promised that 'if people give an opportunity to rule the state for another term, they would consider the Telangana issue seriously'. The people from Telangana did not believe the alliance of TRS, TDP and Communist parties. At the same time, the people of Telangana did not give full consent to the Congress party in the general elections. Congress won a majority seats across the state and formed the government once again with the support of MIM. In light of this background, the comparison of Telangana movement in the decade of 1960s needs to be emphasized with the period from 1990–2012.[18]

Political Parties and Their Response

The ongoing separate Telangana state movement is different from that of the 1960s. There was less participation of intellectuals, artists, writers, but in this phase, there was higher participation of intellectuals, activists and civil society organizations. The first meeting at Warangal in 1994 culminated in an intellectuals' forum. There were already mobilized sections which took part in the Telangana movement in 1960s and created the ground for political mobilization. This phase initially brought all the sections (Dalits, tribals, Adivasis, middle classes, backward classes and other castes) together for the struggle for a separate Telangana state. A lot of literature has come out on several issues. Telangana movement gave scope for growth of Dalit literature, feminist literature, and rewriting Telangana history, the question of tribal, Dalit and women empowerment and the issue of minorities became vital for all political parties. In fact, it is multi-dimensional.[19]

Comparison of the Movement in 1960s and 1990s

In 1960s, the movement was confined to urban areas, but now it has spread to the rural areas. The people of Telangana were angry and even nurtured hatred towards the Andhra people in 1960s, but antagonism is absent in the ongoing movement. Language of Telangana people during the 1969 movement was hesitancy mannered, but now it is lenient. In 1960s, the social dimension was missing, but now it is visible. There was no organization that worked for the cause of Telangana on the caste lines in 1960s but now many organizations and leaders have emerged and represent their castes on par with Telangana movement.[20] In 1960s, it was started by the students in urban areas but now by opinion-makers. The Telangana agitation of 1969 turned out to be a long drawn out struggle using several forms of agitation that have undergone many changes starting from hunger strikes, relay fasts, Satyagraha and courting arrest. The nature of the movement has undergone substantial changes. During the agitations in both 1960s and 1990s, the administration in the state stands paralysed. All the employees, students, political leaders, ministers, advocates, lecturers, trade unions are vertically divided into two groups. The agitation has completely paralysed the routine and normal life in Telangana.[21] These sections have taken the movement to the grassroots. The response of the state and the attitude of the police towards the movement continue to be similar. They resort to arrests, foisting of cases on the activists, constituting committees and delaying the decision. The role of the media, however, is totally different. In 1960s, there were only one or two newspapers and only one TV channel – Doordarshan.[22] There was no scientific agenda or strategy in the movement and no substantive developmental agenda. They demanded implementation of the Mulki-rules, more allocation of funds for the development of the region and employment for the Telangana youth.

It assumed that 'from school children to intellectuals, all are in know about the Government Orders, river water distribution, construction of irrigation projects and comparison of policies and benefits from development activities within the state'. Leaders started mobilizing the people based on two reasons: one could be injustice done to the region and the second, self-respect. It carried different perspectives and democratic heritage is a great resource. All the sections in the region are with TRS. Hence, after formation of the party, it was able to win a majority of seats in the local body elections and an impressive number of seats in the 2004 general elections.[23] The

TRS party, in the initial stage, was trying to be a representative of different groups on the platform of the Telangana movement, but after the 2007 elections, it dropped its initial approach and went to an extent where it did not tolerate any other representative in the name of Telangana demand. But in the 2008 byelections, it started losing the support from these sections because of the monopolistic attitude of its president and the party not being able to hold different organizations together.[24] In the initial phase of TRS, intellectuals played a crucial role. The party got the support from intellectuals but later, it started bypassing them. This led to a gap between the TRS and intellectuals. There was a collapse of dialogue and absence of debate within the party. After 2007, the role of students in the movement became huge as in the 1960s. The participation of students was widespread in 1990s but their role in the decision-making was missing.[25]

The overall perceptions seem to be that people's movements have some sort of commitment, whereas political parties do not have commitment and sincerity on issues. During the 1960s, when the separate Telangana movement reached a stage where the leaders were able to pressurize the government with support of people's organizations, students and employees, leaders like Marri Chenna Reddy and others entered the movement and made use of it for their selfish political ends. After a long gap, the people expected the leadership to carry on a sustained struggle for statehood in this phase. Activists from different walks of life working for statehood were apolitical and were waiting for a political party to take up the demand of Telangana seriously. It was in this backdrop that KCR launched the TRS and got support from all sections in the region. Initially, TRS worked according to the wishes of the people. Hence, the movement got a fillip. Initially, all the sections supported TRS. Most of the leaders from the dominant community protested against the party decision, resigned and joined the Congress party. This resulted in losing its own representation in both the Assembly and Parliament.[26] To get back the support of people it changed its strategy from lobbying to movements after the 2009 general elections.[27] Though people have strong aspirations for a separate Telangana state, ironically leaders from the region from all political parties are working for their own political interests.[28] This is the pathetic story of the Telangana leadership. TRS gradually started moving from its original character and moved closer to individual-centric politics. It believes in the politics of 'lobbying', but failed in getting full consensus in favour of Telangana. No new state in the country attained statehood with full electoral consent and lobbying, though they too had followed the strategy of lobbying, but could not succeed.[29] CPI believes that the demand would be realized through people's movements. The party further maintains that 'Telangana state demand is not merely territorial, but a democratic demand and whoever is working for the cause of a separate Telangana state has to work together, irrespective of the ideological differences. It is natural to have diverse ideas and ideological stands, but when there is a common issue, all shall work together for a democratic cause'. It may not be possible to form a state with a democratic model. These problems would remain even after formation of the state. Unless one could struggle against them, there was no possibility of democratic society. CPI (ML) New Democracy supported and conceived the demand and promised a new democratic society. It believes that the people of Telangana require not merely a territorial Telangana, but a democratic Telangana. The party argues for the initiation of struggle to attain statehood and others democratic demands as well.[30]

The president of the Congress argues that 'Congress Party was not opposed to a separate state, the party thinks that there is a need to consider the sentiments of the other region in case Telangana state is formed'.[31] Sonia Gandhi further promised at an election rally at Bhongir in Telangana that 'if at all there is a party which can deliver Telangana, it is the Congress. People should not trust the TDP-TRS alliance.'[32] The Chief Minister constituted a Cabinet Sub-Committee to study those problems. No opposition party joined the committee as they believed that it was a political gimmick of YSR. In contrast to the announcement in the Assembly, during the general election campaign, he cautioned other regions, despite the Congress party's election manifesto assuring no objection to formation of a Telangana state: 'supporting the TDP meant endorsing the demand for a separate state of Telangana at the expense of the interests of the people in Andhra and Rayalaseema regions'.[33] The contradictions and double standards of political parties, particularly the Congress party, is very evident in this whole process. The result was that the Congress party won in general election with a reduced majority as TDP-TRS alliance failed in convincing peoples in 2009 general elections. YSR became CM for the second time, but he died in an air crash in September, 2009. After the death of YSR, the people and media were not debating about the development or the other problems of the state but about who would be the next Chief Minister and was trying to manufacture consent that Y.S. Jaganmohan Reddy who did openly opposed the statehood for the

Telangana in the Parliament would be the next CM. Another important development took place, i.e., the Supreme Court judgment on Hyderabad. This judgment gave the scope for TRS to start the movement once again.

Fast unto Death and Impact on Students

The Supreme Court of India gave a judgment on Hyderabad zone, stipulating that 'it is not a sixth zone, as it was mentioned in six-point formula, but a free zone'. It argues if it is implemented, unemployed youth from Telangana would lose job opportunities. KCR took advantage of this judgment to strengthen the movement and launched the movement and gave a call to fight against the Supreme Court order. It is true that since 2001, TRS had continued its movement in a peaceful manner without any violence for almost a decade. The political parties like TDP and Congress used this issue for their electoral advantage. This kind of negative response of the state, which is detrimental, once again made the students restive. Three months prior to going on fast unto death, KCR had informed the President of India, Union Government, Opposition leader of the state and Centre. On 29 November 2009, while on his way for a relay hunger strike, the police arrested him, and took him to Khammam Sub-Magistrate. Later, he was shifted to Hyderabad. Until the arrest of KCR, the movement was peaceful and trusting electoral politics, but after the arrest of KCR, it turned violent. It was because of the provocation of the state that the movement turned violent. Against his arrest, TRS gave a call for a Telangana bandh, and people took part in dharnas, rallies, and effigy burnings. APSRTC cancelled its buses and the South Central Railways too cancelled long-distance trains.[34] All sections, irrespective of caste, class, gender, employees and unemployed youth, joined the movement voluntarily. Telangana became the battleground once again.[35] Juluri Gouri Shankar opines that 'the movement acquired upper hand and political leaders and political parties became of secondary importance during the agitation'.[36] One could see relay hunger strikes, fasts unto death, community feasts, signboards and even vehicle registration plates marked with the letters TG, standing for Telangana, in place of the official AP, standing for Andhra Pradesh.[37] These forms of protests indicate that Telangana movement is a peaceful movement and created the pressure on the state and union governments. At last, on 9 December 2009, the union government announced that it will start the process for the formation of Telangana state. Political leaders from Seema-Andhra opposed the decision and within a day a majority of them submitted their resignations to the Speaker of the Assembly.

Counter-agitation by Seema-Andhra Leaders

The representatives from Seema-Andhra opposed the decision of the government of India. In protest, one after the other the leaders threatened to resign from their MLA and MP positions and mobilized the people against the decision and favoured a united Andhra Pradesh. They gave a call for *Seema-Andhra bandh* for 48 hours. It is widely believed that the movement against formation of Telangana was started by the political leaders and not by common people. Irrespective of the parties, all the leaders came together and organized meetings, launched bus *yatras* and a few representatives launched fasts unto death. With the pressure from Seema-Andhra leaders, the Government of India once again went back on its given decision.[38] In this whole process, three groups had taken different stands on Telangana.

There were three responses from Andhra region: Samaiyka Andhra, Jai Andhra and greater Rayalaseema movements. Samaykya Andhra opposed Telangana state and demanded not to bifurcate the state; Jai Andhra supported a separate state for Telangana and a separate Andhra state; Greater Rayalaseema opposed Telangana state, but said, if Telangana state is formed, there should be a Greater Rayalaseema. Haragopal argues that 'those who are supporting the demand for united Andhra Pradesh are divided based on their political interests. Hence, there is a no strong argument for their demand except on the pretext of unity'.[39] After bending to the pressure from Seema-Andhra representatives, the Home Ministry announced on 23 December 2009 'for the initiation of a consultation process on the Telangana issue by convening a meeting at New Delhi with eight recognized political parties from Andhra Pradesh on 5th January 2010'. The Home Ministry observed that 'a large number of political parties are divided on the issue of Telangana. There is a need to hold wide-ranging consultations with all political parties and groups in the state. The Government of India would take steps to involve all concerned in the process.'

On 3 February 2009, the Home Ministry, Government of India announced 'a five-member Committee under the Chairmanship of Justice Srikrishna to have wide-ranging consultations with all sections of the people and all political parties and groups in Andhra Pradesh on the Telangana issue'. The Committee was asked to submit its report by 31 December 2010. Terms of references were given to the Committee.

After the Home Minister's statement, agitations stopped. If Telangana state becomes a reality, it is widely believed that their political, as well as economic, interests would be hit. It is important to understand the nature of leadership and their hidden agenda behind their opposition to the separate statehood.[40] The committee submitted its report to the Government of India after consulting all stakeholders of Andhra Pradesh but the recommendations were not acceptable to people of Telangana, they opposed the recommendations but leaders from Andhra welcomed it. Ch. Hanumatha Rao argues that no such Committee in the country submitted six recommendations to the government with confidential chapter like the committee submitted. This approach, he argues, kills the democratic spirit.

Home Ministry's Second Statement and Its Impact on Telangana Movement

After the Government of India's 'U' turn, the people of Telangana felt that they had been betrayed once again by the UPA government and Congress party. To oppose the move of the government, once again all the sections in the region, irrespective of class, caste and gender, came out on the streets and participated in protests.[41] It was a significant shift for the first time in the history of the Telangana movement. Initially there were no Joint Action Committees, all the parties, associations participated independently but after the move to reconsider the decision by the government, leaders and associations from Telangana region realized that they have to work with unity for the cause of their demand, but not the political parties. It is true that before Central government made the announcement in favour of Telangana, students pressurized their representatives to resign from their elected posts and join the movement, but they did not do so. This response made the people come together and form the Joint Action Committees in Telangana region.[42]

Student Movement, State Violence and the Intervention of Judiciary

KCR's arrest had a major impact on the students in Osmania University. They took active part in the movement. A few students burnt the effigy of the state government and immediately the police entered and lathi-charged the students. The provocation made the students to start a rally with a few students initially started from the Osmania University Arts College but gradually, the number swelled into thousands. The police tried to stop the rally but the students demanded withdrawal of the police camps from the campus. While students were taking out the rally, the police beat them up and assaulted them; even the students who were reading in their rooms. Against the police action, the students protested and to express solidarity, the people of the region launched rallies and dharnas. It was assumed by the local electronic media that KCR had broken his fast unto death as the government had released those video clips. After this news was flashed, the students got outraged. The same students who supported him burnt the effigy of KCR and blamed him for the betrayal of the movement and decided that despite KCR breaking the fast, they would fight on their own till they reached the goal.[43] Participation of students in the ongoing Telangana movement has been substantive. Without their participation, it couldn't have been possible to pressurize the government to initiate the process.[44] The cadre of TRS and the supporters of Telangana movement were arrested and booked under several cases and filed bind-over cases on the leaders of TRS. A lot of pressure from the people's movements had been built on the government.[45] The Home Ministry, Government of India, made the announcement that 'the process of formation of Telangana state will be initiated and request the Chief Minister of Andhra Pradesh to move an appropriation resolution in the State Assembly'. The people of Telangana had celebrated the decision all through the night of 9 December 2009.[46]

When the lathi-charge took place at Osmania University, the court observed that 'to maintain peace in the university, an adequate number of civil police personnel shall be deployed in the university police station' and further the High Court asked students 'not to disrupt classes and exams and warned them that action would be taken against them if they resort to acts of criminal intimidation or violence'. To study the police repression, the SHRC constituted a 10-member committee to look into the matter. The AP government later constituted a Peace Committee with the university professors, police officers and intellectuals to see that the university is peaceful and students maintain discipline.[47] The civil rights activists and intellectuals argue that the police seem to have made a planned and deliberate attack on Osmania University (OU) students to provoke them to indulge in violence and brand them as violent and discredit the movement. Though they have been agitating non-violently, but have been clamped with all kinds of restrictions which they have been able to successfully overcome by tapping their constitutional rights.[48]

It is a sad reflection on democracy in the country. It was widely reported and debated by the student leaders from OU that students faced rubber bullets and tear-gas shells. The ambulances were not allowed inside the campus to carry even the severely injured students and one girl got a bullet injury on her leg and fell down with shock. The enraged students burned down the police tents and drove out the police camp from Arts College in the night. The police targeted media persons, injured six journalists, damaged cameras and disconnected the power supply lines to the campus. The police force had to face stone-pelting students and resorted to tear-gas shelling. A reporter was thrashed by the police. Rapid Action Force and Greyhounds personnel were all present at the scene. Against the police repression, students took out rallies and protested in front of the police station. In support of students, neighbouring colonies of OU supported students and protested against the police repression on the campus but they were also beaten up by the police, who even entered their houses and dragged them out. The JAC asserts that 'they would continue the struggle for separate statehood irrespective of how much blood would flow and how many shocks it might cause'.[49]

In addition to the student agitation, the role of advocates in the ongoing movement is equally impressive. During the second phase of the Telangana movement, they boycotted the courts and joined the protests. They gave a call for '*Parliament Muttadi*' at New Delhi and organized a meeting at Jantar Mantar. Their main demands were equal representation from the region in the posts of Government Pleaders, Assistant Government Pleaders and Standing Counsels. To pressurize the government, three advocates[50] observed fast-unto-death. It is clear that an agitation by any section in Telangana pressurizing the government for statehood and mobilizing and sensitizing the people has a democratic import.[51]

The democratic character of the movement is evident from the resistance and the nature of state's repression. At one stage the police took control of Osmania University campus and when the students approached the High Court, the police were ordered to leave the campus. Justice[52] of the High Court was angry with the DGP and police for not complying with his order on 22 February 2010 to leave the Osmania University campus. The judge directed the Joint Police Commissioner, Hyderabad,[53] 'to appear before the court and explain the police action on OU campus within two days'. The Judge further observed that 'the state police are a lawless lot and accountable to none. It looks that they are acting at the behest of somebody. The CM, as well as the cabinet, appears to be helpless if their statement that they did not witness the incidents on the campus is any indication'. He further observed: 'We do not find such kind of a situation in any other part of the country. It's all the more unfortunate that such things are happening at a time when a renowned former police officer is the governor of the state. His presence should act as a deterrent on the police. But the reverse is happening.' The court ordered 'withdrawal of the forces and removal of the barricades on the OU campus'.[54]

The Judge ordered 'the police forces to withdraw all its Special Forces which have been put up on the Osmania University campus' and ordered the Director General of Police (DGP) and the Police Commissioner, Hyderabad, 'to withdraw forces and vacate the campus'. The High Court was of the view that 'the police in thousands seem to be determined to enter the campus and create tension and insecurity on the campus'. The Judge further reiterated that 'the police force should enter only in case any trouble arises'.[55] The government of Andhra Pradesh challenged the judgment in the Supreme Court[56] and argued that Maoists have infiltrated the movement. The Supreme Court stayed the state High Court's direction for withdrawal of paramilitary forces from OU campus. The Bench stayed the High Court direction till 23 February 2010 and directed the state Home Secretary 'to supervise the paramilitary forces and ensure that they do not misbehave with the students in any manner'. The Apex Court observed that 'we are concerned with the students'. A Supreme Court Bench also constituted a three-member committee comprising the state Home Secretary, Hyderabad Police Commissioner and the V-C of OU to review the law and order situation on the campus on a day-to-day basis and accordingly decide on the deployment of forces.[57] The V-C of OU appealed to the police 'not to enter the campus without informing the university authorities' and advised students 'to maintain peace'.[58] Students' agitation in the movement, the response of the state and intervention of judiciary explains the democratic issues and dilemmas of the state. The movement is almost an experiment and assertion of democratic rights.

It is a new twist to the Telangana movement that the government of Andhra Pradesh rarely gives permission to hold meetings in Hyderabad city. The students of Osmania University held *Vidyarthi Garjana* and KU students too organized the *PoliKeka and Doctors Gharjana* with the permission of the High Court under certain guidelines. OU students got the permission[59] by the High Court one day before. The High Court directed the police to allow JAC to hold the meeting.[60] Contrary to the High Court guidelines, the police stopped vehicles which were carrying students from various districts. JAC leaders alleged that the police violated the court order by arresting students, using repressive measures to foil *'vidyarthigrajna'* (students' roar). Still, the students from the region voluntarily participated. Chukka Ramaiah[61] observed that

'Osmania Vidhyarthi Gargana of OU[62] shows maturity of the students as it started the meeting exactly on time which High Court suggested and stopped the meeting five minutes before the schedule'. He compared 'the Telangana students' agitation with French students' revolution'.[63] Haragopal 'compared the movement with India's independence movement'.[64] These three meetings[65] at Hyderabad demonstrate their strength. These meetings came as a rude shock to the Andhra political leadership, opposing the formation of Telangana state.

Post-December 2009 Agitations and Byelections: Impact on Telangana Movement

The second phase of the agitation is crucial as it gave the compass for the formation of Joint Action Committees (JACs) from the city down to the village level. Despite such intense politicization, it is striking to note that the general trust in political leadership and parties has been very low. JACs were headed by prominent local non-party individuals, like a teacher or a lawyer, and the political party leaders remained in the rear. Several castes, community and other occupational groups joined JACs. Every caste and community has taken part in the *dheekhashibirams*. A new form of solidarity was seen evolving on the Telangana demand, based on community identities and cutting across political differences because of what they felt was the unpardonable demand for a unified Andhra Pradesh and the pessimistic disposition of non-Telangana leaders. Through an interesting discursive mapping, the social and economic crisis in the region and the tragedies of everyday life were brought forth and turned into support to the Telangana issue.[66] Another political turmoil in political JAC was that after constituting the five-member Srikrishna Committee, JAC gave a call to all the representatives from Telangana region to resign. TRS announced that their party MLAs would resign as the terms of reference were against the Telangana people and contrary to Chidambaram's initial statement made on 9 December 2009. In contrast to JAC's decision, the Congress party leaders welcomed it and said they would cooperate with the Committee but not quit their MLA and MP positions. The Congress party had quit the JAC but the leaders from TDP, who were not happy with the terms of references, stayed with JAC and sent their resignations to Kodandaram, Convenor of JAC, but not to the Assembly Speaker as they believed that the Committee will put the issue in cold storage. They argued that they would resign if the Congress representatives resign. After all these developments, the JAC gave a call to the people to pressurize the leaders to resign as MLAs and MPs and if they do not resign, request the people to boycott them socially. In this process, a lot of pressure was built on the leaders, but they did not resign, except TRS and one BJP MLA. With this backdrop, there are several issues that reflect the conflicts and complexities in the political JAC.

After the political turmoil in Andhra Pradesh on the issue of Telangana from November 2009, many political developments took place. All political parties except MIM and Communist parties are a part of the Committee. The Steering Committee of JAC gave a call for resignation of all MLAs and MPs opposing the Union Home Ministry's statement against the formation of a separate state. A majority of MLAs from TDP, TRS and Congress from Telangana region submitted their resignations to the Speaker of the Assembly but the Speaker only accepted resignations submitted by TRS and BJP MLAs. The result was byelections in the Telangana region. TDP candidates lost their deposits and Congress too was defeated, in spite of huge resources and money power that it commanded.

The ruling Congress party and opposition TDP in Andhra Pradesh suffered a massive blow as both the parties drew a blank in the byelections to the seven Assembly constituencies held in 2011. While TRS swept four of the six constituencies in Telangana region, one seat was bagged by a pro-Telangana Independent candidate. It was a clear message that the people of Telangana wanted a separate state. Both the Congress and TDP were rejected by the electorate in the region. The Congress forfeited its deposit in Station Ghanpur, while Telugu Desam lost its deposit in Kamareddy constituency. TRS won the seats of Adilabad, Kamareddy, Station Ghanpur, Mahaboobnagar and Kollapur. Nagar Kurnool seat in Mahaboobnagar district was won by an independent candidate, Nagam Janardhan Reddy, who had resigned from the TDP in protest against the anti-Telangana stand of the party leadership. In Mahaboobnagar constituency, the BJP candidate was declared elected. The victory for the TRS came in Kamareddy (Nizamabad district), where its candidate Gampa Govardhan defeated the Congress party. TDP's deposit was forfeited. In Station Ghanpur (Warangal), T. Rajaiah of TRS won with a majority of more than 32,000 votes, defeating his nearest TDP rival Kadiam Srihari and the Congress candidate lost his deposit. In Kollapur, TRS candidate defeated Congress by a margin of more than 5,000 votes. Except Mahaboobnagar, all the Assembly seats had fallen vacant following the resignation of sitting members. In Telangana, the five sitting members had resigned in support of a separate state, quitting their respective parties and joined the TRS. All of them entered the fray as the TRS candidates looked all set to retain their seats. TRS and BJP won and the supporters of Telangana celebrated the victory of these parties. TRS leaders hailed the results as yet another verdict of the people in support of a separate state.[67] Konda Surekha from Parakala constituency resigned in protest against mentioning of YSR's name in the FIR filed against YS. Jaganmohan Reddy by CBI.

The TRS won the Parakala Assembly seat in the bypolls held on 12 June 2012, defeating the nominees of YSRCP, TDP, BJP and the Congress, and clearly showing that the people of Telangana were in favour of a separate state. Parakala was the only constituency in Telangana region that went to polls in the present byelection. The TRS candidate won with a slender margin of 1,562 votes over his nearest rival, YSRCP candidate Konda Surekha. It was the resignation of Konda Surekha, who joined YSRCP, that necessitated the byelection here. The candidates of both the national parties, the Congress and the BJP, lost their deposits. The BJP contesting the seat was one of the reasons for the split in separatist vote and the reduced majority of the TRS candidate.[68] It is understood that Telangana Political JAC under the leadership of Kodandaram had supported TRS in this byelection, whereas it did not support either TRS or BJP as both the parties were supporting the separate statehood demand in the previous byelection that was held in 2011. It is further argued that Konda Surekha, who resigned her MLA seat and contested again from the same seat, has a strong political base in Parakala constituency and her husband Konda Murali has a factional background. And the person who contested from TRS has no family support, no personal identity as like his opponent in the constituency, no community background and political support, except commitment towards Telangana statehood demand and working for the goal as an activist of TRS. So it was not surprising to see that TRS won by lesser number of votes but winning against Konda Surekha indicated people's support for the Telangana state.

The by-elections in the 12 Assembly constituencies (2011) and one constituency (2012) of Telangana indicate that the separate statehood demand has gone far deeper. Social classes and groups seem to have abandoned their older political affiliations and coalesced around candidates who stand unequivocally for a separate state. The dominant political parties have paid heavily by not taking a clear stand and trying to play the dice. The impressive performance of the TRS in byelections is not much of a surprise for anyone familiar with the dynamics of the ground situation. The miserable performance of the Congress and the

TDP could be seen as symptomatic of the deeper crisis these parties are undergoing in the region. Their response to the electoral outcome has further exposed their confusion on the Telangana issue. This has only given credence to the TRS's claim that its victory is a clear popular mandate for the Telangana state demand. There has not been any significant opposition to this demand either from the political elite or any other civil rights group in the other region of the state. In fact, Dalit and civil rights groups in coastal Andhra extended their support to Telangana, with a view that this would significantly reduce the dominance of the two powerful castes – Reddys and Kammas – and thereby facilitate democratization of the political system in the two regions of the state.[69]

The developments suggest that the Telangana movement got shifted again from the political leadership to people's movements. It is clearly evident that the people are not happy with the political parties and leaders as they are making use of the Telangana movement for the sake of their political career. It is also a new development in the movement that all non-political actors in Telangana came together and formed joint action committees. The second phase of the movement witnessed several forms of struggles: hunger strikes, relay fasts, satyagraha on a mass scale and courting arrest in thousands to exhaust all tactics of mass agitation. Its nature and content underwent substantial changes. All the employees, students, political leaders, ministers, advocates, lecturers, trade unions are vertically divided into two groups on the issue of Telangana. The response of the central and state governments, of course, has been repressive and the Telangana demand for the state continues to be treated as a law and order problem. The attitude of the government towards agitators was that of utter hatred and contempt. It is argued that though the activism of TRS and KCR is a part of democratic process and Dalits, tribals, OBCs and minorities have been promised that after the formation of a separate state, his party would make a Dalit as chief minister and deputy chief minister would be from minorities and ensure fair participation to OBCs. These promises appear to be rhetorical than realistic. Perhaps, these promises are part of political strategies to mobilize the subaltern classes and castes to take part in the movement. One can observe TRS's priority to the territorial state and then the democratic state.

Critical Assessment of Suicides in Telangana Movement

Several studies on democracy movements reveal that till today, no movement in the country, perhaps the world, has witnessed the culture of suicides but the Telangana movement has been witnessing this culture from the last three years. Approximately 800 youths have committed suicides. Though in the first phase of the Telangana movement, around 350 students died in police firing, these cannot be classified as suicides. This culture of suicides in the region engages scholars to assess it critically. From the last one decade, protest movement took a democratic approach without violence. The people participated democratically in rallies, protests and demonstrations and organized meetings in a democratic way as per High Court guidelines and lakhs of people attended the meetings (*OU Garjana, KU Poli Keka, Doctors Garjana*). Leaders have emerged, creative literature has come up, folk culture further strengthened and the consciousness of the people of the region doubled. Notwithstanding these positive aspects, students and youth from the region have been committing suicides. It is understand that majority of them had a professional background. This phenomenon exemplified that it was the failure of the state in dealing with the issue effectively as the state always used force to suppress the movement, instead of solving the problem. Instead of trying to contextualize the problem, probe into the reasons why the people of region were demanding a separate state and solve the problem, the state by constituting committees and using repressive measures was giving scope for the emergence of other problems. This kind of negative approach of the state was one of the important reasons for the suicides committed by the students. The political leadership too is responsible for the suicides. The study argues that a few leaders hailing from Andhra region from the entrepreneur *Kamma* community were indirectly responsible for the suicides in Telangana region because of their economic, political and social interests. Whenever the movement reaches the peak stage, this section mobilizes the people from Andhra against the demand of Telangana state. This negative approach of the state and leadership is responsible for the suicides. This leads to discontent among the people and further tensions among the three regions in the state. This undesirable culture of suicides questions the very basis of democracy, particularly Indian democracy.

Here are a few suicide cases which throw light on the intensity of the movement. The Telangana movement witnessed self-immolations and suicides. As of now, the report of Committee[70] to stop the suicides say that around 800 young students committed suicides for the cause of Telangana statehood during the period of three months. Students like Srikantha Chary, Venugopal, Venugopal Reddy, Swarna and

Yadaiah are cases in point. Even Kistaiah, a police constable, committed suicide at Kamareddy in Nizamabad district by shooting himself with his service revolver after climbing on the top of a cell phone tower in support of a separate Telangana.[71] Laxmaiah (25) set himself ablaze in front of BHEL,[72] demanding that vacancies in the Public Sector Undertaking (PSU) be filled only with locals. He pleaded for formation of a separate Telangana in a suicide note left behind. A student, Siripuram Yadaiah, set himself ablaze while raising pro-Telangana slogans in Hyderabad and died in hospital and wrote a note in favour of statehood.[73] Satish, a student from Osmania University, made an appeal: 'Please try to understand why we are participating in such a struggle. We have no jobs, our parents are in debt, there is no money at home, it is a matter of life and death for us.'[74] Mandadi Yadi Reddy travelled from Bedala Mangalaram village in Rangareddy district of Andhra Pradesh to New Delhi and allegedly committed suicide by hanging himself from a tree outside Krishi Bhavan, in front of Parliament, frustrated at the delay in formation of Telangana.

The students see the movement as a *'do-or-die battle'*. These cases underline the seriousness of the issue and the role of students and youth in the ongoing movement, among others. It is argued that no movement in the country or in the world has witnessed suicides and the Telangana region, which has seen the historical struggles like peasant struggle, left-wing politics, enormous literature, creative writers, intellectuals and active civil society organizations, could not stop suicides by students and youth. It is fact that youth who committed suicides were educated and a few of them were professionals. It is further argued that no movement in the country has been continuing its agitations in one form or the other for the six decades for separate statehood. It is one of the longest movements in post-independent India. Activists like K. Jayasankar Haragopal, Varavararao, Ghanta Chakrapani and Chukka Ramaiah argue that suicides are the result of the negative attitude of the state and the leadership of Andhra Pradesh, particularly Telangana leadership. Instead of solving the problem, the state and leaders have made the issue very complex by postponing a decision. Instead of using the contextual approach, the state has been using a confrontation approach in solving the problem. Hence, frustrated youth have committed, and are still committing, suicides. This approach only gives scope to intensify the movement and use of other democratic forms of agitations, but the state's response is not positive.

Dual Nature of Political Parties and Leaders, Issue of Telangana and Assertion of People

The dual nature of the political parties in Andhra Pradesh on the issue of Telangana has been challenged by the people of Telangana for the last two decades. The Congress, TDP and YSRCP did not take any decision on Telangana. Though TDP promised a separate Telangana state in its election manifesto in 2009 and submitted the report in favour of a separate state to the Pranab Mukherjee Committee, it changed its stand on Telangana after 9 December 2009, when Chidambaram made a categorical statement in favour of Telangana and argued that both the regions were like two eyes for the party. It is fact that the party's opposed to the bifurcation of the state and that its social base is from *Kamma* community from Andhra region, that dominates in all spheres, like socio-economic and political. Hence, TDP does not want to lose the support base from *Kamma* community. TDP tried to escape from the responsibility by blaming the Congress party. The result was that lost in all the byelections which it contested. The senior leaders left the party and joined the TRS and senior leader Nagam Janardhan Reddy formed an organization called *Telangana Nagara*. Whenever there is a visit of Chandrababu Naidu to Telangana, there is a serious resistance from the people to pressurize him to take a decision on the separate statehood demand. The same is the case with the Congress party as it has been ignoring the voices of Telangana for the last six decades by constituting committees, managing the leadership and with its coercive, co-option and consensus methods. The Congress is responsible for 1960s' agitations that left 300 students dead and somehow, the party managed the leadership from Telangana, particularly, Marri Chenna Reddy, and slowed down the movement but it could not stop the agitation permanently. Post 1990s, the Congress once again deceived Telangana people and intellectuals from Telangana argue that the Congress party is responsible for the suicides of students and youth in Telangana.

The dual nature of Congress leaders from the Telangana has seen resistance through the process of elections and through movements by the Telangana society. After the 2009 general elections and KCR's hunger strike, the Congress lost almost all the seats it contested in the byelections in Telangana. The cadre at the grassroots too is facing resistance in villages. The newly-launched YSR Congress party headed by Y.S. Jaganmohan Reddy has the same stand on the demand as TDP. But it is interesting to note that when his father Y.S. Rajasekhara Reddy was the chief minister, he used all the means to stop the bifurcation of Telangana from Seema-Andhra, and tried to provoke the people from Andhra that if Telangana state is formed, they would need a visa to visit Hyderabad. He managed to convince the Congress high command not to give separate statehood. President of YSRCP, being the son of Y.S. Rajasekhar Reddy, is carrying the legacy of his father who tried to divide Telangana leadership, sold land in Hyderabad in the name of SEZs to Seema-Andhra businessmen and tried to stop the Telangana state by dividing Muslims and Hindus in Hyderabad, opposed Telangana statehood in Parliament as an MP representing Seema-Andhra. It is understand that after launching the party, he has been trying to mobilize the people in support of his party in the name of the problems of farmers, but the people of the region – particularly TRS and Joint Action Committees in Telangana – are not allowing him and his party unless his party supports the bifurcation of the state.

The YSR Congress party, which sought to make inroads into the Telangana region by holding a massive demonstration in Sirisilla in Karimnagar district to highlight the problems of weavers, had to face a violent resistance from Telangana. At last, Y.S. Vijayamma visited Sirisilla with full police security to take part in *deeksha* (strike) to support the handcraft community. She witnessed the protests on her way from Hyderabad till Sirisilla. Farmers and agricultural labour protested against her visit and the police lathi charged and fired rubber bullets, and activists were severely injured.[75] Thus, the people of Telangana have taken up cudgels against parties that are opposed to the bifurcation of the state as it is felt that they have to take a stand on whether they support or oppose the demand. It is dangerous for a democratic system not to take any decision. This leads to law and order problems. Hence, the nature of leadership is lumpen, corrupt and not responsive to the problems of the common people. People of one region have been protesting for the last six decades for a separate Telangana but the state has been delaying it and political parties have been trying to make use of this demand for their political interests. The state has been using its legitimized power to suppress the movement. This negative response of the state has resulted in 800 suicides by Telangana youth.

Negative Response of Parliamentary Politics towards Democratic Demand of Telangana

Members of Parliament from the Congress, particularly from Telangana region, have been pressurizing the Congress high command

and UPA-II government to take a decision quickly on the demand of Telangana statehood. Several times during the sessions they have raised slogans in favour of Telangana, stalled the proceedings of Parliament and disturbed speeches of the ministers and members, along with the other members of Telangana, particularly from TRS. However, the response from the government or Congress has been muted; neither is the government responding to the members nor taking any decision on the issue. It is simply delaying the issue. The main opposition party BJP in Parliament supported the demand and gave an assurance that if the UPA government introduces the Bill in favour of Telangana, they would support the Bill. Sushma Swaraj, the Leader of Opposition, spoke in favour of Telangana statehood but the Congress has not been able to take a decision. In Parliament politics, it is the first time that the ruling party suspended its members from Parliament for four days. Whenever MPs try to protest in Parliament, the Congress tries to shut their voices.

Same thing has been reflecting in the Andhra Pradesh Assembly from 2009. MLAs from TRS have been protesting several times with the support of independent MLAs, TDP MLAs and BJP MLAs from Telangana whenever the Assembly is in session. They have stalled, disturbed and boycotted the proceedings of the House. Several times, MLAs from TRS have been suspended from the Assembly by the Speaker of the House and the same thing has been happening in the Council. At times, in protest against the government, the MLAs have voluntarily boycotted the Assembly session too but it is found that the Speaker is in a helpless position to take a decision or suggest to the government to take the decision early. Chief Ministers, be it Rosaiah or N. Kirankumar Reddy, look towards the Congress high command for support as these leaders have not being elected by the people for the position of Chief Minister but by the Congress high command. This culture of parliamentary politics is a sad symptom of Indian democracy. This negative response of the Congress during 1980s and its leadership gave the scope for the launch of TDP by NTR. The Congress party has had to face the same experience once again, for following the same political culture that they followed in the decades of 1970s and 1980s. The failure of UPA to take a decision has led to frustration among the Telangana youths as they have used almost all the democratic methods or forms which are available to them to pressurize the government, but they have not succeeded in convincing the government and political parties. It further led to suicides. Those responsible for the suicides in Telangana are the political parties, particularly Congress and TDP. The negative response of the Union government has pushed the economy of Andhra Pradesh back and raised the question of development. It is witnessing the same politics of 1980s when the Chief Ministers of Andhra Pradesh used to depend on the Congress high command for every small issue. Chief Ministers used to fly to New Delhi and get permission for their decisions. This culture of party politics once again raises the dominance of Centre on the state by taking the advantage of a weak leadership.

Politics/Politrics of Telugu Desam Party and Telangana Statehood Demand

TDP has been playing a dual role on the issue of Telangana and trying to sideline it by maintaining silence and arguing that both the regions are equal like two eyes for the party. The leaders and opinion-makers from Telangana argue that this principle is baseless and that the two eyes should be considered and protected equally. No human being concentrates or is concerned about only one eye and ignores the other. This principle does not apply to the Telangana demand, they point out. They argue that when Home Minister Chidambaram made a statement in favour of Telangana at 11 pm. Instead of welcoming the decision, N. Chandrababu Nadu countered the statement by saying that 'this decision has been taken without consulting the regional parties like TDP and this statement is being made in the night'. His remarks 'indirectly encouraged the leaders from Andhra and Rayalaseema region to oppose the decision of UPA government' to initiate the process of Telangana state. In parliamentary politics, this principle does not stand for a reasonable debate. On one side, the party is arguing that it respects the sentiments and feelings of Telangana people, submits a letter to Pranab Mukherjee Committee in support of the demand and, on the other, it indirectly encourages the leaders of Andhra to raise demands like Seema-Andhra, Rayala-Telanagana and Jai Andhra. The TDP has been trying to sideline the issue by bringing these jumbled and unsolicited demands which are being articulated by the few leaders from Seema-Andhra for their self-interest. It resulted in the TDP not winning polls from 2009 onwards. This negative response of TDP weakened its base in the Telangana region. This kind of dual nature of political parties adds to, instead of solving, problems and weakens the very notion of democratic politics and democratic culture. It gives a fillip to movements, which may become violent. Parties can cheat people for the time being, but they cannot continue doing it for a long time. If the TDP follows the same methodology in dealing with the movement, it will face the same resistance. In July–August, 2012, there was a new demand from the Rayalaseema region under the leadership of Baireddy Rajeshakara Reddy, who is the senior leader of TDP, demanding a separate state for Rayalaseema region. TDP president Chandrababu Naidu, it may be recalled, suspended the leaders from Telangana region when they upheld the demand of Telangana state and demanded that the party leadership take the decision quickly. This dual nature or stand of TDP president has been questioned by the people of Telangana. That's how the Telangana movement has created consciousness among the people and they are able to question and seek answers from the political and administrative setups of Andhra Pradesh.

Politics of BJP and Telangana Movement

The politics of BJP is different from that of other political parties in Andhra Pradesh as it supporting the movement outside and inside Parliament. However, when they were in power at the Centre under the leadership of Atal Bihari Vajpayee with the help of NDA allies, the BJP did not stand by its promise to form a separate Telangana state. The same NDA government created three new states. Now, the BJP is not in power and wants to gain support from Telangana region and hence is actively taking the programme or agitations to put pressure on the UPA government to take a decision on Telangana BJP does not have much support in the region but compared to Andhra region, the party has a reasonable support base in Telangana region. In principle, BJP is for smaller states and it believes smaller sates strengthen the federal structure of the country.

The BJP in its Kakinada Resolution supported the demand for smaller states and stated that they would create Telangana if they form the government at the Centre. NDA had created three new states of Chhattisgarh, Jharkhand and Uttaranchal, but not Telangana as TDP was one of the strongest allies in the NDA and opposed the separate state of Telangana. Though Atal Bihari Vajpayee ruled for five years, BJP ignored its promise to the people of Telangana. In Parliament, Advani as Home Minister said that a solution to the Telangana issue was not a separate state, but development. Hence, BJP too has playing a dual role on the issue of Telangana. When in power it ignored the issue of Telangana and when in the opposition, it is supportive of the demand. This dual nature of BJP has been questioned by the Telangana intellectuals, opinion-makers and students of the region. Another way of looking at BJP politics is that the party has no base in the region except a few urban pockets. In the name of Telangana, the party wants to mobilize, organize and get the support from the people and turn this support into votes and form the government. It is not wrong to have this strategy to form government but the question here is the extent of commitment towards the formation of Telangana state and development of the region as well. Telangana region has witnessed peasants' struggle and Naxalite movement. The ideology of Left plays a major role in mobilizing and organizing the people. Apart from these, activists, students, Dalits, minorities and tribals are with either with Congress, TDP or with other political parties, but certainly not with the BJP. In the light of this, there is not much scope for Right-wing politics in the region which BJP stands for. So, BJP is trying to get a political base in the region in the name of Telangana. Having witnessed the politics of BJP and its approach towards Muslims (Godra massacre in Gujarat), it is a sad indication to Telangana region as the region reflects solidarity and brotherhood among the different religions. If the BJP gets a political base in the region, it will be good for the party but many opinion-makers and activists feel it would not be good for the people of the region. Thus, it is argued that if at all the Telangana state is to be formed, it has to be formed with the help of people's movements or other political parties or organizations solely formed and working for it, but not with the support of communal parties.

TRS Politics: Critical Evaluation

The only political party in Andhra Pradesh apart from the national parties struggling for the formation of a separate state is the TRS, which was formed in 2001 by KCR who came out of TDP, which is opposed to a state. In the initial years after its launch, TRS got support from all sections as it tried to respect all the voices in the region but after the general elections of 2004, TRS started losing its base at the grassroots as it completely believed in lobbying and ignored the agitations and neglected democratic voices in the region. Because of the pressure from individuals, organizations and intellectuals, it changed its strategy and once again followed the same agitational path and tried to gain support from the people. But it had an alliance with TDP in 2009 general elections and lost majority of the seats to Congress. This defeat was a setback for the party and learning from this experience, TRS strived once again to gain people's support. It shifted its strategy from lobbying to agitations and KCR went to the extent where he decided to sit on a hunger strike and built pressure on the Centre and state and succeeded in it. The UPA government formally announced its intention to initiate the process of formation of a separate state. TRS's election manifesto or promises made to the people of the region, particularly Dalits, tribals and minorities, are interesting and appear to be naïve as well. It promised chief ministership to Dalits, Deputy CM post to minorities, important portfolios to OBCs, land to the tribals in the separate Telangana state. However, having witnessed the politics of TRS, it does not get reflected in spirit. There is criticism against TRS of KCR bringing family members to the mainstream electoral politics. Most of the district presidents are from the upper strata and the political nature and approach of KCR itself sometime back was being questioned by the Telangana leadership. Strategy of movement has been questioned, questions raised and his own party leaders have opposed him and joined other parties. The democratic nature and character of the party is missing in its approach and strategy. It is not merely fighting for statehood, but also for the rights of Dalits, tribals and minorities. A political party like TRS has to see that that these rights are given and enjoyed by the subaltern classes in the region. Merely getting geographical Telangana is useful to the political elites and may bring more advantage for the socially privileged classes, but will not mean much for the marginalized communities. Hence, they demand not merely geographical statehood but also democratic statehood in which there shall be distribution of land to the poor, employment opportunities for the weaker sections, gender equality, strict implementation of reservations, social security to the weaker sections and minorities and so on. The role, strategy, programme and approach should benefit the subaltern classes. Otherwise, if the TRS follows the same ideology, approach and political tactics as other political parties, it would not be much different from other political parties. Hence, TRS has to fight for statehood and also for the rights of subaltern classes simultaneously, otherwise people will not support it in future.

Forms of Protests in Telangana Movement and Deepening Democratic Culture

As a part of the movement, the people of Telangana have shown their dissent against the state through several forms of protests. Each form that they have chosen has contributed to the movement, created enormous consciousness among the people and pressurized the state and leaders to take a clear stand on Telangana and take a decision immediately. These are considered as democratic forms and have been different from other movements in the country, though there have been violent acts like pelting buses with stones. These forms united the people from across the social, political, economic and cultural backgrounds. In the light of this, the study evaluates the role of the forms of protests and their contribution in deepening democracy.

Maha Padayatra of Telangana Students

The agitation by students appears to be a part of the democratic process. A majority of Student Joint Action Committees seem to be more committed to a democratic Telangana. They employed several means to pressurize the governments and own leaders from their region at one level and raise popular consciousness at another level. This form of *padayatra* is an attempt to look at the dynamics of public protest. The students from Telangana Universities – divided into two groups: *Doddu Komuranna* group (south Telangana) and *Komuram Bhim* group (north Telangana) – started the march (*padayatra*) from their respective universities and toured the villages and reached Warangal[76] and took part in the *PoliKeka (lion roar)* sabha.[77] The strategy was to mobilize rural people and make them aware of the injustice being done to them by Andhra leaders and create awareness on social issues. One of the participants[78] in *maha padayatra* shared his experience. They started the *padayatra* from Hyderabad on 18 January 2010 and ended it at Warangal on 7 February. They toured 610 kms and emphasized in their speeches on 'what kind of Telangana they desire. Getting just territorial Telangana state is not a solution to all the problems, rather one should fight for a democratic Telangana in which all sections in Telangana shall live with dignity, decent life and equality on all grounds'. They got immense response from the people wherever they entered the villages and towns and during the march, they emphasized 'they want Telangana to live with self-respect, self-rule and develop by themselves'. He recounted that an old woman donated ₹ 500 from her daily-wage earnings, indicating involvement of the people in the movement irrespective of the age. He mentioned that sometimes 'we felt tired and suffered minor ailments but when we saw the response, we forgot those minor ailments and went ahead reassured' and reached Warangal on 7 February 2010.[79]

Tirumali Inukonda argues that the Telangana movement is an expression of the people's democratic yearnings. It is a silent people's revolution for a separate state. The people's protests are taking place in the forms of *dhoom-dhams* (songs and dances), *garjanas* (hullabaloos), and *padayatras* (marches). Sometimes, it involves celebrating *vijayayatras* (victory marches) in anticipation of the Telangana state, and at times taking out *shava yatras* (processions carrying the dead) too. These protest campaigns gathered momentum in the course of the Telangana discourse in the region. They protested in typical Telangana *bonalu*-style (offering to deities), drawing *rangoli,* and *vanta-varpu* (cooking and eating in public places) and, of course, in the tears of (about) 250 mothers whose sons and daughters had died in the last two months. The Telangana service castes expressed their solidarity with the Telangana movement through demonstrative forms of shaving, washing clothes, and in *vanta-varpu,* in public places. Not in the form of the Telangana Rashtra Samithi's agenda, nor by staging theatrics and resorting to political manoeuvres. In different districts, women offered *bonalu* (women's festival of traditional offering to the deity) and playing *batakammas* (a feminine expression of protest specific to Telangana women) as a mark of protest. The doctors treated the patients on roads. The weaker sections constitute 83 per cent of Telangana, the caste associations held relay fasts, drew *rangoli* as protest. Lunch was prepared on the roads in Telangana villages. A procession of bullock-carts was held, *padayatra* was taken out, *dharnas* were conducted in front of police stations. Effigies of local politicians were burnt, *bonalu* processions were taken out as usual and bullock-carts, tractors, bike rallies, *rasta roko* (roadblock) were held in Telangana villages. The women carried *bonalu* and washermen washed clothes on the roads of the several villages. The movement surged at the grassroots. It appeared to be the beginning of a new era of a movement by those who were excluded from the political process. The weaker sections of Telangana, kept outside politics, have now jumped into the movement. It is essentially a new type of 'political movement'. The students, employees, lawyers and various associations, representing the lower stratum, are leading the movement. A massive people's movement is going on in these forms in the villages from the last two years without a semblance of any let-up. These protest forms are rooted in their desire to turn the political system to listen to voices of people as they themselves are leading the campaigns in the villages and towns. The same people's resolute determination scared the politicians to visit their constituencies and forced them to resign from their positions. It is obvious that the students have initiated the present outburst and helped it to spread to the other sections. The urban intelligentsia, like employees, journalists, advocates, teachers and artists, are associating and supporting the mass movement and carrying it down to the towns. In certain districts like Warangal, it has spread to almost all villages. As far as its intensity and mobility is concerned, it is no way lesser than the people's movement in the 1940s.[80] Along with these forms of protests, there are other forms of agitations like Palle-Palle Pattalapaiki.

Palle-Palle Pattalapaiki (Every Village on to the Railway Tracks)

The Telangana Political Joint Action Committee (TPJAC) gave a call for the *Palle Palle Pattalapaiki* (every village on to the railway tracks) as a part of *Sakalajanaula Samme* from 1 March to 2 March. All the Joint Action Committees like TSJAC, TPJAC, Telangana Praja Front, other activists, political leaders, students, youth and common people came on to the railway tracks, played games, prepared food and had their breakfast, meals and dinner on the tracks itself. The protesters completely disconnected the link between North and South India to pressurize the union government to take a decision on Telangana statehood. But the response from the state and Union governments was not positive and they did not respond to this form of agitation to solve the problem, but to bring down the movement, the government arrested many leaders and activists and filed cases against them. This response was seen as undemocratic and activists argued that an informal emergency was on in Telangana region. Despite the police repression, rail roko continued for two days peacefully and democratically without any violence.[81] This form of protest gave the scope to bring thousands of masses from rural and urban localities on to the roads and tracks to take part in the movement. This form completely disconnected South India from North India. It had a major impact on coal mining industries, power generation industries and it adversely impacted railways. The agitators moved on to the roads and tracks near their villages and towns and prepared food there itself. This novel form of protest inspired crores of people from Telangana and elsewhere in the country. This form of protest was considered a historical event in the Telangana movement and gave further encouragement to the people of the region and put additional pressure on the state as well.

Telangana Million March

On 10 March 2011, Hyderabad city witnessed people expressing their anger against the governments and political leaders from Andhra Pradesh. Before the Million March began, the police tried to stop the supporters of Telangana from entering Hyderabad by arresting people and leaders and putting them in jails. However, after turning the entire

Telangana region into an open jail, detaining more than a lakh people and the police virtually laying siege to Hyderabad, the government could not stop the inevitable. Though a million people could not converge, at the end of day, the Million March in support of Telangana state proved to be a big success as the supporters of Telangana walked for several kilometres to gather at the Tank Bund of Hussain Sagar lake in the heart of the city and took a collective pledge to achieve their goal. As the day progressed, hordes of people reached Tank Bund. The agitators pushed back the police, pulled down the iron barricades and removed the barbed wire to make way for those who followed. Groups of doctors rubbed shoulders with drivers and coal miners. Lawyers in black coats took out their own procession. In a reflection of the angry mood of the ordinary people of Telangana, Congress MPs K. Keshav Rao (Rajya Sabha) and Madhu Yashki (Lok Sabha) were attacked when they reached Tank Bund to show their solidarity. The angry crowds pulled down the statues of several historical, religious and literary figures belonging to coastal Andhra, which dot the Tank Bund. The supporters of Telangana pulled down the statues on the pretext that these figures were from Andhra and Rayalaseema regions, there were not many statues on Hussain Sagar of leaders from Telangana region. The police managed to arrest all the top leaders of Telangana movement but could not stop the ordinary people. Though the police and the security forces had sealed the roads in all the Telangana districts, as well as Hyderabad, people from far-off places from Telangana reached the venue of the Million March. Kodandaram said that by gathering in such a large number, despite the police repression, the people of Telangana have delivered their verdict.[82]

The stage was set for a possible showdown between the police and Telangana protagonists in Hyderabad as the Telangana Joint Action Committee (TJAC) vowed to go ahead with the Million March despite ban orders. In an attempt to foil the march and to prevent people from reaching Hyderabad, police in Telangana districts took a large number of activists into preventive custody. As the police denied permission to TJAC for the Million March, barricades were put up in nine districts and on the outskirts of Hyderabad to prevent activists from joining the protest. The TJAC decided to hold the march of a million supporters to demand a Bill in Parliament for the creation of a new state. All the leaders from different political parties from Telangana backed the march, including activists, students and lawyers. The Andhra Pradesh High Court declined to pass any orders to stop the march. On a petition by the organizers, the state human rights commission directed the police not to violate human rights while taking steps to foil the march.[83] The Million March to Hyderabad turned violent as thousands of agitators broke through police barricades to reach the Tank Bund and statues of eminent Telugu personalities erected on the Tank Bund were vandalized and thrown into the Hussain Sagar Lake. Tension started building up in Hyderabad right from the morning with the police virtually sealing off the entire central Hyderabad as the Assembly was in session. Normal life was thrown out of gear with traffic restrictions enforced strictly right from 6 am. But when a group of about 200 agitators managed to reach Tank Bund by the northern end, police contingents remained inactive, paving the way for the breaching of the barricade. Once the barricades were breached, the crowds on the Tank Bund swelled to around 20,000 and the agitators became belligerent. Once news broke that TJAC convener Kodandaram had been arrested. Declaring that they would destroy all statues on the Tank Bund if he was not freed, the crowds went about the job an hour later.[84]

Sridhar Rao Deshpande recalled that normal life of people in Hyderabad was thrown out of gear as police sealed all routes leading towards Tank Bund, where the TJAC planned to hold the Million March despite ban orders. There was a curfew-like situation around the Tank Bund. Police had set up check-posts on all the roads connecting Hyderabad to other districts to stop people from reaching Hyderabad and trains were cancelled to prevent people from heading towards the city. Buses were being checked at every check-post and only those travelling to Hyderabad for purposes other than participating in the Million March were being allowed to proceed. Policemen and the Central paramilitary forces were deployed across Hyderabad. Majority of the forces were deployed around the Assembly and Tank Bund. Osmania University was tense as police sealed the gates while student leaders said they would reach Tank Bund at any cost. Police had already denied permission to TJAC to hold the march and had imposed prohibitory orders banning assembly of four or more people. The march was supposed to be peaceful and was only aimed at drawing the attention of the central government to their demand for a Bill in Parliament to carve out a separate Telangana state. State-owned Road Transport Corporation suspended some services in the city and outskirts and diverted others. MMTS (local) trains were also suspended on majority of routes as a precautionary measure. Police arrested hundreds of people in entire Telangana comprising 10 districts, including Hyderabad, to foil the march. Notwithstanding the denial of permission and ban orders, activists, leaders and students managed to reach Tank Bund in thousands within an hour.[85] This agitation witnessed both repression of the state and the anger and assertion of the people. The message was clear: the state cannot stop the people and their anger forcefully. Despite arrests, people reached the spot and took a pledge in favour of Telangana statehood. This form of protest intensified the movement. The other form of protest movement that was witnessed was Vanta-Varpu (Cook and Eat) programme.

Vanta-Varpu (Cook and Eat) Programme

As part intensifying its agitation for formation of separate state, the TPJAC organized *'Patnam Roadpi Poyyi'* programme in Hyderabad. Hundreds of peoples, including leaders of various constituents of JAC, participated in the unique form of protest in various places of the city amid tight police security. They argued they had taken up the programme to convey their strong desire for a separate state to the union government. The protesters set up kitchens on the main roads. Telangana activists, including women, were seen cutting vegetables, preparing ingredients and cooking food. The protesters also participated in cultural activities. Politicians, freedom fighters, businessmen, government employees, teachers, civil rights activists, daily labour, doctors, lawyers, engineers, IT professions and students came along with their families together on to the roads of Hyderabad for Vanta Vaarpu (cook and eat) agitation to demand a separate state.[86] This form gave a boost to the movement as it further mobilized the youth from Hyderabad city, particularly those working as software engineers, other organized and unorganized employees and workers and employees in the working service sector. Another important angle in this protest was that the people settled in Hyderabad city from Seema-Andhra participated in this agitation. This way, through this form, the organizers of the JAC tried to give an assurance to people settled in Hyderabad from Andhra region. Yet another important and historical form of agitation was the Sakalajanula Samme.

Sakalajanula Samme

The state government employees of the Telangana region went on a general strike – *Sakala Janula Samme* – from 13 September 2011 till 24 October 2011 to press for a separate Telangana state. Most of the political parties of the Telangana region were in solidarity with the general strike. This strike was the brainchild of the Telangana Political Joint Action Committee. On 31 August, the JAC convener[87] announced the timeline of the general strike. In solidarity with this call given by JAC, the TRS called for a *Rail Roko* on 13 September 2011. TPJAC called on for a film theatre bandh and National Highway *rasta* roko. An indefinite general strike began across Telangana. The 36-hour Rail Roko called by the TJAC saw agitators squatting on the rail tracks at several locations. The JAC leaders protested on the rail tracks at several railway stations. MLAs and MPs from Telangana region also took part in the agitations across the region. A few trains were cancelled and a few trains diverted as a precautionary measure. Heavy police force was deployed at several railway stations across the Telangana region. Agitators took the pledge that the agitation would be intensified further.

TNGOs, contract and outsourced employees stopped going to work and stalled the governmental administrative work in the state secretariat. The state government threatened to take action against contract and outsourced workers who were taking part in the indefinite general strike in Telangana. Chief Minister Kiran Kumar Reddy's warned of strict action against agitating employees and notices were issued to outsourcing agencies not to redeploy the workers who were participating in the strike and abstaining from work. For regular government employees who abstained from duties, there would be no pay for the same period. Provisions under GO 177 were enforced. Telangana Congress leaders warned the government not to curb the *Sakalajanula Samme* by invoking ESMA provisions. Workers in the Singareni Collieries actively took part in the Sakalajanula Sammae. They alleged that the workers who were on strike in support of a separate Telangana state were being forced to work by the personnel of CISF deployed at the mines. An all-party delegation met the Chief Minister and submitted a memorandum to withdraw the security forces deployed at the Singareni Collieries. Public transportation took a major hit during the Telangana *Sakalajanula Samme*.

The APSRTC employees joined the general strike. The Telangana Employees Joint Action committee (TEJAC) boycotted duties and joined the strike except in cases of emergency services like power supply and maintenance. Auto drivers too joined the agitation and called for a two-day auto bandh. The TJAC leaders and various political parties in Hyderabad staged *rasta rokos* in the city. A delegation comprising of

TJAC convener M. Kodandaram, TRS president KCR and others met Prime Minister Manmohan Singh and urged him to initiate the process of formation of a separate Telangana state. The Telangana Congress leaders met the Prime Minister to apprise him of the current situation in Telangana. The bandh call given by the TJAC across Telangana evoked a good response as the agitation was peaceful across the region. At last TEJA agreed to call off the strike after a series of negotiations with the government. The *Sakalajanula Samme* (42-day strike) was one of the longest agitations by the government employees in the state. Democratic forms of protests have been taken up like *rallies, rasta rokos*, and demonstrations near houses of Ministers and MLAs in protest against power cuts to farmers in Telangana region, travelling without paying toll gate fee, celebrating *Bathukamma Utsavams* as Telangana festival, *nimajjanam of Bathukamma* in spirit of Telangana festival, burning of Congress effigy and *rail roko*. Other forms of protests included *Rasta Roko* at important junctions all over the region, Bandh by all educational institutions in the region, students and lecturers of various degree and PG colleges taking part in the protests. Employees at various Collectorates in the region locked their offices and staged protests. Lawyers staged a protest in front of the courts.

The Telangana Congress leaders warned the state government of serious consequences if it continue to crush the *Sakalajanula Samme* (General Strike) with an iron hand. Members of Parliament questioned the government on how it can plan to stifle the voices of the Telangana state government employees and their right to agitate for separate statehood. The leaders visited *Godavarikhani* and other mining areas to show their support and express solidarity with the workers taking part in the general strike. The CPI leaders urged the Central government to take immediate steps to solve the Telangana issue before the situation got out of hand. The TJAC leaders and various political parties in Hyderabad staged *rasta rokos* at prime locations in the city. Leaders from Telangana argued that the state government was trying to curb the Telangana movement by pressurizing the employees in Telangana region to resume their duties. Transportation was severely hit. The *Rail Roko* called by the TJAC saw people squatting on rail tracks and present in large numbers at railway stations as part of the *Rail Roko* agitations and several leaders were arrested and booked. The Telangana activists blocked the Hyderabad-Vijayawada highway, which led to disruption of traffic for several hours. The theatres were closed, as were schools across Telangana region, the Singareni Collieries miners also went on strike despite threats by the management, the Secretariat

Telangana Employees Association was also part of the protest. The *Sakalajanula Samme* came to an end after the TEJAC agreed to call off the strike after a series of negotiations with the government.

The decision to call off the strike came after the government broadly conceded nine demands of the TEJAC. Government agreed not to enforce ESMA provisions on the employees who took part in the agitation; agreed to scrap criminal cases filed against the employees who participated in the strike; agreed to pay salaries to the employees for the strike period. It agreed to file an appeal in the AP High Court seeking exemption of employees from GO 177; a panel would be constituted to look into the implementation of GO 610 for contract and outsourcing staff. The representatives of the government said that the issue of separate Telangana was not under their purview and it was for the Centre to take a decision on the same.[88] G. Haragopal said that, irrespective of caste, religion, rich, poor, political, apolitical and ideology, the people of Telangana participated in the *Sakalajanula Samme* and held that it is just not possible to continue the movement for a long time given the nature of the state. Notwithstanding the difficulties, people worked and participated in the movement unitedly. He felt that agitations like *sakalajanaula samme* created enormous confidence, moral power and awareness among the people of Telangana and intensified the movement once again.[89] People from different professions, castes, communities, government and private employees, farmers and, agricultural labourers took part in the *Sakalajanula Samme*. Every section not merely responded to the movement, but also participated actively and voluntarily as per their strength and ability. The unity witnessed among different sections, particularly among the Singareni workers, was exemplary and compelled the Union government to take a decision on Telangana demand. Hence it is the landmark agitation in the Telangana movement.[90]

Telangana Million March (Sagaraharam)

Sagaraharam is the other name of Telangana march[91] and it has witnessed the participation of thousands of activists, several organizations, students, employees, artists and various sections of the region who joined irrespective of the ideology, caste, class and religion at Necklace Road in Hyderabad and demanded the UPA government to form the Telangana state. Hence, the tension prevailed across the region when agitators were furious to cross police check-posts to reach Hyderabad, but the police barred them and used the repressive methods to disperse them and they arrested the Members of Parliament

(MPs)[92] of the ruling Congress party from Telangana region who staged a sit-in in front of the Chief Minister's office to protest against large-scale arrests of people coming to Hyderabad. All the MPs who have been arrested are from the Congress party and they were not even given an appointment to meet the Chief Minister and inform about the repressive nature of the police.[93] To persuade the government, there were hectic negotiations between the ministers from Telangana region and later between the ministers and the JAC leaders. Though initially the Chief Minister had refused to permit the March citing the law and order problem, he agreed later as the JAC leaders promised the government that they would conduct the meeting in a peaceful manner.[94] Hence, the government gave the conditional permission for Telangana march. M. Kodandaram has announced that the march would convey the message of Telangana state formation desire not only to the government but also to the whole world and expressed that the agitation would build massive democratic platform.[95]

Notwithstanding repression of the police, a large number of people reached Hyderabad to participate in the march. The activists who were being stopped by the cops organized '*dhoom dhaam* cultural programme' at the spot where they have stopped and demanded that they may be allowed to proceed to Hyderabad. Kodandaram has said that the march was necessitated owing to the failure of the ministers from the region and negative response from the state. It was the time for the leaders of Telangana to decide either they would be with people of the region or with the *Seemandhra* leaders.[96] He wondered that how the government could grant permission for the march on one side and directs the police to prevent the people from far-flung areas from joining the *Sagaraharam* on other side. Passunoori Ravinder[97] has argued that the conspiracy of the state government got exposed as lakhs of people voluntarily came from the villages and joined the *Sagaraharam*. There is no political party that can claim to be the champion of Telangana cause, but it is the strength and commitment of people.[98] The TJAC seems to have outwitted all political parties and emerged as the sole organization in championing the cause of Telangana state by successfully organizing *Sagaraharam*. TJAC has reached a position where it could dictate the terms to all political parties. The success of Telangana march indicates that the leaders and the political parties have lost the faith and trust of the people and are pretending that they are seriously working for the smaller state but in reality their actions show that either they are against the bifurcation the state or opposed to the Telangana state or directly/indirectly supporting *Seema Andhra*. Hence, the people gave enormous support to TJAC which is an apolitical body headed by an academician with no political motives. In fact, their dual nature has been questioned for the last decade, at least.

Samara Deeksha and Praja Poru Yatra

The thirty-six hour *Samara Deeksha* was organized[99] by the Telangana Political Joint Action Committee at Indira Park in Hyderabad despite the government denied the permission initially. Notwithstanding the denial of permission, several leaders and students tried to attend the *Deeksha* venue and were arrested and the police used the repressive methods to disperse the crowd when they tried to reach Indira Park. After these developments, a lot of pressure had been built up on the government and at last, it granted the permission to hold *Samara Deeksha* in Hyderabad. A large number of civil society activists attended *Samara Deeksha* at the Indira Park and demanded the Congress-led UPA government to resolve the Telangana issue as per the deadline announced by the Union Home Ministry and condemned the dual nature and the negative approach of the Congress leaders.[100] Kodandaram[101] termed the denial of permission to protest at Indira Park as undemocratic and in contradiction to spirit of the Constitution. It is found that whenever there is protest call, students from Osmania University (OU) would be in forefront of the movement and seeing the experience of the movement for the last one decade, students were never allowed either to organize the meeting or to participate in the agitations led by TJAC. Same thing has happened during *Samara Deeksha*.

The situation became tense at the OU campus after students shelled stones on the police when the latter denied the permission to take out a rally to Indira Park. The activists expressed concern over the union government for not keeping their promise and made a demand to decide about granting separate statehood soon or to face the consequences.[102] Apart from the *Samara Deeksha*, under the leadership of Narayana, the CPI organized a-day *Praja Poru Yatra* at Palavancha in *Kammam* district to mount pressure on the Centre to announce a road map for formation of the Telangana state. The CPI state secretary[103] launched two-day *Praja Poru Yatra* at Palvancha in Khammam district and demanded that the ruling Congress party should announce its stand on the statehood issue. He accused the UPA government of trying to evade the issue of bifurcation of state in the name of consensus and blamed that once again the Centre wants to cheat the people of region. He asked the Centre not to test the patience of Telangana people.

Chalo Assembly

TJAC has been giving agitation calls continuously to the people of the region starting from the Telangana march, *Vanta Varpu, Rail Roko, Pattalapaiki Palleloo,* Telangana bandh and other mass protests. This time, to build pressure on both the state and the union governments, it gave the '*Chalo Assembly*' call, as this period happened to be the second last assembly session for these governments and assuming that they could be able to build the pressure on the Congress or UPA government to take the decision on their long pending demand. Hyderabad was tensed with a strong police force blocking off all entry points to the State Legislative Assembly and other places in the city to reach the '*Chalo Assembly*' rally. Pro-Telangana agitators tried to organize the rally against the delay in granting statehood to the region and it resulted in large-scale arrests and the city turned into a war zone and sporadic incidents of violence took place in the city and across the region. The government tightened the security arrangements in such a way that protestors could not reach anywhere close to the assembly as it was made an impenetrable fortress, with gun-toting policemen positioned all around and every link road taken over by police. It is argued that generally CRPF, BSF and other military forces are supposed to save the country from the external threats and fight with neighbouring states, who intend to create the problems in the country but interestingly, the state is deploying the armed forces to handle their own citizens, i.e., agitators, and supress the movement and create some sort of fright and insecurity among the activists, students and people who are fighting for a separate state for Telangana region. The government even cancelled MMTS services to all routes, diverted buses and closed the roads and flyover bridges in Hyderabad to stop agitators. The leaders of JAC, TRS and BJP tried their best to gather at Indira Park to march towards the Assembly. The policemen arrested them and taken into custody and tension prevailed at the site as protestors stoned the policemen deployed in large numbers to prevent gathering. The police have made unprecedented security arrangements across the city and imposed prohibitory orders to ensure smooth functioning of the assembly session. The police had to lob teargas shells to stop the mob from disrupting the services and educational institutions remained closed.

The students from OU have clashed with police by pelting stones for not allowing them to attend *Chalo Assembly* programme and it prompted the police to fire teargas shells. It is interesting to note that the entire region was filled with the police, army, CRPF, BSF and military men so that no single person can come close to the assembly but nobody expected that MLAs from TRS would climb on top of the assembly building. It is argued that this incident indicates the strength of the movement and dedication of its activists. Despite high security, MLAs could to reach the top of assembly to reflect the people's aspirations to the entire nation apart from the state and its machineries. Two legislators belonging to the TRS managed to climb atop the assembly building to plant a black flag. Police forces, however, brought them down.[104] The leaders of TJAC argued that the government had used all repressive measures to prevent the activists who were coming to Hyderabad to reflect the aspirations of Telangana people in a peaceful manner. Apart from these, on par with agitations outside the assembly, TRS and other political parties who are supporting separate Telangana state have not allowed the assembly to function continuously and despite attempts made by the speaker of the assembly to break the impasse, the TRS did not attend the assembly. However, they accused that the government did not allow any adjournment motion of other issues which meant that the Telangana issue was not given priority.[105]

Sansad Yatra and Satyagraha Deeksha in New Delhi

The demand for separate Telangana was again the talk of the town in the national capital with its supporters sitting on hunger strike at two prime spots. While the Congress MPs from Telangana region launched 48 hours' hunger strike[106] at the main gate of Parliament House against the non-fulfilment of the promise by the UPA government to create a separate state and gave the slogans like "Give Telangana and Save Democracy", the TJAC leaders staged a similar protest at Jantar Mantar, New Delhi. TJAC has launched several agitations at the state level to pressurize the state and union government. This time TJAC which has taken the programme called the *Sansad Yatra*[107] at New Delhi to pressurize the union government to take the decision early and influence other political parties and national leaders to support the Telangana state demand. During this time the parliament was in session. The Telangana issue echoed in the national capital, with the two-day *Sansad Yatra* of TJAC commenced at Jantar Mantar inaugurated by Sumit Chakravarty and 48 hours *deeksha* by the MPs from Telangana rocked New Delhi.[108] The activists from TJAC argued that the Telangana issue should be settled during the parliament session and that the Congress party has failed to fulfil its promise on Telangana and argued that due to the negative attitude of the Congress, about thousand people, particularly youth, have had sacrificed their lives for the cause of the separate statehood. The MPs[109] from Telangana said that the Centre should stand by its promise as it was the last chance for the Congress party to take a decision on Telangana.[110] Thousands of activists, political leaders and students went to New Delhi to convince the UPA coalition government and the leaders of national parties to extend their solidarity.[111] BJP leaders[112] have visited the protest camp and extended their party's support and promised that their party would also support the Telangana bill, if it is introduced in the parliament. Etala Rajender[113] has said that if the Congress fails to concede the statehood demand, it has to face the consequences. The general secretary of Congress party had not only extended support to TJAC's *deeksha*, but also announced that his party would join TJAC and work for the cause of Telangana state. He further added that the main objective of the *Sansad Yatra* was to exert more pressure on the Congress-led UPA government to concede to the demand for Telangana state.[114] The *Sansad Yatra* brought social activists and political leaders together. The academicians and intellectuals visited the venue and supported the cause. Thus, based on these findings, it can be argued that the *Sansad Yatra* not merely mobilized the political parties at the national level and made the regional political parties like TDP to concede to the demand and cautioned them not to confuse the people with their double stand but also it gave scope to mobilize the people and create consciousness among them. The MPs urged that the government should fulfil its promise of Telangana state formation. Sushma Swaraj met agitating MPs and showed her solidarity and demanded the UPA government to table the bill in the parliament on Telangana and promised that her party would support it if it comes. MPs from various political parties also expressed their solidarity with the cause.

It is understood that Congress MPs from Telangana have been vocal in raising the statehood demand, sometimes causing discomfiture to the party as it is in power in the state.[115] As many times, the Congress MPs gave the slogans in favour of Telangana and stalled the parliament sessions along with other opposition MPs from the region. It is to be noted that in the history of parliament, the government has never suspended its own MPs from the parliament. But it has happened in the case of Telangana when the speaker of the Lok Sabha suspended the Congress MPs. This one instance is enough to understand and justify the Telangana movement. It is pertinent to mention that MPs who are protesting, not on their own but by respecting the aspirations of the people of the region from where they were elected. It is an embarrassment for the Congress party and its leaders as its own MPs fighting against their own party and the government and getting the support from other opposition political parties. Sushma Swaraj further argues that since the Congress is not fulfilling its promises they are forced to protest. Congress MPs from Telangana region have been vocal in raising the separate statehood demand, sometimes causing discomfiture to the party as it is ruling not only at the Centre but also in the state.[116]

Telangana Sadhana Sabha

After pursuing the demand with the Congress leadership from almost one decade, the party leaders from the region also voiced their demand for the separate state and organized a massive Telangana *Sadhana Sabha*[117] which was attended by almost all ministers, MPs, MLAs, MLCs and other leaders from the Telangana region and expressed the confidence that the separate state would be formed by the UPA government and the Congress party soon. They had tried to send a message to the people of the region that a separate state could be realized only by the Congress party and not by any other political party. D Srinivas[118] argues that in the larger interest of the people, the Prime Minister would take a decision in favour of formation of a separate Telangana state. The meeting passed a resolution that there is no alternative other than the formation of a separate state. It reiterated immense faith in the leadership of the Congress party and demanded formation of the separate state without any further delay.[119] Digvijay Singh, the party's general secretary, said that the decision to create a separate state of Telangana is not an easy task as the Congress leaders have had widest consultations at all levels of elected representatives and political parties on the issue. A final decision is to be taken and he had requested the CM, the Deputy CM and the PCC president to prepare a roadmap keeping both options open as to what should be the strategy and what should be the course of action followed by the decision.[120] He further said that the Centre is in favour of bifurcation of the state and acknowledged the authenticity of the demand. The road map is about 'what should be the strategy and course of action if the state is divided or left united'. He further argues that the decision on Telangana would be taken in the best interests of the state as well as the nation.[121] It is understood that Congress started pretending that the party is serious and want to take the decision as early as possible. Apart from these reasons, sitting MPs[122] and former MP from Telangana have resigned from the Congress party and joined TRS. It is expected that a few more congress leaders would follow suit.

After these political developments in Andhra Pradesh, the Congress High Command called the Chief Minister, Deputy Chief Minister and PCC president of Andhra Pradesh as special invitees to the CWC meeting[123] and they presented their road maps separately one by one. After the CWC meeting, Digvijay Singh said that the process of consultations with the stakeholders is over and decision would be taken soon after the Core Committee meeting of the Congress party. The details of the meeting are confidential and nobody revealed the information which they discussed and what the road maps that the three special invitees from Andhra Pradesh presented but the local and national media – both print and electronic – limelighting according their wish and will or trying to manufacture mass opinion from Andhra region against the Telangana demand or bifurcation of Telangana, particularly the media in Andhra Pradesh, except one or two media channels, all are dominated by the Andhra businessmen and political leaders. It is found that they are really constructing the *Seema-Andhra* demand but actually it is not there among the masses from Andhra region. Again, the second Core Committee meeting of Congress party was held[124] within two weeks and discussed in detail and clarified their doubts with the CM, Deputy CM and PCC president of Andhra Pradesh. After the meeting Digvijay Singh[125] said that 'the consultation process is over and await the decision of the party as well as the (Congress-led) UPA government.' The final call would be taken by the Congress Working Committee (CWC). On other side, MLAs from YSR party once again started resigning to their MLA positions in opposition to the bifurcation of the state and MLAs and ministers from Andhra region even threatening to resign from their respective positions – both party and government. They have issued an ultimatum to party president that they would quit their ministerial posts in case the party opts to divide Andhra Pradesh. This kind of negative approach of a few leaders from upper castes and business community from Andhra region of the state creates the problems for the people of the state, by confusing them, threatening their party and trying to stop the formation of Telangana state.

The Congress party had to speed up the Telangana issue because of the continuous fight, sacrifice of lives of the region and commitment of the opinion makers and of course political force – TRS. All these forces have been relentlessly mobilizing and educating the people on the demand of Telangana for last one decade. All the protests/resistance forms that they have chosen are Gandhian forms of protests. The Telangana movement used this democratic resistance to attain their long pending demand of a separate Telangana state from Andhra Pradesh.

Though the people have been protesting democratically without any violence through several forms of protests, the leadership from Andhra Pradesh, especially Telangana region, maintains dual nature on the demand and has been trying to sideline the issue or working on party lines. This nature of political leadership created new problems and indirectly drove many youth to commit suicides.

II

Separate Telangana State Movement: The Question of Democratic Rights

It is understood that the debate on the politics of parties is confined to the territorial statehood for Telangana though there are some voices raising the question of democratic rights of Dalits, tribals, minorities and other subaltern classes in the separate state. In the last section, the study focused on territorial statehood, nature of the state, political leadership and forms of participations. It argued that the first priority could be merely a territorial state and the question of democratic rights, social inequalities, tribal rights and political power for marginalized could follow. Nevertheless, political parties like TRS came up with a manifesto that after formation of the state, the party would give an opportunity to a Dalit to become the Chief Minister, land to the tribals and so on but these promises do not seem realistic but are only for mobilizing these sections. That said, territorial Telangana state is not enough as it would cater to cater the interests of the political elites of the region only.

This study evaluates the relevance of Dr B.R. Ambedkar. His argument for the desirability of smaller states was prophetic and he welcomed the recommendations of the States Reorganization

Commission in 1955 for the creation of Hyderabad state consisting of Telangana region as a separate state. Further, he envisaged the division of Uttar Pradesh into three states (Western, Central and Eastern); Bihar into two (North and South or present Jharkhand); Madhya Pradesh into two (Northern and Southern); and Maharashtra into three (Western, Central and Eastern). He was for linguistic homogeneity of a state in the sense of 'one state-one language' and not 'one language-one state'. This is an absurd formula and has no precedent for it. It must be abandoned. A people speaking one language may be part of many states as done in other parts of the world as smaller states facilitate efficient administration, cater to the needs of different areas, provide assurance to the sentiments of different areas, and the domination of the majority on the minority can be stopped in smaller states. Ambedkar argued that larger the state, the minority living within it is lesser understood and 'larger the state, smaller proportion of minorities are bound to be submissive to their fellow majorities in terms of economic, political and social power'. Hence, in larger states, minority is going to be dominated by the majority. He contended that no single state should be large enough to exercise undue influence in the federation. The smaller states were in the best interests of a healthy federalism and socially disadvantaged sections were likely to be subjected to greater discrimination in bigger states because of the consolidation of socially privileged or dominant groups. Further, he maintained that 'a smaller stone of consolidated majority placed on the chest of the minority may become borne. But the weight of a huge mountain, it cannot bear. It will crush the minorities. Therefore, creation of smaller states enhances minorities to enjoy their rights'.[126]

Renowned writer Arundhati Roy supports the demand for statehood for Telangana region in principle while raising the question: what would be the contours of the state after formation of Telangana? She maintains that one would expect a developmental model in favour of poor people in a smaller state. All the governments are following the developmental model based on LPG, SEZs and cutting of employment opportunities, withdrawing from their responsibilities and opening doors for free market and corporate industrialists. She adds that states in which the Congress party is ruling have opened up free market and job security has been removed. If the same policies continue in Telangana state, what will be the use of having a separate state? She argues that there should be a developmental agenda for a better society that is missing in this model. What kind of leadership is promoted is also important to see that the state follow an egalitarian model of development. She holds that people do not need merely a geographical, but a democratic state, in which all Dalits, tribals and Adivasis would live with dignity. The fundamental rights and democratic voices must be protected. She wants that one should reflect about the culture, history and level of consciousness of the people of the region, identities and geographical conditions as they are all preconditions of development. For Arundhati Roy, a Telangana that meets all these conditions is desirable. She opines that political parties and organizations must fight for *jal* (water), *jungal* (forest) and *jameen* (land). She maintains that in the name of democracy, media is manufacturing people's consent and has been dominated by a few corporate agents and elite class. This mode of media is being reflected in Andhra Pradesh politics. The media is not able to reflect people's aspirations and problems. Roy fears that these unjust developments are dangerous to the very notion of democracy and cautions that Telangana people should be careful and keep a close watch on their own leaders and developmental process.[127] She, however, cautions that the separate state should not fall into the same trap as the other newly-formed states, which she alleges have been vying to suppress people's movements. Societies do have a right to self-determination and the demand for Telangana is a valid democratic demand. She hopes that Telangana should not end up like Chhattisgarh, Jharkhand and Uttarakhand, which are oppressing people's movements. She called upon writers to ensure that the dream does not turn into a nightmare. 'I hope that the people of Telangana have such a long and remarkable history of resistance, whose women deserve standing applause for how much they have suffered and for the victories they have won'.[128]

Balachander Mungekar[129] holds that the demand for a separate Telangana is legitimate and justifiable. When justice has been denied in the combined state, the people are bound to articulate their demand for a separate identity on the basis of region, caste, ethnicity or language. That's what happened in the case of Telangana. He said if the present model of development was pursued further, there would be greater demands for smaller states. Drawing a comparison between Vidharbha and Telangana, Mungekar maintains that development in the regions has been uneven and unequal both in Maharashtra and Andhra Pradesh. The one-language, one-state theory is neither justifiable nor practicable; he cites the example of more than two Hindi-speaking people. He argues that though Hyderabad has 10 universities, no one should consider that the Telangana people benefited from these universities. Out of 15 lakh jobs in the state, Telangana got only three lakh jobs. As per the population, the Telangana people deserved 40 per cent jobs. The

Telangana dialect was not found in the textbooks as it was considered inferior. Hence, he argues that such kind of cultural sub-ordination and feeling of discrimination leads to the demand for separate states. He pleads that the movement should be non-violent, suggesting that the ruling class would force violence and impair instruments of agitation. He cautions the rulers of the Telangana state that 'once Telangana state is realized, it should not pursue the same exploitation to its own people from vulnerable communities and classes in the separate state'.[130] Devender Goud[131] argues that every movement should run with people's active participation, without which it cannot succeed. He feels that the participation of students, youth, employees and common people is required in the movement to protect the democratic spirit and believes that these sections work with enormous commitment and without any political motives. He adds that 'the movement has to simultaneously take social issues, create awareness on rights among the weaker sections'. This method could be useful for both the movement and development of these sections. He thinks that 'this kind of participation leads to strengthen the spirit of democracy'.[132] He feels that 'the demand should not be confined to mere separate statehood but go beyond the statehood issue. Every problem should be considered as a Telangana problem: Dalits, students, farmers, workers, poor people, and craftsmen, unemployment, untouchability, landlordism and corruption'.[133]

Perceptions from the grassroots have been reflected on different democratic concerns that protect the democratic rights in Telangana region. The people of Telangana in terms of education have not developed. He further reiterates that all the sections in the region should enjoy social, economic and political equality enshrined in the Indian Constitution. If it does not happen, there is a scope for people's movements against the dominant sections.[134] Ongur Srinivas[135] believes that if a separate Telangana is formed, there is a possibility of demanding more funds from the Union government. The political parties could demand equitable irrigation facilities and equitable distribution of water to the region as that would legally enable them to represent their demand to the Water Tribunal or Award Committees. It is not possible to represent their problems as there is no such statutory provision in the Constitution for intra-regional demand for a share in water. He says if Telangana state is formed, only a few elite castes would dominate the political economy of Telangana as the lands and resources are in their hands but there is bound to be strong resistance from the people as there is high political consciousness.[136] When the consciousness of people gets intensified, involvement of the people increases. The relationship between political parties and civil society organizations in a democracy is inter-related and interdependent. Political parties are craving for political power whereas people's organizations are working without any political ambition. It is held that the Telangana movement is a result of failure of political parties in dealing with the demands and they have made use of it for their political ambition. Media plays a major role in articulating the demand. He feels that since the media is in the hands of Andhra business class, it is neither supportive to the Telangana demand nor addressing people's expectations. It resulted in launch of the electronic (T News) and print media (Namaste Telangana) to focus on the news of the movement in the region. After formation of the state, it depends on whom the people elect as their representatives and on what basis they elect. The level of assertion in this region is much higher compared with the other regions.[137] Apart from these assertions from the respondents from grassroots, there is also the important cultural aspect, which is considered as a powerful tool in mobilizing the people.

Telangana Movement: The Role of Cultural Aspects

Every movement can be built based on history, economy, social issues, literature and culture. For every identity movement, there is a common culture and symbols. They unite the people and make them work till they reach the goal. The Telangana movement has all these positive symptoms. The parties, organizations or individuals who are a part of the movement can think on all these grounds and come up with a substantive agenda to build the movement through which they could pressurize the state.[138] Numerous cultural fronts have been formed by artists and writers to protect and promote the language and culture of the region. These fronts argue that the culture of Andhra and Telangana are different and distinct and they are on their way to reconstruct their cultural and literary histories. Several groups from Telangana argue that in the name of *Telugu language* and *Telugu Talli*, the culture of Telangana has been undermined. Hence, they mapped the concept of *Telangana Talli* on to the political stage. This concept has been used as a slogan of the movement. This helps in broadly assessing the democratic dimensions of the ongoing movement. Thus, installing idols of *Talli Telangana,*[139] celebrating *Batakamma (goddess)* festival, Telangana *Sambaralu*, and *Moharam* festival, all constitute a part of restoration of self-respect. The cultural awareness in the region during 1960s was not much compared to the ongoing movement. The 1960s movement did not have much of an ideological resonance and lacked political strategy. The movement was violent unlike the second phase in which many artists participated with greater clarity and in a more democratic way.[140] There are many groups like the intellectuals, academicians and human rights activists have been raising their voices in support of separate statehood. Andhra Pradesh Civil Liberties Committee (APCLC), Human Rights Forum (HRF), Viplava Rachaitala Sangam (Revolutionary Writers Association) and Lother revolutionary groups in support of the cause and argue that statehood for Telangana is a democratic solution to the problems of the region.[141] *Telangana History Forum* holds that the history of Telangana has been undermined and recount their cultural and political landmarks.[142] All these groups formed their own Joint Action Committees to participate in the ongoing movement.

Artists and writers endowed with creative abilities emerged and the cultural movement became a part of the movement. The Telangana region has seen artists like *Gaddar, Goreti Venkanna* and *Andesree*. The movement produced writer-cum-singer *Andesree*, who is illiterate and hails from a bonded labour family but has written songs and got an honorary doctorate from Kakatiya University. One of his songs[143] became a march – song for the movement.[144] These trends indicate that the artists, singers and writers coming from different socio-economic backgrounds of Dalits and other subaltern classes advance the democratic ethos that, in turn, may lead to an egalitarian society. Singers, writers and people's organizations believe that movements do not merely try to solve the problems, but also throw up creative individuals and groups who keep working for strengthening of democracy. Though artists in the movement are not educationally qualified and hail from rural and weaker sections, but the way they communicate the demand to the grassroots is effective and their knowledge on all political developments is rich and very creative. It is widely believed that[145] artists take up issues and air them, pen the songs in local language and communicate them in a simple language which local people speak and try to pass on the message to the people effectively.[146] All the political parties are trying to use the traditional symbols[147] to evoke the Telangana sentiment, and narrate the history of Telangana, its culture, and socio-economic conditions of vulnerable sections.[148] In the light of this aspect, it is indispensable to focus on the phenomenon of Gaddar.

Phenomenon of Gaddar in the Movement

Gaddar is a revolutionary singer and writer who was part of the Naxalite movement and now is active in the Telangana movement. He has been continuing the culture of folk culture as a part of the movement, which is considered as a powerful tool to attract the masses. He has written innumerable songs on Dalits, tribals, working classes and women, apart from Telangana songs which focus on the plight of the Telangana people. Starting from 1990s, before the formation of TRS, he has been taking part in the movement, mobilizing and organizing the people and pressurizing the state with the support of songs, public demonstrations and dances. The culture of *Dhoom-Daam, Dappu* and revolutionary songs is the brainchild of Gaddar. Thousands of people who are writing, singing songs and taking part in the movement actively have been inspired by Gaddar. Most of these singers are from rural, weaker sections, with little education. This culture has been playing a major role in the Telangana movement. Though there are other singers and writers, they themselves claim that they are followers of Gaddar and his phenomenon. Gaddar believes in a democratic Telangana and not merely a territorial Telangana. He argues for the distribution of land to the poor, employment to jobless youth, irrigation facilities to farmers, and construction of houses for the marginalized and weaker sections in the region. Apart from these, measures have to be taken to annihilate the caste system, feudalism and the dominance of a few elite sections on the rest, particularly the marginal. He has started organizations like *Telangana Aikya Vedika* and Telangana Cultural Front to mobilize the masses. Gaddar also had a marathon walk from Hyderabad to Khammam. During the *padayatra*, he argued for *jal, jamin and jungle* to the poor people. He was critical about KCR's strategy, approach and his political interests. He argues that the dream of separate statehood is possible with the help of movements, but not with the help of lobbying, petitions and requests. Hence, he believes that people should pressurize all the political parties and governments to take a clear stand on Telangana. His presence in the movement encouraged masses, artists, writers, singers and other democratic voices to take part, which shaped the movement as a democratic one. But the drawback of Gaddar's strategy is his radical background and working with the conventional political parties like BJP does not match his stature, given his ideological and political background. The other negative aspect is that the state always looks at his activities and programme with suspicion. His presence in the movement though has strengthened the democratic culture and encouraged people from among the masses to take part in the movement actively.

Separate Telangana Movement: The Question of Democratic Rights

The Telangana movement can be seen from the Ambedkarite perspective. Ambedkar argued that formation of separate states would diffuse the monopoly of the dominant castes and pave the way for the minorities to take over the state power that was long denied to them.[149] By participating in a separate Telangana movement, Dalits are aspiring to get justice in a separate state and they believe that it would lead to an inclusive democracy. There is a demand coming from backward classes: what kind of Telangana – geographical or democratic? If Telangana becomes a separate state, which sections would enjoy political power? A few scholars have called for distribution of land and financial support to Dalits to cultivate their lands and irrigation projects to the region to be ensured. Unless feudal social dominance is fought, there is no possibility of development of Dalits. It is held that Dalits should be mobilized and united to lead a Dalit movement on par with the Telangana movement. It would give rise to new leadership from Dalit community and strengthen them politically. It could enable them to bargain for political power after formation of a separate state. Hence, Dalits started asserting their rights and demanding their share in political power. Another section of Dalit scholars argues that they do not want Telangana to be a separate state, but want to live with self-respect and their rights should be protected. A third section of Dalit group is supporting and actively participating in the movement and argues that if a separate state is formed, dominant castes may get weakened in terms of political and economic power, as they do not have support from their fellow communities from the others regions. It maintains that caste and cultural composition, caste oppression, atrocities on Dalits and domination of upper strata is similar in all the three regions. The elite sections in all the regions are strong in terms of landholdings, economy, polity and social domination. The Telangana statehood movement has witnessed wide-ranging democratic agitations and created men and women of courage and conviction. The Telangana people's movement is rooted in a historical context and a faulty development model. This entire direction of imbalanced development has sharpened the contradictions and created new tensions.

The ongoing Telangana movement is a search for some resolutions to the contradictions.

The Telangana movement initially saw activists and the leaders from the elite class taking part. As there was not much representation of activists from among Dalits, tribals and Adivasis, they were not politically enthused. But after 1980s, leaders, activists and artists from Telangana started participating in the movement as they got initiated to the movement by the writers and the people's movements.[150] Dalits are politically conscious and are aware of developments which are evident by the fewer occurrences of atrocities in the region, unlike the Andhra region. There were not many atrocities in Telangana as the influence of revolutionary movements in the region is strong.[151] He added that if Telangana state is formed, the rich class in the region would get lesser support while Dalits will get additional support from the other regions in political and economic terms to struggle against the dominant sections. Apart from this, the population of weaker sections in the region is high, they are conscious about political and cultural issues, that leads to strengthen them further.[152]

Artists undertook a 400-km '*padayatra*'[153] from *Manuguru* in *Khammam* district for the cause of a separate Telangana under the banner of *Aikya Cultural Front*.[154] The people of Telangana do not want a geographical Telangana merely, but they want a democratic Telangana state. In a separate Telangana, 'surplus land has to be distributed to the landless, the system of landlordism should be eliminated and feudalistic nature of the rulers should be fought'. It is argued that the factories, natural resources, investments and industries have to be taken over from the ruling and feudal classes. All the sections should fight together for a separate Telangana state, which is possible only through people's movements. It is only then that a majority of people will get a leverage, including political power. There shall be a movement against social evils like untouchability, caste oppression and humiliation on par with Telangana movement. Irrigation projects have to be constructed. Further, he reiterates that 'governments shall consider social justice as high priority to Dalit and women. Muslim minorities shall be given reservations based on their population. The small-scale industries have to be started, right to work should be guaranteed, and avenues for self-employment have to be provided to the educated youth'.[155] The political parties, beyond promising political positions to the Dalits, should think about the basic problems faced by the Dalits and tribals. It is necessary to focus on the sources of these problems and try to identify them and have a strategy to solve the problems with commitment. Priority should be given to free education, health care, social security and employment. Unless one concentrates on these issues, he believes, it is useless in getting a separate state.[156] The demand should not be confined to mere statehood but a fight against the lumpen political class and exploitation.[157] These political developments indicate that there are contradictions and complexities in the movement. There are disparities arising between the elite class and Dalits. These developments have to be understood in the right perspective.[158]

The Telangana movement intensified the scope for the assertion of tribals in the region and led to an idea of a separate state, i.e., *Manya Rastram*. It is believed that a separate tribal state is the solution for the problems of tribals and that in such a state, they will have similar culture, history and geography[159] and reiterates that self-rule is a solution to their problems. Although they have lived in the forests for centuries, that life has eroded as the policies of governments led to degradation of forests and selling of the lands to the industrialists. Instead of giving the land rights to the tribals, in the name of SEZs and construction of dams, the governments are taking the land from the poor and bartering it to the elite classes.[160] This kind of articulation of the rights of tribals, however, suggests the vibrant nature of the movement. Political parties like TRS promised the development of tribals in the separate Telangana state and the party would give high priority to develop the tribals and take initiative to set up statues of tribal leaders like *Komaram Bhim*, 12 per cent reservations will be given to them. All *tandas*[161] would be recognized as panchayats, distribution of 3 acres of land with irrigation facilities and loan will be given for a year without interest. Birth and death anniversaries of tribal leaders will be observed. The TRS party has a political agenda to solve the problem of Naxalism after formation of a separate Telangana state. It is argued that the movement is not an ethnic struggle to target the people of coastal districts. It is a democratic movement striving for the interests of people of the backward region, who are being exploited and ignored. Hence, it will not good to violate the rights of any region or section in the state. If it targets the settlers in Telangana state, the movement will lose the human angle. TRS engineered slogans like 'development is the civic right of people and separate state is their birthright' and 'development is no substitute for self-respect and self-administration'.[162] Hence, one has to see the Telangana movement from the rights point of view as they are demanding civil, political, economic and cultural rights that are enshrined in the Indian Constitution.

At this juncture, it is significant to have a look at the political scenario of Muslims in the region of Telangana. After formation of Andhra Pradesh, the dominance of Andhra elite class got accentuated in the city of Hyderabad and the development model adversely affected all the professions of Muslims. Over a period of time, small business, industries, employment and land got affected. As a result, a large section of Muslims in Hyderabad lost their livelihood and were rendered helpless. After the 2001 attacks on the World Trade Center, Muslims of Hyderabad came under surveillance and their activities were looked at suspiciously by the governments. They are politically marginalized, culturally eroded and economically deprived. The political leadership from Seema-Andhra is not aware of the hurdles of Muslims as they had never faced such problems. Hence, they believe, the development of Muslims is possible only in a separate state. It is the responsibility of political parties and other organizations to support them in terms of economic, political, social and cultural aspects.[163] It is further argued that the united Andhra State not only abandoned Urdu language but usurped several thousands of acres of Wakf land – 829 acres were sold for ₹ 444.4 crores by the state government. Liberation of the state following the police action in 1948 and thereafter formation of Andhra state in 1956, have both cumulatively resulted in targeting Muslims and their interests by vested interests in a systematic manner. In the integrated state, many Muslims lost job opportunities in industries like Azam-Jahi cotton mills and Allwin Company and most of the Muslims in the region depend on small business. They feel that they got displaced by the Andhra businessmen. Post-police action and thereafter formation of Andhra state resulted in ousting of 38,000 Muslim employees of the state government in one stroke.[164] Muslim employment in the state government dwindled to 3 per cent as per Sachar Committee report of November 2006.[165] Other Muslim groups[166] have also come up to spearhead the movement. The issue of Muslim participation in the Telangana movement has always been crucial as they constitute nearly 20 per cent of the population in the region and were mostly concentrated in Hyderabad and other urban centres in Telangana. They argue that Telangana state should be formed on the basis of justice, equality, fraternity and liberty. If Telangana state is formed, their language could be revitalized, their culture should be revived and the politico-economic rights must be given priority.[167] Ultimately, the positive approach of the state towards minorities leads to an egalitarian society. In fact, this progressive development will lead to solidarity and fraternity among all religious communities in the region.

After assessing the movement critically, it is maintained that the movement has two dimensions: territorial Telangana state and democratic Telangana. Political parties and leaders are arguing merely for a territorial state and the question of rights in Telangana would be approached after the state is formed. The other sections in the movement are people's organizations, social activists, Dalit activists and Marxist parties, including revolutionary parties, demanding a democratic Telangana state. They argue that merely getting a territorial state is not useful for the economically poor and socially marginalized and politically undermined sections. The exploitation, feudalism, caste system, violation of rights and same developmental model will continue in the separate state. So, territorial statehood is not useful for these sections and they are arguing for a democratic Telangana. It is understand that there are serious differences, including on the strategy of the movement that the political parties particularly TRS are following, though they are working for the same cause: a separate state. Both the political parties like TRS and people's organization are strengthening the democratic culture and creating consciousness among the people and this creative and critical culture strengthens and deepens democracy. The democratic rights and values seem to be good, but are very difficult to implement because of preconceived notions of the political and administrative leadership. Hence, it is argued that people have lost trust in the political and administrative leadership but still believe there are or will be administrators working for the subaltern classes. The presence of such administrative leaders, their concerns and commitments are required to help and support the subaltern classes in a separate Telangana state. Here is the case of an administrator who passed away recently whose administrative culture and approach reflects the developmental agenda of the poor, Dalits and tribals in the country.

The Relevance of S.R. Sankaran's Model of Administration in the Separate Telangana State

Witnessing the lumpen and corrupt political and administrative leadership in Andhra Pradesh, particularly Telangana leadership, it is indispensable to take into account the bureaucratic model of S.R. Sankaran. The late distinguished member of the civil service was an institution. He demonstrated an abiding concern for the upliftment of the vulnerable segments of society. The Constitution was his goal and the law was his tool to enhance the space for the poor. His administration altered the image of the adversarial relationship between the people and the bureaucracy. Throughout his service, he shaped and humanized power so as to build a sensitive institution. He moved from the elitist on the horseback status administrative culture inherited from the ICS, which distanced the officers from the masses, and created a new ethos which responded to the poorest of the poor. His administration was vigilant to put the marginalized on to the developmental agenda. Through his pro-poor intervention and pioneering work in designing and delivering anti-poverty programmes, he brought about striking changes in the lives of the poor. Sankaran's model in civil service had an indigenous social context and culture, and needs to be studied in greater depth. S.R. Sankaran suggested measures for enhancing the quality of Dalit rights, that included land restructuring, better wages, an equitable share in emerging opportunities and well-targeted socio-economic programmes, backed by effective implementation of special laws in their favour, not just 'safety nets' or measures with a 'human face'. Taking the spirit of S.R. Sankaran, many parties started preparing an action plan encompassing various aspects like compulsory education, common education school system, and provisions of irrigation sources to Dalit families for cultivation of lands and involving Dalits in decision-making. Even in the absence of legal-rationale, the moral gets penetrated. The penetration of this moral is seen in the formation of the Committee of Concerned Citizens (CCC) – a body that was formed after his superannuation. The CCC is a body through which he was striving continuously to democratize not only the state, but also the civil society and the people's movements. Today, in Andhra Pradesh, CCC is one of the prominent democratic voices. The ongoing negotiations demonstrates the legitimacy that he enjoys – from the state, civil society and the people's movement. Thus, the relevance of S.R. Sankaran's model is a prerequisite in a separate Telangana state as earlier values in the administration are shrinking, political morality has been dwindling and civil society organizations are gradually moving close to state, which is not really concentrating to develop marginalized communities. After the formation of Telangana state, administrators, policy-makers and societal organizations need to take note of S.R. Sankaran's humanistic model and his rigorous practice of morality has to be carried forward and practised in their activities in helping the poor and needy. Otherwise, getting a separate

Telangana state will mean little to the lower-middle class, particularly, Dalits, tribals and other subaltern classes in Telangana. Not merely committed administrators are required, but there is also a need to protect the rights of settlers from Andhra region who stay in Hyderabad. The apprehensions need to be elaborated.

Apprehensions of the People of Andhra Region if Telangana State is Formed: What are the Safeguards?

The apprehensions of the people from Andhra region on the issues like water, capital city and the land raised by the political leaders and business elites from Andhra region in Hyderabad and outskirts of Hyderabad city are simply because of their personal economic and political interests. Their worries if a separate state is formed are understandable but these fears are not concerned with the common, poor, middle and lower middle class. Their problems and apprehensions are different. The worries of the common people of Seema-Andhra are about employment guarantee, settlement, and sentiments on the capital city. Issues of life security, housing and health facilities are also raised by them. One has to take these issues seriously and understand their apprehensions and try to give the feeling of 'we' ness, the security. Particularly, the people who are fighting for the smaller state have to create conditions which give more chances to the people from Andhra region, particularly students, common people and youth, to get education and employment in Hyderabad city. As a citizen of the country, one can live wherever he/she wants. This right applies equally to all regions and citizens. Thus, it is the responsibility of people of Telangana to give an assurance of security. A positive approach always leads to fraternity and brotherhood and further leads to an egalitarian society. Both the regions can live happily as different states with common concerns.

Conclusion

Andhra Pradesh's political economy is an example. The Government of India constituted the Justice Srikrishna Committee to study the demand of Telangana, but the intellectuals felt that the Committee did not consider ground realities and grassroots feelings and experiences. It is widely felt that the government constituted this Committee to delay the issue and sideline the problems. It further gave scope for people's agitations. Instead of solving the problem, the state aggravates the problem. The constitutional provisions or formal arrangement do not get enforced effectively. Thus, the role of movements seems to be more to protect rights as there is a gap between the formal and substantive components of democracy. The second phase of the Telangana movement has been in vogue for more than a decade. After a decade of struggle, the movement picked up. It led to assertion by students, advocates, teachers, employees, communities, trade unions, women, labour, retired Army personnel and NGOs. These groups formed Joint Action Committees (JACs) and participated in the movement. The state employed repressive methods. This response indicated that the state had not yet matured enough in politically handling the movement. The state considers the movement as a law and order problem. Such an approach creates more problems and widens the gap between the state and the people. The study also indicates that the people of the region do not have faith in their leaders as the latter stopped respecting their feelings and sentiments. Hence, the people from all sections without any political background came forward to participate in the movement. This response has come in the form of mass agitations in the entire Telangana region, irrespective of their socio-economic background.

The leaders from Seema-Andhra region threatened to resign their MLA and MP position, if the demand for Telangana state was conceded. The Telangana political leadership was not quick to respond, nor was it united on the demand. This failure of the formal political leadership of the Telangana region made the Central government go back on its announcement. This led to a series of assertions and heightening of the political movement in the Telangana region. There was a spurt in emergence of JACs literally from every walk of life. All these developments suggest the seriousness of the demand and indicate that electoral politics did not respond to the problem the way they should have forcing the people to go in for agitations. Many civil society organizations emerged and used several forms of protests to pressurize the state. Political parties too formed a JAC under the leadership of apolitical man, though he has a different ideological stand. The apolitical groups became crucial in electoral politics. Political parties and institutions have not been effectively functioning and political leadership is not concerned about the problems and democratic demands of the people. In reality, procedural democracy has not been able to address the democratic demands and people opted for agitations to fulfil their democratic urges. The state responded to the movement through coercive and cooption modes. It is found that the state has been delaying the issue. This approach made the people of the region

impatient and assertive, that led to the demand for separate state rather than an integrated state. Political parties and leaders have not been representing the people's aspirations but using the demand of a separate state for their political ends. The people lost confidence in political parties and leaders. These organizations have not been merely working for the demand of a separate state, but raising several questions like rights of Dalits, tribal, minorities, and women. Political parties and leaders failed in addressing these democratic demands but people's organizations are trying to address these issues. Political parties have maintained dual standards in making use of the movement for their political gains. This dual nature of political leadership and state made the youth and the students of Telangana commit suicides as they were frustrated with the state's response and believed that there was no hope of seeing a separate state. Hence, this irresponsive state and the leadership is a sad symptom of democracy. This is a serious question as the younger generation contributes its services to see that India's democracy is a success. Hence, it is argued that democracy is facing serious problems like religious intolerance, regional imbalances, social disharmony, gender inequalities and so on and these need to be critically looked into.

The political leadership has been lumpenized as many people who have been entering politics in the state of Andhra Pradesh for the last two decades have been from the real estate business, liquor mafia and elite classes. They emerged from the leakages of huge resources that the state invested in irrigation, roads, public enterprises, mining and other infrastructural development projects. This pattern of public expenditure through contractors gave rise to a neo-rich class and a wide range of middlemen as they were the direct beneficiaries of the leakages of public funds. These sections are not concerned about the poor and needy and are solely working for promoting their own political interests. Thus, a set of opportunistic, money-hunting power elite have been let loose by a faulty developmental model. They have become an important component of the political processes of the state. The same leadership is considered as representative of the people as well as movements in Andhra Pradesh. Thus, failure of the leadership made the general masses and opinion-makers take the responsibility to fill this gap in the polity and movements.

It is clear from all the byelections that people from all castes, religions, rural and urban regions are taking part in the Telangana movement and that people do not believe in the leadership of the Congress and TDP as they have not taken any clear political stand on Telangana. In the by-elections, candidates of both political parties lost their deposits. Prior to KCR's hunger strike, the leadership was confined to a few sections. Though certain sections took recourse to agitational politics, there has been a rise of non-formal political processes when many new students' organizations and joint action committees have come up. They included caste-based and profession-based organizations that participated in relay strikes all over Telangana region. The students from schools to universities have been supporting, justifying, participating and forming human chains across the region in support of the movement. They argue that fruits of the movement should reach the most disadvantaged sections. It is widely felt that territorial statehood is not adequate to meet the democratic aspirations as it would only benefit political parties, elite sections and leaders. Political dominance of a few elite sections has always been there. This led to the demand for a democratic state. Hence, the study advocates a parallel Dalit or tribal movement on par with the Telangana movement. The demand for statehood passed through several ups and downs but the aspirations by people have gained momentum and the cause has struck deeper roots. The demand that found articulation, to start with by the students, was picked up by the political elite and they carried it forward, but not far enough. The ball moved back to the people's organizations and activist groups who energised not only people, but also political parties. One significant trend that is seen in this statehood demand is the very limited capacity of the political elite and their estranged creativity. The Indian democracy and its future do not seem best when entirely left to the political parties. The people's direct involvement and their active support seem to be a necessary condition for the political parties to function and democracy to survive.

At the grassroots level, there are widespread democratic concerns. They feel that just a separate state is not enough for the weaker sections unless it responds to the feelings of the weaker sections. What emerges from the study is that though Indian democracy formally is constitutional, there are provisions to end poverty, disparities, and inequalities. In a real sense, these have not been on serious agenda of the elite classes. This gap between promise and performance is obvious. It is such movements which are likely to make the constitutional arrangement relevant not only in terms of their vision, but in realizing that vision. The Telangana movement is in the process of filling the gap between electoral politics and people's aspirations.

Critical Assessment of Telangana Movement

Though the Telangana movement is democratic and political parties, political leaders, organizations and individuals are working together, unity among all these stakeholders has often been found missing. Many political leaders, have been found lacking in being committed to the cause and several have been trying to make use the movement for their political interests. There are leaders who are genuine and committed to the cause but their number is very less, so their voices have been ignored in the movement. Another aspect is that the Telangana movement does not have any ideological base to unite different groups in the region towards the movement. A drawback is that there is no substantive participation of Dalits and tribals in the movement and their participation is confined to agitations and in the process of politics of Telangana, their role is minimal. Also, the strategy of the movement is not that unique as the movement appears to be sessional. Whenever there are elections, the movement gains momentum and whenever the political parties give a call for an agitation, there is a response from the people and other people's organizations. This is one of the important reasons, they are not able to get success because the state is making use of the weakness and differences among the parties and groups to dilute the movement and cause delay. It is further argued that the Telangana movement is not trying to adopt the strategies of the other movements in the country or elsewhere in the world. The political parties and organizations need to have a plan of action and policies for the weaker sections, tribals and Dalits in a separate Telangana state as getting geographical Telangana would help the cause of only political elites of the region. Hence, there should be future plans for development of the subaltern sections.

Notes

1. They ruled the state which comprises Telangana, Bidar and Mysore.
2. M.D. Tajuddin, 'Role of State and NGOs in Issues of Food Security: A Case Study of DDS', Medak district, Unpublished dissertation, Centre for Regional Studies, University of Hyderabad, Hyderabad, 2004, pp. 5–6.
3. K. Srinivas, *Caste, Class and Social Articulation in Andhra Pradesh: Mapping Different Regional Trajectories*, Overseas Development Institute, London, 2002, pp. 1–6.
4. *Human Development Report 2007*, Andhra Pradesh, Centre for Economic and Social Studies (CESS), Vidhya Graphics, Hyderabad, 2008, pp. 19–21.
5. G. Haragopal, 'Telangana People's Movement: The Unfolding Political Culture', *Economic and Political Weekly*, Vol. XLV, No. 42, 16 October 2010, p. 56.
6. Educated people, teachers, writers, singers, poets, academicians and intellectuals.
7. Interview with Prof. K. Jayasankar, former Vice-Chancellor, Kakatiya University, Warangal, Andhra Pradesh, interviewed on 20 November 2009 at Hyderabad.
8. Ibid.
9. On irrigation, which explains how Telangana was undermined in the developmental activities like constructing irrigation projects. He especially focused on Nagarjuna Project construction. How the rulers were trying to dilute the left canal water to Krishna district. In the light of this paper, G.S.

Melkote, Member of Parliament, raised the same question in the Lok Sabha and even issue was highlighted in the Parliament news.

10. Ibid.
11. G. Kodandaram, Convenor of JAC (Telangana Political Joint Action Committee).
12. Ibid.
13. (One) respecting the recommendations of first SRC, which kept the option of forming the state of Telangana open; (two) in the event of conceding the demand of Telangana state, the possibility of similar demands being raised like that of Vidarbha; and (three) the possible need to set up the second SRC to sort out certain problems.
14. On 11 March 2004 at Karim Nagar; 'in case the Congress party returned to power both at the Centre and the state, the hopes and aspirations of the people of Telangana will be fulfilled'.
15. Ibid.
16. Ibid.
17. Ibid.
18. Ibid.
19. G. Krishna Reddy, Professor and Director of Centre for the Study of Exclusive and Inclusive Policy, University of Hyderabad, delivered a lecture on 'Separate Telangana Statehood Movement: Past, Present and Future', organized by the Bahujan Students Front, University of Hyderabad, Hyderabad on 24 September 2009.
20. Potturi Venkateshwar Rao, senior journalist.
21. G. Ram Reddy, *Regionalism in India: A Study of Telangana*, Concept Publishing Company, New Delhi, 1979, p. 15.
22. Potturi Venkateshwar Rao, Hyderabad, 2 March.
23. Ibid.
24. Ibid.
25. Ibid.
26. Bhoomaiah, Palamuru University, Mahaboob Nagar.
27. Mahatma Gandhi University, Sathavahana University, Palamuru University and Telangana University.
28. Bhoomaiah, Bandamedi Pally, Mahaboob Nagar, interviewed on 23 September 2009.
29. Ibid.
30. State Committee, CPI (ML) New Democratic, Pratyeka Telangana: CPI (ML) New Democratic Vaikari, Navya Printers, Hyderabad, 2009, pp. 57–66.

31. Sonia Gandhi promised in the public meeting.
32. *Eenadu Daily News*, 'Separate Telangana will be a Safe Haven for Naxals', 6 February 2009.
33. *Express News Service*, 'YSR Shocks Telangana', 17 April 2009.
34. *Eenadu Daily News*, 'Rajukunna Agni', 2 December 2009, p. 1.
35. Interview with Deshapathi Srinivas, writer and singer, on 15 February 2009 at Hyderabad.
36. *Andhra Jyothi*.
37. Anant Maringanti, 'Telangana: Righting Historical Wrongs or Getting the Future Right?', *Economic and Political Weekly*, Vol. 45, No. 4, 23 January 2010, p. 33.
38. *Eenadu Daily News*, 'Telanganaku Jai', 10 December 2009.
39. G. Haragopal, HMTV live telecast at Warangal.
40. N. Venugopal, writer and editor.
41. *Telanganapai Vestrutastai Charchalu: Andariki Bagaswamyam*, Eeedu, 24 December 2009, p. 1.
42. *Andhra Jyothi Daily News*, 'Seemnadra Pratinidula Rajinama', 11 December 2009, p. 2.
43. *Eenadu Daily News*, 'Osmanialoo Teevra Udriktha, Veedyarthulapai Virigina Lathi', 30 November 2009, p. 1.
44. *Eenadu Daily News*, 'Jailulone Deksha', 30 December 2009, p. 1.
45. *Andhra Jyothi*, Medak district News, TRS Leader Iapaina Baindovarcasulu, 27 November 2009, p. 2.
46. *http://www.indianexpress.com/news/centre-says-a-guarded-yes-to-telangana/552114/*
47. *Eenadu News*.
48. Speech by Varavara Rao at Vidyarthi Gharjana, Osmania University, on 3 January 2010.
49. Interview with N. Kumaraswamy, OU-JAC leader, on 28 February 2010 at Hyderabad.
50. S. Satyam Reddy, Jyothi Kiran and Vijay Kumar Goud.
51. 'Govt Bows to T-Advocates', *The Times of India*, source: *http://timesofindia.indiatimes.com/city/hyderabad/Govt-bows-to-T-advocates/articleshow/6582910.cms#ixzz12mP75ZPl*
52. L. Narasimha Reddy.
53. P.S.R. Anjaneyulu.
54. *Eenadu*, 'Chattamante Gouravam Ledu', Aayana DGPya, 17 February 2010.
55. Ibid.

56. Argued on 24 February 2010.
57. *http://beta.thehindu.com/news/states/article113984.ece*
58. *Eenadu Daily News*, 'Vidyartile Kavvincharu', Sabitha Indira Reddy, 18 February 2010.
59. 2 January 2010.
60. *Eenadu Daily News*, 'Shartulato Gharjanaku OK: High Court', 3 January 2009, p. 1.
61. Educationist and Member of Legislative Council, Andhra Pradesh.
62. Held on 3 January 2010.
63. Edi Vumukti Gharjana, Nootana Shakti Masa Patrika, January 2010, p. 26.
64. Civil rights activist, live discussion on HMTV at Warangal on 2 January 2010.
65. HMTV Dasha-disha programme, 25 January 2010.
66. K. Srinivasulu and D. Satyanarayana, 'Byelections and Telangana Agitation', *Economic and Political Weekly*, Vol. XIV, No. 33, August 2010, p. 12.
67. Mohammed Siddique, 'Pro-Telangana Candidates Sweep Andhra Pradesh By-polls', source: *http://www.rediff.com/news/report/pro-telangana-candidates-leading-in-andhra-by-polls/20120321.htm*
68. 'TRS Wins Parakala Seat, BJP and Congress Lose Deposits', Friday, 15 June 2012, source: *http://www.siasat.com/english/news/trs-wins-parakala- seatbjp-congress-losses-deposit*
69. K. Srinivasulu and D. Satyanarayana, op. cit., p. 13.
70. Ganta Chakrapani, Chairman of Committee, Professor from Dr B.R. Ambedkar Open University, Hyderabad.
71. He was associated with the Machareddy police station. He climbed a mobile phone tower in Kamareddy and raised slogans in support of Telangana policemen. Civilians who gathered there tried to persuade him to come down but he shot himself with his service revolver. He wrote in the suicide note, 'I am dying for the cause of separate Telangana. Drive out people of Andhra from Telangana and fight for separate statehood'. He also made an appeal to the OU students not to stop their fight for separate statehood and said: 'Telangana is more important than your studies. You get jobs only in a separate state. Fight for it.'
72. On 26 February.
73. A note found in his bag stated that the government was not responding to the demand for Telangana. 'People like me will get jobs if Telangana state is formed. I am giving my life for Telangana and please don't stop this movement till Telangana is achieved.'
74. Student from Osmania University, interviewed on 25 February 2010 at Hyderabad.

75. R. Srinivasa Rao, 'Telangana Town Tense as YSRCP and TRS Workers Clash', source: *http://indiatoday.intoday.in/story/telangana-town-tense-as-ysr-congress-trs-workers-clash/1/209867.html*
76. Headquarter of Warangal district where Kakatiya University is located.
77. 7 February 2010.
78. Temaji Deongre, research scholar from University of Hyderabad, interviewed on 25 February 2010 at Hyderabad.
79. The students who have taken part in *padayatra* are from different universities that include Osmania University, Kakatiya University, Mahatma Gandhi University, Satavahana University and University of Hyderabad. The students of Palamuru University launched a bus yatra and toured Mahaboob Nagar district. Both the yatras became a landmark in Telangana movement. Most of the students who have taken part in padayatra are from SC, ST, minority and backward classes.
80. Inukonda Thirumali, 'Lessons from the Telangana Movement', *Mainstream*, Vol. XLVII, No. 14, 27 March 2010, pp. 19–21.
81. Kranthi, *Palla Palle Pattalapaiki, Nadustunna Telangana*, No. 1, March 2011, p. 17.
82. *http://telanganastudents.blogspot.in/2011/03/telanganas-million-march-gets-huge.html*
83. 'Hyderabad Braces for Telangana Million March', IANS, Hyderabad, 9 March 2011, source: *http://www.deccanherald.com/content/144463/hyderabad-braces-telangana-million-march.html*
84. 'Million March Turns Violent in Hyderabad', source: *http://www.hindu.com/ 2011/03/11/stories/2011031158870100.htm*
85. Sridhar Rao Deshpande, *Telanganaloo Kukutunnavi Gevitalu, Nadustunna Telangana*, No. 1, March 2011, pp. 19–21.
86. 'Vanta-Varpu on Roads in Hyderabad', 19 June 2011, source: *www.andhraheadlines.com/statevanta-varpp-on-roads*
87. Prof. M. Kodandaram.
88. 'Highlights of Agreement', source: *http://www.telangananewsonline.com/2011/October/24/Telangana-Government-Employees-call-off-42-day-old-Strike.htm*
89. G. Haragopal, *Namaste Telangana*, Saturday, 21 July 2012, p. 4.
90. G. Haragopal, *Chaitnyam Veleginchina Samme, Negadu*, Research Centre, Hyderabad, December 2011, pp. 7–9.
91. Was organized by TJAC on 30th of September 2012.
92. G. Vivek, Manda Jagannatham, Rajaiah, Gutta Sukendhar Reddy.
93. Thousands attend Telangana march amid clashes.

94. http://articles.timesofindia.indiatimes.com/2012-09-30/hyderabad/34176894_1_telangana-march-jac-convenor-m-kodandaram-telangana-joint-action-committee
95. http://www.aegindia.org/2012/09/sagara-haram-dandu-yatra-tank-bund-turn-violent-supress-telangana-jac/213859.html
96. 'T' March named 'Sagara Haram' http://www.andhraheadlines.com/state/27t27_march_named_27sagara_haram27-4-106059.html
97. Writer and poet from the Telangana region.
98. Did JAC Kodandaram hijack T-cause and Isolated TRS? http://www.siasat.com/english/news/did-jac-kodandaram-hijack-t-cause-and-isolated-trs
99. 36-hour '*samara deeksha*' protest on January 27, 2013.
100. 36-hour T-Deeksha continues at Indira Park, Hyderabad, January 28 http://news.chennaionline.com/newsitem.aspx?NEWSID=e94e4d6a-dad3-4512-8001-c7f005f4b125=South
101. TJAC chairman.
102. Pro-Telangana activists hold 'samara deeksha' protest in Hyderabad http://truthdive.com/2013/01/28/pro-telangana-activists-hold-samara-deeksha-protest-in-hyderabad.html
103. K. Narayana.
104. Hyderabad remains tense as pro-Telangana supporters start 'Chalo Assembly' rally http://www.thehindubusinessline.com/news/states/hyderabad-remains-tense-as-protelangana-supporters-start-chalo-assembly-rally/article4813685.ece
105. Telangana- What is at stake today?June 14, 2013 http://vickynanjapa.wordpress.com/2013/06/14/telangana-what-is-at-stake-today/
106. April 29–30, 2013.
107. Ibid.
108. Editor of *Mainstream* weekly.
109. Ponnam Prabhakar.
110. http://www.sakshipost.com/index.php/news/state/17701-jac-steps-up-telangana-movement-in-delhi
111. Over demand for separate state http://truthdive.com/2013/04/28/Telangana-activists-begin-march-to-Delhi-over-demand-for-separate-state.html
112. Prakash Javedkar and Sushma Swaraj.
113. TRS floor leader, Legislative Assembly, Andhra Pradesh.
114. TJAC's Sansad Yatra heats up Delhi on Telanganahttp://newindianexpress.com/states/andhra_pradesh/TJAC%E2%80%99s-Sansad-Yatra-heats-up-Delhi-on-Telangana/2013/04/30/article1568065.ece

115. Five Congress MPs from Telangana on 48-hour sit-in at Parliament Gate http://indiatoday.intoday.in/story/telangana-issue-congress-mps-protest-outside-parliament/1/268345.html
116. Sushma Swaraj meets Andhra Congress MPs protesting over Telangana statehood issue; http://indiatoday.intoday.in/story/telangana-issue-sushma-swaraj-andhra-congress-mps/1/268321
117. June 30, 2013.
118. Former AP Congress president Congress leader.
119. Former AP Congress president Congress leaders demand formation of separate Telangana state; http://timesofindia.indiatimes.com/india/Congress-leaders-demand-formation-of-separate-Telangana-state/articleshow/20848675.cms
120. Decision on Telangana not an easy one, says Digvijay Singh http://in.news.yahoo.com/decision-telangana-not-easy-one-says-digvijay-singh-140937950.html
121. http://economictimes.indiatimes.com/news/politics-and-nation/telangana-statehood-congress-readying-a-proposal-which-will-satiate-trs/articleshow/20905064.cms
122. G. Vivek, Manda Jagannatham and former APCC president and former Congress Working Member.
123. July 12, 2013.
124. 26 July 2013 at New Delhi.
125. Congress general secretary in-charge of Andhra Pradesh.
126. B.R. Ambedkar, *Dr Babasaheb's Writings and Speeches*, Vol. I, Part II – *On Linguistic States*, Education Department, Government of Maharashtra, Bombay, 1979.
127. Booker Prize winner and activist, interviewed on 12 July 2010 at Hyderabad.
128. 'Arundhathi Roy Extends Support to Telangana', source: *http://missiontelangana.com/arundathi-roy-extends-support-to telangana/*
129. Former Member, Planning Commission of India, and Member of Parliament in Rajya Sabha.
130. Former Member of Planning Commission and Member of Parliament in Rajya Sabha, delivered the 14th Prof. G. Ram Reddy Memorial Lecture at the Centre for Economic and Social Studies (CESS) on 'Regional Dimensions of New Economic Paradigm: The Case for Telangana', at Hyderabad on 6 March 2010.
131. TDP leader, former Home Minister, Government of Andhra Pradesh, and presently, Member of Parliament from Rajya Sabha.
132. President, Nava Telangana Praja Party, Telangana Vidyarthi Sadassu, Chakali Ilaimma Pranganam, Osmania University, 9 August 2008.

133. Ibid.
134. Ibid.
135. Ongur Srinivas, Bandameedi Pally, Mahaboob Nagar, interviewed on 24 September 2009.
136. Niranjan, Bandameedi Pally, Mahaboob Nagar, interviewed on 22 September 2009.
137. Kailash, Venkat Rao Palli village, Karim Nagar district, interviewed on 20 February 2010.
138. Editor, *Andhra Jyothi*, delivered a lecture at CPI (ML) New Democratic, Pratyeka Telangana: CPI (ML) New Democratic Vaikari, Navya Printers, Hyderabad, 2009.
139. Mother of Telangana.
140. Interview with Nernela Kishore, singer from Telangana, interviewed on 21 February 2010 at Hyderabad.
141. S.R. Sankaran, Negotiating Peace, Committee of Concerned Citizens, Hyderabad, 2006, pp. 1–2.
142. Yadava, Gouda, Vaddera, Poosala, Boya, Vansaraj (Pichchakuntla), HoliaDasari, BudagaJangala, Mondi, MunnuruKapu, Rajaka, Dakkali, NayiBrahmana, Budabudakkala, Lambadi, Madiga, Uppari, Mala, Mudiraj, Gangaputhra, Bhatraju, Weavers.
143. *Jai Telangana … Jai Jai Telangana.*
144. Kakatiya University awarded Andesree with an honorary doctorate in 2007.
145. Ibid., interviewed on 14 December 2008 at Hyderabad.
146. Eppuri Somanna, artist and activist from Nalgonda district participated in Telangana Separate State movement, interviewed on 12 December 2008 at Hyderabad.
147. The idols of *Telangana Talli, Samakka and Sarakka Deities, Moharam (Peerulu)*, martyrs of Telangana movement and the symbol of Komaram Bhim.
148. Ibid.
149. Seminar on People's Telangana, organized by People's Telangana Foundation, Saturday, Hyderabad, 30 June 2007.
150. Belliah Naik.
151. Bellaiah Naik, President of Lambadi Hakkula Porata Samithi, interviewed on 16 August 2008 at Hyderabad.
152. President, Telangana Sangarshana Samithi, interviewed on 12 December 2008 at Hyderabad.
153. As part of his programme, Gaddar undertook a 'cultural peace march'.

154. He comes from a radical political background, is a revolutionary singer and president of Telangana Praja Front (TPF).
155. Gaddar, Lecture at Telangana Diary–2009 inauguration meeting at Ravindra Bharati, Hyderabad on 4 January 2009.
156. Sanjay was interviewed on 24 September 2009 at Hyderabad.
157. Ibid.
158. Gogu Shyamala, writer and activist, interviewed on 15 November 2008 at Hyderabad.
159. Tribal state.
160. Sripathi Ramudu, *Bahujana Keratalu*, Vol. 2, No. 7, July 2010, Ongole, p. 15.
161. Tribal localities.
162. Delivered a lecture in a round-table discussion on 'Relevance of Smaller States Demand', organized by Academic Staff College, University of Hyderabad, on 4 February 2008 at Hyderabad.
163. M.D. Waheed, 'Telanganaloo Tellavarani Muslimla Batukulu', Pooru Telangana, Hyderabad, December 2007, p. 21.
164. Hails from the city of Hyderabad, belongs to Muslim community, Chairman of Telangana Muslim Joint Action Committee, Hyderabad.
165. Ibid., report submitted to Sri Krishnan Committee, constituted by Government of India, 2010, source: *http://www.ummid.com/news/2010/April/18.04.2010/telangana_and_MUSLIMS.htm*
166. Muslim Forum for Telangana and Telangana Muslim Front.
167. Belongs to the Muslim community, Venkat Rao Palli village, Karim Nagar district, interviewed on 16 December at Hyderabad.

8 Conclusion

Democracy and human rights are interrelated and interdependent. As a result of sacrifices of several people, revolutions and wars, humanity today is enjoying a larger degree of human rights and democracy. There are several international human rights organizations apart from governmental institutions which are striving for promotion and protection of human rights. India too is a part of this historical process. The Indian freedom struggle gave a boost to the evolution of the rights discourse and it has had a major impact on the Constitution, which emphasized on social, economic, political and cultural freedoms. But into the seventh decade of independence, there is a gap between formulation and implementation of constitutional values. This gap gives scope for people's agitations. The study indicates that income inequalities, scale of poverty, incidence of hunger, and unequal distribution of means of production, gender inequalities, caste discrimination, lack of education entitlements, poor access to health, unemployment, globalization and commercialization of social services and agrarian crisis can lead to people's agitations. The right to agitate turns into a major democratic instrument as the system fails in responding to people's aspirations through conventional modes of politics or institutional arrangements which are generally apathetic towards equitable development and enlargement of justice. The state also gradually shifts its responsibilities to non-state actors: national and international. The first phase of the Telangana movement took place when there was spurt in regional imbalance due to green revolution and as a result of this, development was confined to a few regions that were already prosperous and it ignored and pushed the backward regions further backward. Hence, due to an imbalanced development approach, it gave the scope to the demand for a separate state. Telangana separate state movement could be seen from that angle. Even the second phase of the movement that started in the

1990s was due to the adverse impact of globalization on backward regions and poor and common people. Hence, once again, the negative development model gave the scope and reiterated the demand for a separate state of Telangana as the region suffered due to globalization.

The study indicates that democracy cannot confine itself to a few elites but has to involve all the sections and have institutional arrangements that ensure individual rights and promote freedom. This is possible through collective action which promotes self-confidence and, dignity, which, in turn, leads to enlargement of the scope of rights.

The study evaluated formal and substantive forms of democracy and found that the spirit of freedom struggle in India is gradually shrinking, memories of independence are dwindling and leadership is tending to become self-centred. Electoral politics has provided more opportunities to elite sections than poor people. This leadership, by and large, is not working for the holistic development of communities. This callous attitude of leadership led to violation of human rights and inevitably gave rise to people's agitations. India is considered a formally democratic country but lacks substantive content as it is suffering from several limitations like ethnic identities, caste, religion, regional, religious orthodoxy, cultural variations and geographical differences. The study holds that Indian democracy is facing several hurdles and there is great pessimism among the people and disappointment with the institutions. Many leaders who occupy positions in these institutions lack constitutional principles. The study further holds that there has been a decline of morality in public life with rampant corruption and growing of an unclean political climate. There has been a sharp increase in social disharmony and, therefore, caste conflicts and casteism have become the key factors of expression of dissent. The findings of the analysis on the nature of protest movements from 2004–05 suggest that they are not only against the government but also against certain powerful sections of society. For instance, the protest movements of one sub-caste against another sub-caste, group of individuals against another group and one region against another region. These movements or counter-movements do pressurize the government or administration to reformulate the policies. The state, caught between the pressure and counter-pressure, is finding it increasingly difficult to decide and govern society. Strikes by MRPS, APSRTC and junior doctors indicate that as governance is becoming complex, and political executive is not able to respond, the judiciary is stepping in. The judiciary is respected as it symbolizes justice. In a democracy, the faith in the impartiality of the institutions is important. The legislature and executive face a credibility crisis; if the faith in judiciary gets reduced, the crisis of democracy will be far deeper and in the long run counter-productive. It is time that Indian democracy learns to respond to the macro and micro-movements in time and in favour of the people. These cases reflect the irresponsive picture of India's democracy.

It also witnessed that the state has been gradually shifting its responsibilities to non-state actors: national and international. It has been depending on experts to study problems and suggest solutions. This strategy has been used either to dilute the issue or delay the process and escape from its responsibilities. These expert committees have been giving their reports often based on their pre-conceived notions. The state is encouraging the experts who believe in the neo-liberal model of development and are from a corporate background and trained abroad. This is a sad symptom of Indian democracy. These people give advice to the governments that are not based on the welfare model of development. Andhra Pradesh is an example. The Government of India constituted the Justice Srikrishna Committee to study the demand for Telangana, but the intellectuals felt that the Committee did not consider ground realities. It is widely felt that the government constituted this Committee to delay the issue and sideline the problems. Thus, the people of Telangana lost trust on experts as their recommendations do not reflect the aspirations of the people. It gave further scope for people's agitations. Thus, instead of solving the problem, the State aggravates it. It is also seen that the constitutional provisions or formal arrangements do not get enforced effectively. Thus, the role of movements seems to be more to protect rights as there is a gap between the formal and substantive components of democracy. The neo-liberal model of development has further widened the inequalities and became metropolis-centric. Consequently, the disparities particularly between the regions, instead of being bridged, are further accentuated. The episode of the Telangana regional movement is a fallout of these shortcomings of the democratic experiment of India.

The second phase of the Telangana movement has been in vogue for more than a decade. After a decade of struggle, the movement picked up. It led to assertion by students, advocates, teachers, employees, communities, trade unions, women, labour and TNGOs. These groups formed Joint Action Committees and participated in the movement. The state employed repressive methods, considering it as a law and order problem. Such an approach creates more problems and widens the gap between the state and the people. The study also indicates that the people of the region do not have much faith in their leaders as they stopped respecting the feelings and sentiments of people. Hence, people from all sections without having any political background came forward to participate in the movement. This response has come in the form of mass agitations in the entire Telangana region, irrespective of their socio-economic background.

The leaders from Seema-Andhra region threatened to resign their MLA and MP position, if the demand for Telangana state was conceded. The Telangana political leadership, however, was neither quick to respond nor united on the demand. This failure of formal political leadership of the Telangana region made the Central government go back on its announcement. This led to a series of assertions and heightening of the political movement in the Telangana region. Students from all universities started relay hunger strikes and some committed suicide. There is a spurt in emergence of Joint Action Committees (JACs) literally from every walk of life. All these developments suggest seriousness of the demand and do indicate that the electoral politics did not respond to the problem the way they should, forcing the people to go in for agitations. Many civil society organizations, caste-based organizations, workers, employees, students, women and intellectuals have been participating in the agitations. They have used several forms of agitations like fast-unto-death, relay strikes, blockade of roads, dharnas, and boycotting educational institutions and courts. Leaders from different political parties in the latter stage came together and participated in the movement along with other organizations and individuals though they have different ideological stands. Several people – youths, students and young women, including a police constable – committed suicide. Government employees resigned from their posts. Junior doctors and advocates participated too, giving a moral boost to the movement. Though the political leaders took part in the movement, it was only when the demand came from the JAC to quit their posts. Though they resigned because of pressure from the people, the Speaker of the House did not accept their resignations. So, people of the region realized that the state was not sensitive towards the democratic demand and was using repressive methods to contain the movement.

Instead of solving the problem, the state's attitude got further hardened, giving rise to the gap between the state and people. With this backdrop, they preferred to commit suicide. The TRS and one BJP MLA stuck to their decision of resigning, causing byelections. During the byelection campaign, all the JACs campaigned for the candidates and this active participation led to the stunning victory of their candidates. The role of people's organizations, intellectuals, students, youth and other sister organizations and human rights groups became crucial in the electoral politics. These sections did not merely participate actively in the movements, but became crucial factors in winning or losing. In all the byelections held after 1999, the political parties who are opposed or did not take a clear stand on the statehood demand were defeated. This is a clear indication that people's movements are in a position to influence the election results. This positive sign of movements, it is thus argued, strengthens democracy.

Political parties and institutions have not been effectively functioning and the political leadership is not seemingly concerned about the problems and democratic demands of the people. In reality, procedural democracy has not been able to address the democratic demands and people opted for agitations to fulfill their democratic urges. In Andhra Pradesh, several political parties have been dominating and a few powerful communities have hijacked these parties. Outside formal politics, there were several movements like anti-liquor movement, Dalit movement, Naxalite movement and other identity movements, including the Telangana and Jai Andhra movements. The separate Telangana Movement especially has been active for the last six decades. Several political parties and people's organizations emerged for the cause of a separate state and mobilized people in support of the cause. The state responded to the movement through coercive and cooption modes. It has been delaying a solution by constituting committees, arriving at agreements. No agreement though has been fully implemented. This approach made the people of the region impatient and assertive, leading to the demand for a separate state. As people lost confidence in political parties and leaders, it resulted in formation of non-political organizations like caste-based organizations, professional organizations, advocates' organization, and teachers, TNGOs, students and youth came forward and formed into Joint Action Committees and started organizing people without any 'political' motives. These organizations have not been merely working for the demand of a separate state, but raising several questions like Dalit rights, tribal rights, minorities' rights and women's rights. Political parties and leaders failed in addressing these democratic demands, but people's organizations are trying to address these issues. In a way, people's movements for substantive democracy have created conditions for a creative and democratic society. On par with the Telangana movement, there should be Dalit and tribal movements to protect and promote the rights of these sections. The parallel movements give an opportunity for these sections in bargaining for their equal share in the polity and economy and demand equal status at the societal level along with the elites in the region. It is not that somebody provides opportunities to them but they have to achieve the rights through their struggles and assertions. This assertion makes the subaltern classes confident in the process of striving for the rights of their fellow subalterns in the region.

The Telangana statehood movement has witnessed wide-ranging democratic agitations and has seen the emergence of men and women with courage and conviction. The Telangana people's movement is rooted in a historical context and a faulty development model. This entire direction of imbalanced development sharpened the contradictions and created new tensions. The ongoing Telangana movement is a search for some resolution to the contradictions. Caste and cultural composition, caste oppression, atrocities on Dalits and domination of upper strata is similar in all the three regions. The elite sections in all the regions are strong in terms of landholdings, economy, polity and social domination. It also found that for the last six decades, there were not many efforts made to develop this region. Different political formations were formed exclusively to champion the cause of a separate state in this region. A few parties succeeded partially in mobilizing the people in support of the demand but quite a few of them have been confined to electoral politics, which have no adequate potential to respond. Political parties have started maintaining dual standards in dealing and making use of the movement for their political gains. Large sections of the political leadership have been lumpenized as people who have been entering politics in the state of Andhra Pradesh for the last two decades have been from the real estate business, liquor mafia and elite classes. They gained from the leakages of resources that the state invested in irrigation, roads, public enterprises, mining and other infrastructural development projects. This pattern of public expenditure through contractors gave rise to a neo-rich class and a wide range of middlemen as they were the direct beneficiaries of the leakages of public funds. These sections are not concerned about the poor and needy and solely work for promoting their own political interests. This leadership has been questioned by the people's organizations in the Telangana region. The lumpen or mafia lack a basic value framework in public affairs. Thus, a set of opportunistic, money-hunting power elite have been let loose by a faulty developmental model. They have become an important component of the political processes of the state. The same leadership is considered as representative of the people as well as movements in Andhra Pradesh. Thus, the failure of the leadership made the general masses and opinion-makers take the responsibility to fill this gap in the polity and movements.

In the Telangana movement, it is clear from the byelections that people from all the castes, religions, rural and urban regions are taking part. Prior to (2010) KCR's hunger strike, the leadership was confined to a few sections. Though there were people's organizations, activists, intellectuals, students and youth who took recourse to agitational politics, there has been a rise of non-formal political processes when many new students' organizations and JACs have come up. They include caste-based and profession-based organizations who participated in relay strikes all over Telangana region. The students from schools to universities have been supporting, justifying, participating and forming human chains across the region in support of the movement. The movement has not only merely strengthened the voice of people but created awareness too. It has also led to creation of new literature and saw the birth and rise of new writers, singers, women activists and young boys and girls. The movement further witnessed several forms of agitations which not only pressurized the state, but created consciousness among the people and deepened the very notion of democracy.

The movement has witnessed two dimensions: the demand for a democratic and territorial statehood. Most of the opinion-makers from weaker sections do not want a mere territorial Telangana but a democratic state in which rights of weaker sections are protected and respected. They argue that fruits of the movement should reach the most disadvantaged sections. It is widely felt that territorial statehood is not adequate to meet the democratic aspirations as it would only benefit political parties, elite sections and leaders. Political dominance of a few elite sections has always been there. This should change. This has led to a demand for a democratic society, which means that welfare policies have to be implemented in a substantive manner and change social relations. A few opinion-makers want a policy on land distribution to develop weaker sections and evolve a proper mechanism to implement pro-poor policies in an effective manner. In Telangana state, they also yearn for genuine bureaucrats who really strive for the well-being of the poor masses.

Those taking part in the movement are not merely pressurizing the state, but are also engaged in educating the people and themselves. Artists who are relatively less educated and are hailing from rural and weaker sections are able to communicate the demand powerfully at the grassroots level. Their knowledge on several issues is extensive. These developments indicate that movements help in creating a new political culture. As political parties failed to mobilize the people, this void has been filled by the Joint Action Committees. Strategies like lobbying proved inadequate to pressurize the state and the agitations from the grassroots level have become necessary. The study observed that the views of opinion-makers from urban areas are similar to that of grassroots responses. At the grassroots, there are widespread democratic concerns. They feel that just a separate state is not meaningful for weaker sections unless it responds to their feelings. What emerges from the study is that though Indian democracy formally is constitutional and there are provisions to end poverty, disparities, and inequalities, in reality, they have not been on the serious agenda of the elite classes. This gap between promise and performance is obvious. It is movements such as that for a separate state of Telangana which are likely to make the constitutional arrangement relevant not only in terms of its vision, but in realizing that vision. The Telangana movement is in the process of filling the gap between electoral politics and people's aspirations. The movement is on-going and many political developments have been taking place as part of the movement. There is a noticeable tension between the formal democratic parliamentary political process and the substantive socio-political demands through the non-parliamentary JACs and other people's organizations. The question that the movement poses is: whether the substantive democratic urges would make a difference to parliamentary politics or the latter will marginalize the democratic process? The future research on democratic theory and practice may have to probe into this new and emerging domain of knowledge.

Postscript

The Formation of Telangana State and the Social Inclusive Development: The Role of Opinion Makers

The people of Telangana used several forms of democratic resistance from almost six decades to attain their long pending demand of separate Telangana state. It is due to their pressure and the political compulsions of the party that the Congress Working Committee (CWC), the highest policy-making body, resolved[1] to request the Central Government to take steps in accordance with the Constitution of India to form a separate state of Telangana with Hyderabad the capital city within a definite time frame.[2] As a result, there was resistance from the people of Seema-Andhra against the CWC resolution for the bifurcation of Andhra Pradesh and the creation of Telangana as the 29th state of India. The Congress party has constituted a committee with A.K. Antony, Union Defence Minister, as the chairperson, to address the problems of Seema-Andhra region. Despite the protests of masses and resignations of the MPs and MLAs from the party from the Seema-Andhra region, the Central Government stood by its decision and maintained that the decision is final as it has already consulted all the stakeholders. The UPA government has also constituted Justice Srikrishna Committee to resolve the Telangana issue and subsequently an all-party meeting was convened by the Union Home Minister at New Delhi, in which most of the parties, expect CPI(M) and MIM, favoured the creation of separate Telangana state. These parties have earlier been demanding time and again the Government of India to take the decision as early as possible.

In contrast to their earlier commitment for the formation of Telangana state, the regional parties of the state opposed the decision of central government. The party presidents of two political parties (TDP- Chandrababu Naidu; YSRCP-Y.S. Jaganmohan Reddy) went on hunger strike in the name of justice for both the regions and raised the issues like security of Andhra people who settled in Hyderabad, status of Hyderabad, employment, education, water distribution, Telugu identity etc. In fact, while forming any new state, all these issues are be dealt by a Group of Ministers (GoM), constituted by the Government of India, after consulting the concerned state government, people's representatives and experts. In the case of Telangana too, the leadership of both these parties, who are protesting and undergoing hunger strikes, was consulted and both had committed for the formation of the state.

Digvijay Singh, the General Secretary, AICC and in charge of party affairs of Andhra Pradesh, argues that the regional parties may have changed their views which they expressed earlier. However, the Congress party, as a national party and having a long history, will not change its views on the formation of Telangana state like regional political parties. Whatever the consequences, the party is ready to face. Therefore, as he clearly mentioned, the formation of Telangana is reality now. After almost two months of passing the CWC's resolution, the Government of India constituted a GoM under the chairmanship of Sushil Kumar Shinde, the Home Minister. The GoM clearly gave an assurance that they would solve all the problems/issues, i.e., education, employment, water distribution and capital city that Seema-Andhra leaders and people are raising. Already, the GoM has started its work and interacting with the stakeholders and requested the people of Andhra Pradesh and the political parties to cooperate with it in the formation of Telangana state.

It is further felt that several people's associations, joint action committees, singers, writers and political parties, which committedly struggled for the cause of Telangana, have to continuously represent the people's aspirations in their own state and fight against the domination, deprivation and denial of the rights of subaltern classes through their writings, cultural activities and movements. It is believed that the for proposed Telangana state, the government has to take all associations, individuals, institutions and apolitical organizations into the confidence during the time of policy making and implementation as these groups interacted, worked and lived with weaker sections at the grassroots. Therefore, these sections certainly facilitated the state to overcome the problems and gave an assurance to the people of the newly formed Telangana state.

It is to be noted that the people's movements always play a major role in the development of democracy. Both the state and the political leadership should respect the aspirations of the people and concede their demands. If the demands of the people are genuine and their forms of agitations are democratic and within the purview of constitution, the strategies of the movement are scientific and honed, and commitment of the leadership is unquestionable, the state should respond positively towards the demands that the people raise. In this case too, not only the Telangana statehood movement became the laboratory to interrogate Indian democracy and human rights, it proved that the people's aspirations and concerns are more important. The vibrant leadership that was developed during the Telangana movement from subaltern classes had enormous influence on the political leadership. The forms of movements that were taken up by the people's organizations like Sakalajanula Samme, Iailbaro, Telangana Million March, March to Hyderabad, Vanta Vaarpu, Pattalapaiki Pallelu, besides the emergence of the joint action committees from village to city, creative cultural assertions and using the local symbols to create the consciousness among the people, dedicated activists from the beginning contributed a lot to the movement. Apart from these, a political party, i.e., Telangana Rastra Samithi (TRS), which was formed on the issue of Telangana, continuously raised it either in the parliament or assembly. The political pressure from TRS also forced other political parties to take a stand on Telangana. All these issues, concerns, individuals, institutions and democratic forms of agitations played a major role in influencing the central government to take decision to form the Telangana state.

The issues that the employees, NGOs, youth and stakeholders are raising also need to be addressed. It is a greater opportunity for the people of both the regions (Telangana and Seema-Andhra) to develop their own states, and bargain for their due share with the central government. The natural resources can be properly utilized as per the rules and regulations framed by their respective governments and the central government should support them in an equitable manner. Both the states can utilize science, technology, manpower and their innovative and creative faculties which are available within their purview. Already existed vibrant political and civil society organizations, intellectuals and those working for the protection and promotion of human rights can also play an important role in deepening and substantialization of formal democracy in the both the states. In fact, the Telugu-speaking people of both the states can continue their language identity and strengthen their relations further and respect each other's cultures, festivals, political affiliations, interchange of intellectual capabilities, sharing of technological progress, etc. In both the states, poor and middle classes would enjoy greater privileges as there would be decentralization of powers, and the capital city will be nearer to their native places. Therefore, they can physically go to their state secretariat and pursue their grievances personally. It will be not required for general masses to take the assistance of others, i.e., *pyaraveekars* or middlemen and brokers.

The Telangana movement is considered to be the democratic movement relentlessly fought against the injustice and domination, economic, political and cultural hegemony of the ruling class and for land, water and forests (*jal, jamin* and *jangal*). It is the time for the political leadership of Telangana to become more democratic and learn to respect the rights of the weaker sections of their region. Whoever comes to the power, they have to see that there should not be discrimination of any person based on his or her socio-economic status, and implement the land reforms effectively, generate and provide employment to unemployed youth, free education to all till the higher education and introduce the common school education system. Special measures should also be taken to improve the status of women and strict implementation of the constitutional provisions to heighten their self-respect. At the same time, religious tolerance should also be protected. The rights of SCs, STs, minorities and women need to be protected and special measures to be taken to develop these sections politically, economically and culturally. There has to be strict implementation of reservations as per their population. The egalitarian values like equality, liberty and fraternity should also be protected and promoted in the new state. It is a great test for the people of the Telangana to show their maturity in choosing their leadership. If they choose good leadership, who are committed and dedicated towards the welfare of the poor and the weaker sections in the initial phase of the formation of state, the new Telangana state would develop substantially. And they are not able to choose such leadership, once again, they will be betrayed by their own leadership in their own state. In this whole process, the opinion makers of Telangana can play a major role in sensitizing the people, particularly underprivileged sections, and caution the political leadership about their holistic role in the new state of Telangana. It is important to note that the committed political and administrative culture, inclusive model of development and the creative role of the opinion makers are vital to fulfil the aspirations of the people of the new state. During the Telangana movement, the people demanded not merely territorial state which benefits only rich and elite political class, but aspired for a democratic state in which the rights of dalits, tribals, minorities and women would be protected and promoted. It is also noted that the subaltern classes like dalits, tribals and minorities should take active role in constructing democratic Telangana state by participating in policy making and implementation. The intellectuals and opinion makers from these sections should raise their voices against the injustice, domination and deprivation done in any form. Of course, the civil and human rights movement is very much vibrant in Andhra Pradesh for a long time. The human rights groups fought for the rights of subaltern classes and contributed in the protection and promotion of rights of these sections which are enshrined in the Indian Constitution. Their role once again would be prominent in the newly proposed Telangana state and their battle will be continued till the attainment of the Telangana state.

Notes

1. To establish, simultaneously and within a definite time frame, institute mechanism to address the concerns of the people of the regions of Andhra, Rayalaseema on matters relating to (but not limited to) the sharing of river waters, generation and distribution of electricity, safety and security of all residents in all the three regions, and the guarantee of the fundamental rights of all residents. The CWC resolution also has declared that Hyderabad will be the common capital of both states for ten years after the formation of Telangana and to put in place legal and administrative measures to ensure that both state governments can function efficiently from the common capital during the said period; to assist in building a new capital for the residuary state of Andhra Pradesh within a period of 10 years; to declare Polavaram project as a national project and to provide adequate funds to complete the same; to identify special needs of the backward regions/districts of Andhra Pradesh and to provide adequate funds for the development of those areas; and to assist the government of Andhra Pradesh and, after the formation of Telangana, assist both state governments to maintain law and order and ensure peace and harmony in all the regions/districts; the CWC acknowledges that the decision to form Telangana has not been an easy decision. The decision taken was taken after the widest possible consultations and after taking into account the chequered history of the demand for Telangana since 1956.
2. Congress Working Committee resolution on Telangana.

Bibliography

Ackerly, Brooke A. 'Is Liberalism the Only Way towards Democracy?', *International Journal of Political Philosophy*, Vol. 33, 4 August 2008.

Akhtar, Majeed. *Regionalism: Development Tensions in India*, New Delhi: Cosmo Publications, 1984.

Alam, Javeed. *Who Wants Democracy?*, New Delhi: Orient Longman, 2004.

Ambedkar, B.R. 'Annihilation of Caste', in *Ambedkar: Writings and Speeches*, Vol. 1, Bombay: Government of Maharashtra, 1976, pp. 38–67.

Ambedkar, B.R. *B.R. Ambedkar's Writings and Speeches*, Vol. 3, Bombay: Government of Maharashtra, 1976.

Amin, Samir. 'Democracy in the Third World', in *The Multiverse of Democracy: Essays in Honour of Rajni Kothari*, edited by D.L. Sethi and Ashis Nandy, New Delhi: Sage Publications, 1994.

Balagopal, K. 'Post-Chundur and Other Chundurs', *Economic and Political Weekly*, Vol. 26, No. 42, 1991, pp. 2397–99.

Bandopadhyay, D. 'Grassroots Justice: Law, System, and People', *Economic and Political Weekly*, Vol. 26, No. 39, 1991, pp. 2240–42.

Basu, Amrita. 'The Dialectics of Hindu Nationalism', in *The Success of Indian Democracy*, edited by Atul Kohli, Cambridge: Cambridge University Press, 2001.

Basu, D.D. *Introduction to the Constitution of India*, Nagpur: Wadhwa and Company Law Publishers, 2001.

Baxi, Upendra and Bhikhu Parekh. *Crisis and Change in Contemporary India*, New Delhi: Sage Publications, 1995.

Baxi, Upendra. 'State and Rights Movement in India', *Mainstream*, Annual Issue, 1987.

Bayley, David H. 'Public Protest and Political Process in India', *Pacific Affairs*, Vol. 62, No. 1, 1969.

—— 'Violent Agitation and Democratic Process in India', Unpublished Ph.D dissertation, Princeton: Princeton University Press, 1961.

Beetham, David. *Democracy: A Beginner's Guide*, Oxford: Oneworld, 2006.

—— *Max Weber and the Theory of Modern Politics*, Cambridge: Polity Press, 1989.

Berthold, Kuhn. *Participatory Development in Rural India*, New Delhi: Radiant Publications, 1998.

Bharathi, M. 'Transforming of Structure, Development Projects and Rights of Human Being', *Indian Journal of Human Rights*, Vol. 9, Nos 1–2, January–December, 2005.

Birch, Anthony. *The Concepts and Theories of Modern Democracy*, London and New York: Routledge, 1993.

Brenkert, George G. *Political Freedom*, London: Routledge, 1991.

Calman, Leslie J. 'Women and Movement Politics in India', *Asian Survey*, Vol. 29, No. 10, October 1989, pp. 940–58.

—— *Protest in Democratic India: Authority's Response to Challenge*, Boulder: Westview Press, 1985.

Carter, Ian. *A Measure of Freedom*, New York: Oxford University Press, 2004.

Chatterjee, Partha. 'Indian Democracy and Bourgeois Reaction', in *A Possible India: Essays in Political Criticism*, New Delhi: Oxford University Press, 1998.

—— *State Politics in India*, New Delhi: Oxford University Press, 1997.

—— *Transforming India: Social and Political Dynamics of Democracy*, New Delhi: Oxford University Press, 2000.

Chatterjee, Rakhahari. 'Democracy and Opposition in India', *Economic and Political Weekly*, Vol. 33, No. 17, 1988, pp. 843–47.

Chiranjivi, Nirmal J. *Human Rights in India: Historical, Social and Political Perspectives*, New York: Oxford University Press, 2005.

Chomsky, Noam. *Deterring Democracy*, London: Vintage Publications, 1991.

—— *Manufacturing Consent: Political Economy of Mass Media*, London: Vintage Publications, 1991.

—— *The Washington Connection and Third World Fascism*, Cambridge: South End Press, 1989.

Chousalkar, Ashok. *Indian Idea of Political Resistance*, New Delhi: Ajanta Publications, 1990.

Cranston, Maurice. *Jean-Jacques Rousseau: Social Contract*, Harmondsworth: Penguin Books, 1977.

Cuzan, Alfred G. 'Resource Mobilization and Political Opportunity in the Nicaraguan Revolution: The Praxis', *American Journal of Economics and Sociology*, Vol. 50, No. 1, 1991.

Dandekar, V.M. 'Making Rights to Work', *Economic and Political Weekly*, Vol. 26, No. 12, 1991, pp. 667–708.

Dasgupta, S. and Mohammad Yasin. *Indian Politics: Protests and Movements*, New Delhi: Anmol Publications, 2003.

Davis, Howard. *Political Freedom: Association, Political Purposes and the Law*, New York: Continuum Publications, 2000.

Deol, D. *Liberalism and Marxism: An Introduction to the Study of Contemporary Politics*, New Delhi: Sterling Publications, 1976.

Desai, A.R. '"Public Protest" and Parliamentary Democracy', in *Studies in Indian Democracy*, edited by S.P. Aiyar and R. Srinivasan, Bombay: Allied Publishers, 1965.

—— *India's Democracy: Analysis of State-Society Relations*, New Jersey: University Press, 1991.

—— *Protest Movements in Two Indian States*, New Delhi: Ajanta Publications, 1987.

—— *Repression and Resistance in India*, Vol. 1, Mumbai: Popular Prakashan, 1990.

—— *Rethinking of Democracy*, New Delhi: Orient Longman, 2005.

—— *Social Movements in India: A Review of Literature*, New Delhi: Sage Publications, 2004.

—— *State against Democracy: In Search of Humane Governance*, New Delhi: Ajanta Books International, 1998.

—— *The State and Poverty in India*, Cambridge: Cambridge University Press, 1985.

—— *Violation of Democratic Rights in India*, Vol. 1, Mumbai: Popular Prakashan, 1988.

Doctor, A.D.H. 'Low Caste Protest Movements in 19th and 20th Century in Maharashtra: A Study of Jyotirao Phule and B.R. Ambedkar', *Indian Journal of Political Science*, Vol. 4, No. 2, 1991, pp. 199–222.

Dreze, Jean and Amartya Sen. *Indian Development: Selected Regional Perspectives*, London: Oxford University Press, 1997.

Dreze, Jean. 'Dr Ambedkar and the Future of Indian Democracy', *Indian Journal of Human Rights*, Vol. 8, Nos 1–2, January–December, 2005.

Eisenger, P. 'The Conditions of Protest Behavior in American Cities', *American Political Science Review*, Vol. 81, 1973.

Elickstein, H. and T. Gurr. *Patterns of Authority: A Structural Basis for Political Inquiry*, New York: John Wiley and Sons, 1975.

Elliot, C.M. *Civil Society and Democracy*, Oxford: Oxford University Press, 2004.

Evans, Tony. 'If Democracy, then Human Rights?', *Third World Quarterly*, Vol. 22, No. 4, 2001.

Fields, Belden. *Rethinking Human Rights for the New Millennium*, New York: Palgrave Macmillan, 2003.

Frank, Bealey. *Democracy in the Contemporary State*, Oxford: Clarendon Press, 1988.

Frankel, Francine. *India's Political Economy (1947–2004): The Gradual Revolution*, New Delhi: Oxford University Press, 1978.

Gamson, W. *The Strategy of Social Protest*, 2nd Edition, Homewood, Illinois: Dorsey Press, 1990.

Ganguly, Sumit and Marc F. Plattner. *The State of India's Democracy*, Baltimore: Johns Hopkins University Press, 2007.

Ghosh, Arun. 'Marxism, Socialism, and Democracy: Issues Relevant for India Today', *Economic and Political Weekly,* Vol. 26, No. 50, 1991, pp. 2850–52.

—— 'Right to Work: Why and the Wheretofore', *Economic and Political Weekly,* Vol. 26, No. 33, 1991, pp. 1893–94.

Ghosh, Arunabha. 'Probing the Jharkhand Question', *Economic and Political Weekly,* Vol. 26, No. 18, 1991, pp. 1173–80.

Gill, Sucha Singh. 'State, Democratic Movement and Human Rights in India', *Indian Journal of Human Rights,* Vol. 1, No. 2, 1997, pp. 638–39.

Gladstone, J. *States Parties and Social Movements,* New York: Cambridge University Press, 2003.

Gouba, O.P. *An Introduction to Political Theory,* Delhi: Macmillan India Limited, 1981.

Granville, Austin. *Working of Democratic Constitution: A History of Indian Experience,* New Delhi: Oxford University Press, 2003.

Gudavarthy, Ajay. 'Dalit Movement and Naxalite Movement in Andhra Pradesh: Solidarity and Hegemony', *Economic and Political Weekly,* Vol. XL, Nos 1–53, December 2005, pp. 17–24.

Guess, Reymond. *History and Illusion in Politics,* New York: Cambridge University Press, 2001.

Gupta, Dipankar. 'Civil Society or the State', in *Institutions and Inequalities,* edited by Ramchandra Guha and Jonathan Parry, New Delhi: Oxford University Press, 1999.

Gurr, T. *Why Men Rebel,* Princeton: Princeton University Press, 1970.

Guru, Gopal. 'Ambedkar's Idea of Social Justice', in Ajit Bhattacharjea (ed.), *Social Justice and the Constitution,* Shimla: Indian Institute of Advanced Study, 1997.

—— 'Misreading Ambedkar', *Economic and Political Weekly,* Vol. 26, No. 41, 1991, pp. 2348–52.

Haragopal, G. 'Limits of Amartya Sen's Three R's of Reform', *Economic and Political Weekly,* Vol. XL, No. 24, June 2005, pp. 2453–2454.

—— 'Rights in a Transitional Society: A Re-look at Philosophical Foundations of Human Rights', *Indian Journal of Human Rights,* Vol. 7, Nos 1–2, 2003.

—— *Political Economy of Human Rights: Emerging Dimensions,* Bombay: Himalaya Publishing, 1992.

Harriss, J. 'Political Participation, Representation and the Urban Poor: Findings from Research in Delhi', *Economic and Political Weekly,* 12 March 2005, pp. 1041–54.

Held, David. *Models of Democracy,* Cambridge: Polity Press, 1987.

Illaiah, Kancha. 'The State Oppressed and Weaker Sections', in *Development of Weaker Sections,* edited by Chandu Subba Rao and D. Francis, Jaipur: Rawat Publications, 2000.

Jagannatham, B. 'Bonded Labour and Education: The Question of Human Rights', in *Education and Social Empowerment in India*, edited by Ghanta Chakrapani, New Delhi: Milind Publications, 2008.

—— 'Indian Democracy: Values and Reality', in *Dynamics of Change and Continuity in the Era of Globalization*, edited by B.V. Muralidhar and Jaya Kumar, New Delhi: Sunrise Publications, 2009.

—— 'Mahatma Jyothirao Phule: A Revolutionary Social Reformer', *Indian Journal of Political Science*, Vol. LXXI, No. 2, April–June 2010, pp. 399–412.

—— 'Politics of Participatory Democracy: A Case Study of Protests in Hyderabad City', *Indian Journal of Human Rights*, Vol. 9, Nos 1–2, January–December, 2005.

—— 'The Human Rights Implications of Dalit Self-assertion in India', in *Locality, History, Memory: The Making of the Citizen in South Asia*, edited by Rila Mukherjee and M.N. Rajesh, UK: Cambridge Scholars Publications, 2009.

Jagannatham, B. and G. Haragopal. 'Terrorism and Human Rights: Indian Experience with Repressive Laws', *Economic and Political Weekly*, Vol. XLIV, 11 July 2009, pp. 11–17.

Jayal, Niraja Gopal. *Democracy and the State: Welfare, Secularism and Development in Contemporary India*, New Delhi: Oxford University Press, 1999.

Jayaram, N. *On Civil Society: Issues and Perspectives*, New Delhi: Sage Publications, 2005.

Joseph, Sarah. 'Neoliberal Reforms and Democracy in India', *Economic and Political Weekly*, Vol. 42, No. 31, 4–7 August 2007, pp. 3213–17.

Kaase, M. and S.H. Barnes. *Political Action: Mass Participation in Five Western Democracies*, Beverly Hills: Sage, 1979.

Kamble, J.R. *Rise and Awakening of Depressed Classes in India*, New Delhi: National Publishing House, 1979.

Kannabiran, Vasanth. 'Caste and Gender: Understanding Dynamics of Power and Violence', *Economic and Political Weekly*, Vol. 26, No. 37, 1991, pp. 2130–32.

Kohli, Atul. *Democracy and Discontent: India's Growing Crisis of Governability*, London: Cambridge University Press, 1991.

Kothari, Rajni. *Caste in Indian Politics*, New Delhi: Orient Longman, 1971.

—— *Politics and the People: In Search of Humane India*, Vol. 11, New Delhi: Ajanta Publications, 1989.

Kumar, Ashutosh. 'Exploring Democracy', *Economic and Political Weekly*, Vol. 33, No. 11, 2003, pp. 1242–61.

Kumar, K.G. 'Dilemmas of Measuring Human Freedom', *Economic and Political Weekly*, Vol. 26, No. 47, 1991, p. 2672.

Lassman, Peter. *Politics and Social Theory*, London: Routledge, 1989.

Lipsky, Michael. 'Protest as a Political Resource', *American Political Science Review*, Vol. 62, No. 4, December 1968, pp. 1144–58.

Lodha, Sanjay. 'Caste and Two Party System', *Economic and Political Weekly*, Vol. 33, No. 34, 6 February 2009, pp. 3344–48.

MacEwan, Arthur. *Neo-Liberalism or Democracy: Economic Strategy, Markets, and Alternatives for the 21st Century*, London: Zed Books, 1999.

Macpherson, C.B. *Democratic Theory: Essays in Retrieval*, Oxford: Clarendon Press, 1973.

—— *Real World of Democracy*, New York: Oxford University Press, 1996.

Mahajan, Gurpreet. 'Civil Society and its Avatars: What Happened to Freedom and Democracy', *Economic and Political Weekly*, Vol. 34, No. 20, 15 May 1999, pp. 1188–96.

McCarthy, J. and M. Zald. 'Resource Mobilization and Social Movements', *American Journal of Sociology*, Vol. 82, No. 6, 1996, pp. 1212–41.

Mehta, Pratap Bhanu. *The Burden of Democracy*, New Delhi: Penguin Books, 2003.

Migdal, Joel S. *Strong Societies and Weaker States*, Princeton: Princeton University Press, 1998.

Mill, J.S. *On Liberty*, London: Penguin Books, 1984.

Mishra, Tilottam and Udayan Mishra. 'Movements for Autonomy in India's North-East', in *Region, Religion, Caste, Gender and Culture in Contemporary India*, edited by T.V. Sathyamurthy, New Delhi: Oxford University Press, 1998.

Mitram, Subrata K. *Democracy and Social Change in India*, New Delhi: Sage Publications, 1999.

—— *Power, Protest and Participation: Local Elites and the Politics of Development in India*, London: Routledge, 1992.

Mohanty, Manoranjan, Partha Nath Mukherjee and Olle Tornquist. *People's Movements and the State in the Third World*, New Delhi: Sage Publications, 1998.

Nayak, Pulin B. 'On Equality and Distributive Justice', *Economic and Political Weekly*, Vol. 26, No. 11, 1991, pp. 583–90.

Noorani, A.G. 'Civil Liberties, Violence and Civil Rights', *Economic and Political Weekly*, Vol. 26, No. 50, 1991, p. 2853.

—— 'Freedom of Expression in Universities', *Economic and Political Weekly*, Vol. 26, No. 41, 2001, pp. 2335–36.

—— 'Soviet Union, Human Rights and Amnesty', *Economic and Political Weekly*, Vol. 26, No. 34, 1991, p. 1952.

—— 'Stifling the NGOs', *Economic and Political Weekly*, Vol. 36, No. 29, July 2001, pp. 2731–32.

—— 'Student's Rights', *Economic and Political Weekly*, Vol. 26, No. 33, 1995, p. 1892.

Norman, Richard. *Free and Equal: A Philosophical Examination of Political Values*, London: Oxford University Press, 1975.

Norris, Nippa. *Democratic Phenomix*, London: Harvard Press, 2004.

Omvedt, Gail and Bharat Patankar. 'Movement for Water: Takari Peasants' Struggle', *Economic and Political Weekly*, Vol. 26, No. 15, 1991, pp. 955–63.

Omvedt, Gail. 'Gandhi and Ambedkar', *Economic and Political Weekly*, Vol. 26, No. 18, 1991, pp. 1154–55.

—— *Dalits and Democratic Revolution: Dr Ambedkar and the Dalit Movement in India*, New Delhi: Sage Publications, 1994.

Oommen, T.K. 'Sources of Deprivation and Styles of Protest: The Case of Dalits in India', *Contributions to Indian Sociology*, Vol. 18, No. 1, May 1984, pp. 45–61.

—— *Nation, Civil Society and Social Movements: Essays in Political Sociology*, New Delhi: Sage Publications, 2003.

—— *Protest and Change: Studies in Social Movements*, New Delhi: Sage Publications, 1990.

Paine, Thomas. *Rights of Man*, London: J.M. Dent and Sons Limited, 1954.

Patrick, Heller. 'Degrees of Democracy: Some Comparative Lessons from India', *World Politics*, Vol. 52, No. 4, 2000, pp. 484–519.

Pennock, J. Ronald. *Democratic Political Theory*, New Jersey: Princeton University Press, 1979.

Perkins, John. *Confessions of an Economic Hit Man*, Portland: Berrett-Koehler Publications, 2004.

Peterson, V. Spike. 'Whose Rights? A Critique of the "Givens" in Human Rights Discourse', *Indian Journal of Human Rights*, Vol. 3, Nos 1–2, 1999.

Petras, James. 'Unemployed Workers' Movement in Argentina', *Economic and Political Weekly*, Vol. 36, No. 45, 2001, pp. 4261–69.

Prezeworski, Adam. *Democracy, Accountability and Representation*, New York: Cambridge University Press, 1999.

Rudolph, S.H. and L.I. Rudolph. 'New Dimensions of Indian Democracy', *Journal of Democracy*, Vol. 13, No. 1, January 2002.

Sankaran, S.R. 'Bureaucracy and Human Rights: Repressive State or Responsive State', *Indian Journal of Human Rights*, Vol. 1, No. 1, 1997, pp. 38–52.

Scott, John. *Weapons of the Weak: Everyday Forms of Peasant Resistance*, New Delhi: Oxford University Press, 1989.

Shah, Ghanshyam. 'Social Backwardness and Politics of Reservations', *Economic and Political Weekly*, Vol. 26, No. 11, 1991, pp. 101–610.

—— *Social Movements and the State*, New Delhi: Sage Publications, 2002.

Shanker, Gopal. 'American Anti-globalization Movement', *Economic and Political Weekly*, Vol. 36, No. 34, 2001, p. 3326.

Sharma, Kumud. 'Contemporary Women's Movement in India: Its Dialectics and Dilemmas', *Indian Journal of Political Science*, Vol. 5, No. 1, 1992, pp. 1–33.

Sharma, Shalendra D. *Development and Democracy in India*, Jaipur: Rawat Publications, 2003.

Shatrugna, M. 'Road to "Raktakshetram" Report from Chundur', *Economic and Political Weekly*, Vol. 26, No. 34, 1991, pp. 1967–69.

Sheth, D.L. 'Globalization and New Politics of Micro Movements', *Economic and Political Weekly*, Vol. 39, No. 39, January–February 2004, pp. 47–59.

Shyamlal. *Caste and Political Mobilization*, Jaipur: Panchsheel Prakashan, 1981.

Simon, Charles. 'Evaluating Dalit Leadership: P.R. Venkatswamy and the Hyderabad Example', *Economic and Political Weekly*, Vol. 37, No. 52, 2002, pp. 5237–43.

Singer, Sir Hans. *Globalization, Technology and Trade in the 21st Century*, New Delhi: B.R. Publishing Corporation, 2001.

Singh, Dilip. 'Protest Movements in India', *Indian Journal of Political Science*, Vol. 52, No. 4, 1991.

Singh, Yogendra. 'Contemporary Social Crisis in India and its Dimensions', *Man and Development*, Vol. 12, No. 10, 1984.

Sinha, Assema. 'Economic Growth and Political Accommodation', in *The State of India's Democracy*, edited by Sumit Ganguly, Larry Diamond and Marc F. Plattner, Baltimore: Johns Hopkins University Press, 2007.

Sorenson, George. *Democracy and Democratization*, Oxford: Westview Press, 1998.

Tandon, Yash. 'Political Economy of Struggles for Democracy and Human Rights in Africa', *Economic and Political Weekly*, Vol. 26, No. 25, 1991, pp. 1154–61.

Tibbitts, Felisa and I.A. Rehman. 'The Principles and Values of the Universal Declaration of Human Rights', 12 June 2003.

Vanaik, Achin. *Communism Contested*, New Delhi: Vistaar Publications, 1997.

—— *India in a Changing World*, Hyderabad: Orient Longman, 1995.

—— *The Painful Transition: Bourgeois Democracy in India*, London: Verso, 1990.

Weiner, Myron. *The Indian Paradox: Essays in Indian Politics*, New Delhi: Sage Publications, 1989.

Wilson, J.Q. 'The Strategy of Protest: Problems of Negro Civic Action', *Journal of Conflict Resolution*, Vol. 5, September 1961, pp. 291–303.

Yadav, Yogendra. 'India's Third Electoral System', *Economic and Political Weekly*, Vol. XXXIV, Nos 34–35, 21–28 August 1999, pp. 2393–99.

Index